Mastering Intrusion Detection for Cybersecurity

Edited by Akashdeep Bhardwaj

Published in London, United Kingdom

Mastering Intrusion Detection for Cybersecurity
http://dx.doi.org/10.5772/intechopen.1005986
Edited by Akashdeep Bhardwaj

Contributors
Abdul Latif Memon, Adiba Sania, Ch. Likhitha Sowmya, Chelumala Sreshta, Faheem Yar Khuhawar, Fahim Umrani, Floriano De Rango, Hyder Bux Mangrio, Irfan Halepoto, Kangbin Yim, M. Haarika, Mahdi Sahlabadi, Mattia Giovanni Spina, Mauro Tropea, Md Rezanur Islam, Munkhdelgerekh Batzorig, Omar Bani Fayyad, Ricardo Mogro, Rizwan Ali Shah, Silvana Gamboa, Subhash Parimalla, Tarana Aliyeva, Tayyaba Shaikh, Waleed Almuseelem, Yagati Vaishnavi

First published in London, United Kingdom, 2025 by IntechOpen
IntechOpen is the global imprint of INTECHOPEN LIMITED, registered in England and Wales, registration number: 11086078, 167-169 Great Portland Street, London, W1W 5PF, United Kingdom

For EU product safety concerns: IN TECH d.o.o., Prolaz Marije Krucifikse Kozulić 3, 51000 Rijeka, Croatia, info@intechopen.com or visit our website at intechopen.com.

British Library Cataloguing-in-Publication Data
A catalogue record for this book is available from the British Library

Mastering Intrusion Detection for Cybersecurity
Edited by Akashdeep Bhardwaj
p. cm.
Print ISBN 978-1-83634-422-3
Online ISBN 978-1-83634-421-6
eBook (PDF) ISBN 978-1-83634-423-0

Meet the editor

Dr. Akashdeep Bhardwaj is working as a Professor at UPES, Dehradun, India. An eminent IT Industry expert in Cybersecurity, Digital Forensics and IT Operations areas, Dr. Akashdeep mentors graduate, master's and doctoral students and leads several industry projects as the Head of Cybersecurity (Center of Excellence). Dr. Akashdeep is a Post-Doctoral Fellow from Majmaah University, Saudi Arabia, and a Ph.D. (doctoral) in Computer Science. Dr. Akashdeep has over 150 international publications (including SCI, Scopus, WoS papers, Copyrights, and Patents) and has authored several books. Dr. Akashdeep served as a Technology Leader for several multinational organizations during his tenure in the IT industry. Dr. Akashdeep is certified in multiple technologies, including Compliance Audits, Cybersecurity, and industry certifications in Microsoft, Cisco, and VMware technologies.

Contents

Preface

In an era where cyber threats are increasingly complex and relentless, the need for robust and intelligent intrusion detection systems (IDS) has never been greater. *Mastering Intrusion Detection for Cybersecurity* emerges as a timely and practical contribution to the field, offering both foundational knowledge and cutting-edge advancements to professionals, researchers, and students dedicated to strengthening digital defenses.

This book is a collaborative effort that brings together insights from diverse experts across academia and industry. The chapters provide a hands-on, application-oriented perspective on the evolving landscape of intrusion detection, covering a spectrum of techniques, from classical anomaly detection to sophisticated machine learning, deep neural models, and human-in-the-loop systems.

Key topics explored include detecting advanced persistent threats (APTs), utilizing convolution-based optimizers with Hadoop for scalable anomaly detection, and deploying reinforcement learning in network defense. The volume also explores insider threat detection through user and entity behavior analytics (UEBA), cybersecurity in intelligent transportation systems, and the distinct challenges of intrusion detection in cloud and industrial network environments.

By combining theoretical underpinnings with real-world applications, the chapters in this book aim to equip readers with practical tools and innovative strategies for tackling modern cybersecurity challenges. Whether you're enhancing vehicle IDS frameworks, analyzing malicious web pages, or integrating security awareness into operational systems, the insights presented here offer a valuable foundation and a forward-looking vision.

It has been a privilege to curate and edit this collection, and I am confident it will serve as a meaningful resource in the ongoing effort to safeguard our interconnected world.

Akashdeep Bhardwaj
Centre for Cybersecurity,
School of Computer Science, UPES,
Dehradun, India

Section 1

Foundations and Perspectives in Network Intrusion Detection

Chapter 1

The Evolution of Network Intrusion Detection Systems: From Legacy to Programmable Networks

Mauro Tropea, Mattia Giovanni Spina and Floriano De Rango

Abstract

This chapter explores the transformation of Network Intrusion Detection Systems (NIDS) following the evolution of networks from traditional, static infrastructures to programmable entities. Legacy NIDSs are conceived as static, fixed perimeter-based hardware appliances that rely on patterns to detect malicious activities. As cyber threats evolve, these systems become inadequate, unable to keep pace with dynamic, high-speed environments. The rise of Network Function Virtualization (NFV) and Software-Defined Networking (SDN), which made the networks programmable as software, allows for more flexible, adaptive intrusion detection. Using real-time data analytics and machine learning, they enable the rapid identification and mitigation of sophisticated threats. This evolution is crucial in addressing modern cybersecurity challenges, as programmable networks open up to enhanced visibility, scalability, and proactive threat management. Trying to highlight this transition and also providing a practical deployment scenario, this chapter focuses on the innovations that make modern NIDSs more robust by exploiting the evolutionary leap that the network is undergoing.

Keywords: network security, cybersecurity, intrusion detection system (IDS), network function virtualization (NFV), software-defined network (SDN)

1. Introduction

In traditional networks, the structure consists primarily of switches and routers, which include two levels of abstraction: the control plane, which is responsible for decision-making, and the data plane, which executes the instructions provided by the control plane. The control plane can be likened to a "pilot" guiding the data plane, which corresponds to the hardware that performs the required operations. However, this structure has several disadvantages that limit the flexibility and efficiency of traditional networks [1]. The role of Intrusion Detection Systems (IDS) in traditional networks is crucial to ensuring the security and integrity of network traffic. In these networks, IDSs perform several fundamental functions: (i) *Traditional and Static*

Architecture. IDSs in traditional networks operate in environments characterized by rigid and static infrastructures, where changes in network architecture require significant time and effort. IDSs are integrated at the network or host level and often follow predefined approaches, such as signature-based detection or detection based on predefined behaviors; (ii) *Passive Detection*. The primary function of IDSs is to passively monitor traffic to identify suspicious activities. Detection is based on known patterns (signature-based) or the analysis of anomalous behaviors (anomaly-based). However, the lack of adaptability to emerging threats is a limitation compared to more flexible and dynamic solutions; (iii) *Perimeter Security Focus*. In traditional networks, the security approach focuses on controlling incoming and outgoing traffic at the perimeter of the network. IDSs act as a "barrier" that monitors traffic, detecting intrusions or attacks on the perimeter, and alerting administrators to security events; (iv) *Limited Integration with Other Security Systems*. IDSs in traditional networks often function as standalone tools or with limited integration with other security components such as firewalls and Intrusion Prevention Systems (IPS). This reduces their ability to address complex threats or scenarios requiring a coordinated response.

As networks expand in size, their vulnerability to cyberattacks increases. Attackers may infiltrate a network to access sensitive information that can then be used for malicious purposes such as in Link Layer Discovery Protocol (LLDP) [2]. These attacks can originate both externally and internally within an organization, necessitating a robust security approach. However, traditional networks face significant security challenges due to their static and inflexible nature. In large traditional networks, characterized by thousands of devices with varied configurations, infrastructure complexity becomes a barrier to effective management and security. Their distributed and static architecture poses challenges in implementing uniform and dynamic security measures to protect the network. The main challenges of traditional networks include the complexity of control, inconsistencies among routers, and the constraint of using proprietary devices. These limitations of traditional networks are efficiently addressed by the approach of programmable networks, specifically through the Software-Defined Networking (SDN) architecture. The SDN architecture utilizes two main devices [1]: *switches* (also referred to as "blind devices") that do not make independent decisions and operate solely by following the controller's instructions; *controllers* (considered the "brains" of the network) that manage the network's overall operation. This structure enables centralized and dynamic management, simplifies network administration, and enhances security. In SDN programmable networks, the separation of the control plane from the data plane represents a fundamental shift in the implementation of IDSs. The SDN controller, acting as the "brain" of the network, facilitates centralized control and comprehensive management of data flows. This centralized control allows IDSs to analyze traffic more thoroughly than before, as all network information can be observed and managed from a single point. The adoption of IDSs in programmable networks has brought about several significant changes [3]. A key aspect is the ability to proactively and dynamically detect and respond to threats. Through programmability, rules and detection algorithms can be updated without the need to physically replace network devices. This agile approach enables a rapid response to emerging threats and reduces the time that attacks remain inside the network. Another change is the ability of IDS to employ advanced techniques, such as Machine Learning (ML), to analyze traffic in real time, improving the detection of complex multistep attacks. The integration of ML models enables IDSs to automatically learn normal traffic patterns and identify deviations that may indicate an intrusion. Moreover, implementing IDSs in an SDN environment requires greater attention to latency and computational efficiency, as excessive data processing could degrade overall network performance. Consequently, it is crucial to adopt load balancing and resource management strategies to ensure that IDS integration does not compromise performance. Programmable networks have revolutionized the telecommunications landscape by introducing a new management model based on the separation of traffic control from the physical infrastructure that supports it. The core characteristic of programmable networks is the ability of control software to operate independently of hardware, transforming the network into a more dynamic and flexible system. Before the introduction of programmable networks, network management required complex and direct configurations on each hardware device. Network administrators used Command Line Interfaces (CLIs) to manually configure parameters and functions on routers, switches, and other devices. This approach was practical for small-scale networks but became unsustainable as the networks grew in complexity and size [4]. IDSs can be applied to different network architectures, ranging from Internet of Things (IoTs) [5] to Flying Ad-hoc NETworks (FANETs) [6, 7], passing from Vehicular Ad-hoc NETworks (VANETs) [8] or Wireless Sensor Networks (WSNs) [9]. **Table 1** summarizes the differences between IDS in traditional networks and programmable networks.

Aspect	IDS in traditional networks	IDS in programmable networks
Architecture	Rigid and static networks, with slow and complex modifications. IDS integrated using predefined approaches.	Dynamic networks with separated control and data planes. Centralized SDN controller for global and flexible IDS management.
Threat detection	Passive detection based on known patterns or anomalies. Limited adaptability to new threats.	Proactive and dynamic threat detection and response. Real-time detection and continuous adaptation using ML.
Perimeter security	Focus on controlling inbound and outbound perimeter traffic.	Global traffic management with centralized visibility. Capability to update rules and defenses in real time.
Automation	Manual configurations and direct intervention on each device.	Automated security processes (rule updates, segmentation) to reduce human error and improve consistency.
Traffic visibility and control	Fragmented and decentralized traffic management, with complex anomaly monitoring.	Centralized visibility with continuous monitoring and real-time analysis of all traffic.
Advanced technologies	Traditional detection methods, with challenges in identifying complex and zero-day attacks.	Use of ML to identify threats in real time and adapt to new attack patterns.
Operational efficiency	Potential slowdowns due to network complexity and static management.	Load-balancing strategies to ensure optimal IDS performance without compromising the network.

Table 1.
IDS in traditional networks vs. programmable networks (SDN/NFV).

2. The software-defined networking paradigm

With the advancement of technologies, companies began to demand an infrastructure capable of adapting more rapidly to their ever-changing needs. Existing automation techniques, which relied on scripting or configuration copies, were no longer effective in supporting centralized management. Network programmability has thus enabled the overcoming of these limitations by centralizing control and allowing for the automated and simultaneous configuration of various network devices through a single management software, known as the controller. Thanks to this solution, it is now possible to implement large-scale configurations in reduced timeframes and with an unprecedented level of flexibility. Programmable networks laid the foundation for the concept of SDN, which quickly supplanted the term "programmable network" as the industry standard in networking [4]. SDN represents a leap forward in network management, introducing an architecture in which the control plane is separated from the data plane. In this structure, the logically centralized controller manages traffic flow and sends instructions to switches, which are limited to forwarding packets based on the policies set. SDN switches, therefore, perform functions such as routing, firewalling, address translation (NAT), and traffic optimization, all of which are centrally configurable through forwarding tables managed by the controller. With the adoption of SDN, companies have been able to reduce the time and costs associated with network management and optimize the performance of their infrastructures based on specific business needs. Centralized network management through an SDN controller has also improved network security, as control of security policies, performance, and Quality of Service (QoS) can now be centralized [10].

The SDN architecture consists of three main layers:

1. Data plane: Positioned at the lowest level, it is responsible for the physical forwarding of traffic.

2. Control plane: Handles routing decisions and network management.

3. Application plane: Located at the highest level, it includes all applications that interact with the controller to implement specific services, such as security management, traffic monitoring, and analysis.

Communication between the controller and network devices occurs via the Southbound Interface (SBI), while the controller interacts with applications through the Northbound Interface (NBI). This modular structure allows the control and application planes to be updated or modified without directly impacting the data plane, offering greater flexibility in enterprise network management. Due to the separation of planes, the SDN model enables networks to adapt to the specific needs of each application. Network applications can now implement policies that address advanced security requirements, traffic management, quality of service, and more. This level of centralized control also allows organizations to deploy new features quickly and securely without requiring hardware infrastructure modifications [10].

The advantages of SDN over traditional networks are numerous and significant [1]:

- Logically centralized control plane: In an SDN environment, a single centralized control plane manages and directs traffic across the entire network. This eliminates the problem of inconsistency among routers, ensuring uniformity of policies and operations across all network nodes.

- Global network view: With SDN, the controller provides a centralized view of the entire network, allowing monitoring from a single point. This approach facilitates the detection of anomalies and immediate response to potential threats.

- Enhanced security: The centralized nature of SDN networks simplifies software-based traffic monitoring, allowing effective identification and analysis of security threats. This is a significant improvement over traditional networks, where distributed management complicates uniform traffic control.

- Dynamic update of forwarding rules: In SDN networks, forwarding rules can be updated in real time, with changes applied instantly to all nodes connected to the controller. This greatly simplifies the update process compared to traditional networks, where updates require significantly more time and resources.

3. The network function virtualization paradigm

Network Function Virtualization (NFV) solutions have become an essential component of the SDN model. Network virtualization primarily refers to software-based overlay solutions, which operate by layering a virtual network over the physical one. Among the most popular network virtualization solutions are VMware NSX, Nuage Networks' Virtual Service Platform (VSP), and Juniper's Contrail. These systems provide a flexible network infrastructure characterized by the ability to decouple virtual resources from the underlying physical network, enabling more centralized and agile management. A crucial aspect of network virtualization solutions is the use of overlay protocols such as VxLAN (Virtual Extensible LAN) [11]. These protocols allow the creation of network connectivity that links virtual switches based on hypervisors, thereby ensuring Layer 2 continuity among virtual machines distributed across different physical hosts. The use of overlay protocols enables the establishment of a virtual network independent of the physical network configuration, which can operate at Layer 2, Layer 3, or in a hybrid mode. This connectivity model simplifies the integration of virtual networks with existing physical infrastructures, offering greater flexibility and the ability to efficiently scale the infrastructure. Although the overlay is a central component of the implementation of network virtualization solutions, these systems go beyond simply enabling the virtual interconnection of switches. Comprehensive solutions include advanced functionalities such as network security, load balancing, and integration with physical systems through a centralized controller. Network virtualization also enables the use of Layer 4–7 services, such as firewalls, load balancing, and security tools, thereby ensuring more granular control and greater adaptability to the specific needs of enterprise applications. Operational agility is enhanced by the use of a centralized control platform, which facilitates the dynamic and automated configuration of virtual switches and appliance services, reducing the need for manual configurations. With network virtualization, this process is greatly simplified by using Graphical User Interfaces (GUIs), centralized CLIs, and Application Programming Interfaces (APIs) that allow programmatic modifications. This makes the network infrastructure highly scalable and adaptable, offering more efficient management and the ability to respond in real time to the dynamic demands of the IT environment [12].

4. The role of the SDN controller in the NFV IDS

In the context of SDN network security, the controller plays a crucial role within IDS systems. The diversity of SDN implementations and their openness to programmability provide advantages in network management but also introduce significant security challenges. Network-based IDS (NIDS) leverages the SDN controller to analyze traffic in real-time, scanning the infrastructure for suspicious activity and promptly notifying the operator in the event of identified threats. Intrusion detection in this context relies on a thorough analysis of traffic to identify punctual, collective, or contextual anomalies. Punctual anomalies represent isolated events that clearly stand out from the rest of the traffic; collective anomalies occur when a group of elements exhibits suspicious behavior when considered together, though they may appear normal individually; finally, contextual anomalies appear suspicious only in specific contexts, such as particular temporal or spatial conditions. Through centralized control, the SDN controller can distinguish and classify these anomalies, ensuring that responses are appropriate to the severity and type of threat [13]. Despite the advantages offered by centralized control in SDN networks, this structure also introduces significant vulnerabilities. As the system's critical point, the controller is an attractive target for attackers, as compromising it can have widespread repercussions across the entire network. In particular, the open programmability of the SDN architecture exposes the controller to a range of threats, such as Distributed Denial of Service (DDoS) attacks aimed at overloading the controller's resources and reducing its responsiveness, or "man-in-the-middle" attacks that exploit open interfaces between the control and data planes. To mitigate these risks, the introduction of ML algorithms has been explored as a method to enhance the security of SDN controllers. The ML approach applied to intrusion detection allows for the prediction of attacks and abnormal behaviors by analyzing historical traffic patterns and identifying emerging threats. Various categories of ML algorithms, including supervised, unsupervised, and Deep Learning (DL), are trained on datasets that represent known network behaviors historically associated with attacks. Thanks to the implementation of ML, the controller can dynamically adapt to network traffic and prevent risks arising from new attacks. Since Deep Neural Networks (DNNs) can autonomously analyze large amounts of data and detect anomalies, the use of DL enables the SDN controller to develop more advanced detection and response capabilities, reducing the likelihood of false positives and improving network response [14]. With regard to emerging NFV technology, it has radically changed the approach to managing essential network middleboxes such as IDSs, network address translators, and firewalls. Thanks to NFV, these functions, traditionally tied to dedicated hardware, can now be implemented as software applications running on standard servers. This approach provides significant benefits in terms of programmability, scalability, and management, allowing administrators to organize network defenses more dynamically and effectively to adapt to a variety of cyberattacks [15]. However, commonly adopted NFV solutions present certain limitations. Virtualized IDS implementations are often treated as monolithic software, where the entire system functions as a single entity to detect and mitigate intrusions. This approach introduces significant constraints in cloud-based applications, limiting overall efficiency. The monolithic structure prevents flexible distribution of IDS components, generating inefficiencies in resource allocation and limiting opportunities for sharing and distribution across different systems [16].

5. Benefits of programmability in network security

With the evolution of telecommunication networks, technologies such as SDN and NFV have revolutionized the approach to network management and security. The programmability provided by these technologies enables flexible and dynamic management of network resources, allowing rapid responses to threats and enabling novel defense strategies against increasingly sophisticated and adaptive attacks. The benefits of programmability are described below and summarized in **Table 2**.

5.1 Simplified and centralized management

The programmability offered by SDN enables centralized network management through logical and direct control of the data plane via well-defined APIs. This allows administrators to easily configure security policies and dynamically optimize network resources, significantly reducing the human effort required [17, 18]. Furthermore, the virtualization of security functions through NFV facilitates unified resource management via a central controller, enabling automated and reactive interventions [17].

5.2 Reduction of operational costs and increased flexibility

The adoption of commodity servers for virtualizing security functions, instead of traditional hardware-based middleboxes, results in a significant reduction in implementation costs. These servers allow for flexible activation or deactivation of security functions during runtime, allowing administrators to quickly adapt to dynamic attack patterns [17]. Virtualization also reduces hardware dependency, allowing for more cost-effective and versatile implementation in traditional network environments [18].

5.3 Enhanced security and anomaly detection

The integration of SDN and NFV, known as SDNFV, significantly improves the detection and mitigation of security issues. Machine Learning-based solutions leverage network programmability to identify anomalous flows and suspicious behaviors, increasing the effectiveness of defense strategies. Furthermore, this architecture supports the development of software-based IDS and other distributed security functions, such as edge-based firewalls [19].

5.4 Support for innovation and adaptability to new scenarios

SDNFV programmability promotes the implementation of new security mechanisms designed to adapt to an ever-evolving landscape of network services and applications. Innovative applications developed on SDNFV include dynamic access control, load balancing, and caching in IoT contexts, demonstrating its adaptability to diverse scenarios [18, 19].

5.5 Integration of networking and virtualization

The SDNFV architecture combines the traditional network management capabilities of SDN with the virtualization of network functions provided by NFV, simplifying resource utilization and optimizing services. This integrated approach efficiently addresses security concerns related to applications or services within the network [19].

Benefit	Description	Practical implications for IDS	Enabling technologies
Simplified centralized management [17, 18]	SDN enables centralized management via APIs, optimizing network resources and simplifying security policies. NFV facilitates unified management through a central controller.	Enhances control and dynamic updates for IDS by centralizing network monitoring and configuration.	SDN, NFV
Reduction in operational costs and flexibility [17, 18]	Commodity servers virtualize security functions at lower costs compared to hardware middleboxes, allowing dynamic adaptation to threats.	Enables cost-effective implementation of scalable IDS, adaptable to changes in traffic and attack patterns.	NFV
Improved security and anomaly detection [19]	SDNFV supports advanced detection through ML solutions and enables distributed IDS and edge-based firewalls.	Empowers IDS with ML models for proactive anomaly detection and effective distribution of security functions.	SDN, NFV, ML
Support for innovation and adaptability to emerging scenarios [18, 19]	SDNFV fosters innovative security mechanisms and applications to address the evolving network landscape.	Allows the development of customized IDS for specific scenarios, such as IoT and dynamic environments.	SDNFV
Network and virtualization integration [19]	SDNFV integrates network management with virtualization, simplifying resource utilization and optimizing services.	Supports optimized IDS deployment by leveraging virtualized resources and improving operational efficiency.	SDNFV

Table 2.
Benefit of programmability in network security.

6. Integration of IDS with artificial intelligence (AI)

AI integration has revolutionized IDS, addressing the limitations of traditional methods like feature recognition and anomaly detection in handling complex attacks. Techniques such as ML, pattern recognition, genetic algorithms, neural networks, and DL models significantly enhance detection and response capabilities in modern network security. AI-powered IDS systems excel in rapid, efficient threat detection, minimizing resource usage while enhancing performance. Grid algorithms optimize monitoring by dividing networks into manageable zones, improving coverage, and reducing system strain. Automated threat management further enhances precision and bolsters overall network security. The main advantages of AI-powered IDS include [20]:

Robust information processing capabilities. AI-enhanced IDS systems can monitor and analyze large volumes of network data, ensuring high accuracy and authenticity of the information. This capability is crucial, as modern networks generate an ever-growing amount of complex and uncertain data that traditional methods struggle to process effectively. AI allows IDS to handle this information with precision, enabling rapid threat identification without compromising monitoring quality.

AI-network management collaboration. AI introduces a high level of coordination and consistency in network management, significantly improving IDS performance. As network infrastructures expand and are applied in a growing number of everyday applications, the complexity of managing these networks increases. AI enables multi-level management, automatically adapting to network changes, and ensuring consistency in security and operational processes.

Resource consumption optimization. The ability of AI to analyze network data and make real-time decisions optimizes resource utilization. By reducing the complexity of the processed data and improving the processing speed, AI minimizes resource consumption, facilitating a more efficient use of network infrastructure. The integration of AI within IDS therefore represents a paradigm shift, providing enhanced scalability, adaptability, and robustness in protecting modern dynamic network environments.

6.1 AI techniques used in IDS implementations

Below are some of the many AI techniques used in network security, which are subsequently summarized in **Table 3**.

Support Vector Machine (SVM). SVM is a widely used classification technique in the machine learning literature, known for its high performance in classification and prediction tasks. The fundamental principle of SVM is to map the input vector into a higher-dimensional feature space and obtain the optimal separating hyperplane in this higher-dimensional space. When the two classes are not separable, slack variables are introduced, and a cost parameter is assigned to the overlapping data points [22, 30].

K-Nearest Neighbors (KNN). KNN associates new data with existing ones based on similarity using metrics such as Euclidean distance. Widely used in pattern recognition, classification, and regression, recent applications have combined KNN with clustering to improve attack detection by selecting a limited number of features. Despite its high accuracy in controlled scenarios, the method suffers in the presence of large or dynamic datasets [22, 23].

Random Forest (RF). RF uses multiple decision trees to make collective predictions, which proves particularly useful for intrusion detection in network and cloud environments. This technique has been tested on datasets such as DARPA for complex attacks, demonstrating superior accuracy and efficiency with large datasets such as network traffic. However, high processing times may limit its use in real-time applications [22, 24].

Fuzzy Logic (FL). FL techniques are applied in the context of cybersecurity and intrusion detection by assigning data to one or more clusters based on a membership score. This approach has proven to be effective in classifying attacks on datasets such as KDD99. Although its accuracy is better than other clustering methods, detection is limited to a modest percentage of total attacks and suffers from variable stability [22, 27].

Artificial Neural Networks (ANNs). ANNs mimic the structure of the human brain through multiple interconnected layers, offering a simplified representation of the nonlinear relationship between input and output, combined with high computational speed [26]. Used in areas such as intrusion classification and the detection of hidden weapons, ANNs can classify data as normal or abnormal. However, performance may depend significantly on the quality and size of training data [22].

Hybrid classifiers and ensemble techniques. To enhance IDS monitoring capabilities, many researchers suggest a hybrid approach that combines anomaly detection and signature-based techniques. Anomaly detection techniques help identify new (zero-day) attacks, while signature-based methods detect known attacks. Ensembles,

AI technique	Description	Applications in IDS	Pros and cons
Support Vector Machine (SVM) [21, 22]	Uses a hyperplane to separate data classes, mapping input vectors x into a high-dimensional feature space Z through nonlinear mapping.	Classification of normal and anomalous traffic, selection of relevant features, detection, and prediction of attacks.	Pros: High classification accuracy; Cons: Unsuitable for complex datasets.
K-Nearest Neighbors (KNN) [22, 23]	Classifies based on similarity to existing data.	Widely used in pattern recognition, classification, and regression.	Pros: High accuracy in structured datasets; Cons: Ineffective in environments with large data volumes.
Random Forest (RF) [22, 24]	Combines decision trees to make robust and accurate predictions.	Detection of complex attacks in networks and cloud environments.	Pros: Efficient with large datasets; Cons: High processing time for real-time data.
Fuzzy Logic (FL) [22, 25]	Clustering with fuzzy membership to handle imprecise or uncertain data.	Classification of intrusions grouped by similar characteristics.	Pros: Higher precision compared to other clustering methods; Cons: Requires accurate fuzzy boundaries.
Artificial Neural Networks (ANNs) [22, 26]	Multilayer networks mimicking human neural processes for complex analysis, simplifying nonlinear input-output relationships.	Classification of intrusions and detection of complex anomaly patterns.	Pros: Autonomous learning of relationships in data; Cons: Highly dependent on training and data quality.
Machine Learning (ML) [25, 27]	The ability of a system to improve its performance on a specific task through learning from data.	Used for classifying and predicting new attacks, continuously adapting to evolving network data.	Pros: Continuous learning; Cons: Complex management and requires labeled data for training.
Neural Networks (NNs) [27, 28]	Models that learn complex patterns from data using learning algorithms.	Predict anomalous behaviors based on past attack data, detecting variations and anomalies.	Pros: High tolerance to imprecise data; Cons: Requires training and may suffer from overfitting.
Hybrid classifiers [27, 29]	Systems combining multiple ML methods to enhance detection capabilities and reduce false positives.	Improve detection across all attack classes, achieving better performance for known and novel attacks.	Pros: Comprehensive detection; Cons: Potential implementation complexity and risk of overload.
Knowledge-based expert systems [20]	Systems using predefined rule databases to analyze user behavior and identify suspicious activities by comparing them with known intrusions.	Used for rule-based intrusion detection, ensuring immediate actions like blocking unauthorized access.	Pros: Accurate detection of known threats; immediate response; Cons: Limited handling of new threats not in the database.
Deep Learning models [20]	DNNs analyzing local characteristics of data packets using convolutional and pooling layers to reduce data complexity.	Advanced intrusion detection through detailed traffic analysis; adaptation to new threats via DL.	Pros: High precision; adaptive capability for new threats; Cons: Requires large datasets and computational resources.

Table 3.
Comparison of AI techniques applied to IDS.

composed of multiple classifiers, have been proposed to address the issue of detecting all attack classes with an acceptable false positive rate. The use of multiple classifiers, as in the work [31], has shown that the ensemble approach can improve the performance in classifying intrusions using specific datasets such as KDD 1998 [27].

Deep Learning models. Deep Learning models, such as Convolutional Neural Networks (CNNs), represent an advanced level of intrusion detection evolution. CNNs apply advanced mathematical models with multiple network layers, including convolutional and pooling layers, allowing the system to deep learn the characteristics of data packets. Convolutional algorithms are capable of analyzing local features of network traffic in detail, reducing the impact of data complexity and high dimensionality. The adaptive capability of the model thus improves the detection accuracy and allows a faster response to new threats [20]. This trend is further improved by recent advancements in distributed AI techniques, such as the Federated Learning technique [32, 33].

7. SDN-based IDS implementation in a programmable network

In this section, a practical example of IDS deployment leveraging SDN-based programmable networks is detailed.

7.1 Preliminary theoretical background for implementing SDN-based IDS

The integration of programmable networks and AI-based IDS leverages the SDN controller's holistic view to deploy ML/DL models. By analyzing packet flow patterns, the controller detects and infers malicious activities in the network. In this deployment, the function to be considered on the controller is not only limited to the ML/DL model. In fact, AI models must be fed with specific features that are capable of properly representing the domain of interest. In other words, a function that permits moving from the domain of "flows of packets" to the domain of "network features" is needed. An example, in this sense, is using a batch of gathered packet header information to compute network features, like inter-arrival times or average packet size, to model a particular behavior (e.g., malicious or not). In this regard, let F denote a set of network flows such that: $F = \{f_1, f_2, \ldots, f_i, \ldots, f_n\}$. A generic flow $f_i \in F$ can be defined as the set of packets that share the same 5-tuple γ. More specifically: $\gamma(f_i) = \{src\_ip^{f_i}, dst\_ip^{f_i}, src\_port^{f_i}, dst\_port^{f_i}, protocol^{f_i}\}$. The γ function that determines the unique association between packets and the flow to which they belong must then satisfy the following property:

$$\forall f_1, f_2 \in F, f_1 \neq f_2, \gamma(f_1) = ft_{f1}, \gamma(f_2) = ft_{f2} \ s.t. \ ft_{f_1} \neq ft_{f_2} \tag{1}$$

To optimize memory storage, the 5-tuple is then hashed in order to create, for each flow $f \in F$ a unique identifier:

$$\begin{aligned} id^{f_i} &= Hash(\gamma(f_i)) \ where \\ \gamma(f_i) &= (src\_ip^{f_i}, dst\_ip^{f_i}, src\_port^{f_i}, dst\_port^{f_i}, protocol^{f_i}) \end{aligned} \tag{2}$$

Once each flow of the network can be indexed using this approach, packets can be collected per flow, and the extraction of the flow-relevant feature can be executed. More specifically, a feature extractor can be defined as a function $\theta : F \rightarrow \Psi$, where Ψ defines the set of network features considered for the computation. Ψ is a finite set whose size is fixed and determined by the network administrator, or it can depend on the dataset used to train the ML/DL model. Finally, once extracted, the set of network features is used to feed the ML/DL model that can also be defined as a function M:

$$M : \Psi \rightarrow C, \ with \ C = \{Benign, Malicious\} \tag{3}$$

Finally, **Figure 1** shows the architectural organization of an SDN-based AI-driven deployment denoting the functions defined in this section, along with their interactions and required data.

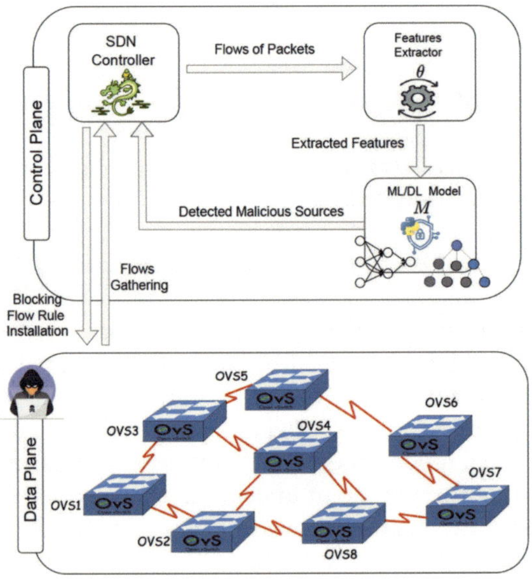

Figure 1.
SDN-based AI-driven deployment setting.

7.2 Implementation

A practical implementation of the architecture described in **Figure 1** is provided. The system is composed of an SDN controller implemented using the Python3 Ryu SDN controller, properly modified to accommodate the γ and M functions. More specifically, γ has been implemented using the cicflowmeter feature extractor [34]. The M function, i.e. the ML/DL models, have been implemented using Scikit-Learn and TensorFlow Python 3 libraries. Two types of AI models have been tested: Random Forest (RF) and Deep Neural Network (DNN). These models have been trained and tested using the CSE-CIC-IDS 2018 dataset [35] with a train-split ratio of 0.7–0.3. Concerning the models, a Random Forest composed of nine decision trees, each with a maximum depth of seven, has been considered. These values have been chosen after performing a five-fold grid search driven by performance indicator metrics such as accuracy, precision, recall, and F1-score. For the DNN, we inspired [36] a simple but powerful architecture that achieves good performance when dealing with anomaly detection. The model is composed of three hidden layers with 12, 6, and 3 neurons, respectively. The hidden layers, enhanced with the ReLu activation function, end up at the output layer that uses the *softmax* activation functions to compute the probability that a flow is malicious or benign. After pre-processing the dataset by removing non-important features using feature selection and importance techniques, such as Pearson Correlation and Mean Decrease Impurity Random Forest method [3], 72 input features from the dataset have been considered, on which both AI models have been trained and tested. The parameters used to conduct the experimental campaign are summarized in **Table 4**.

7.3 Analyzed IDS dataset

The CSE-CIC-IDS2018 dataset [35] is a comprehensive intrusion detection dataset designed to emulate real-world network traffic and modern attack scenarios. It was developed collaboratively by the Canadian Institute for Cybersecurity (CIC) and the Communications Security Establishment (CSE). The dataset is a cornerstone for research in IDS, particularly for evaluating machine learning-based approaches. The dataset was generated using a testbed simulating a realistic corporate environment with multiple users, servers, and other network elements. It includes traffic generated by normal users performing typical activities such as browsing, email, file transfers, and other legitimate operations. The dataset was collected over 5 days (Monday to Friday), where specific attacks were executed at scheduled times while normal traffic was maintained consistently. A simulated testbed included multiple subnets, servers (e.g., web servers, email servers, file servers), and client machines, mimicking a realistic enterprise network. The dataset consists of 80+ features derived from network flow statistics. These features fall into categories such as basic attributes like packet size, duration, and protocol. But also time-based (inter-arrival times, flow duration) and statistical (means, standard deviations, and counts of packets and bytes) attributes. Finally, the dataset contains various and up-to-date attack types, reflecting real-world threats in modern networks. Some major attack types include: brute-force attacks, Denial of Service (DoS), Distributed Denial of Service (DDoS)

Setting	Information
AI models	RF, DNN
Simulation time	300 s
Benign hosts	150
Malicious host	150
SDN controller	Ryu
Injected malicious and benign flows	Wednesday-14-02-2018_TrafficForML_CICFlowMeter
	Wednesday-21-02-2018_TrafficForML_CICFlowMeter
	Wednesday-28-02-2018_TrafficForML_CICFlowMeter
Training and testing dataset	Friday-16-02-2018_TrafficForML_CICFlowMeter
	Friday-23-02-2018_TrafficForML_CICFlowMeter
	Friday-02-03-2018_TrafficForML_CICFlowMeter
	Thursday-15-02-2018_TrafficForML_CICFlowMeter
	Thursday-22-02-2018_TrafficForML_CICFlowMeter
	Thursday-01-03-2018_TrafficForML_CICFlowMeter

Table 4.
Experimental setup information.

attacks [37], web attacks, and botnets. This cybersecurity dataset is extremely utilized in academic research due to the nature of the captured data, which represents real network traffic patterns.

7.4 Results

We evaluated the capabilities of both RF and the considered DNN against metrics such as accuracy, F1-score, False Positive Rate (FPr), and False Negative Rate (FNr). In particular, the last two metrics are paramount when it comes to malicious anomaly detection. While the first represents the number of benign flows wrongly classified as malicious—causing additional overhead for the system—the latter is a more critical and severe issue. In fact, FN denotes malicious flows wrongly classified as benign. These are malicious traces that are allowed to pass through the security system and flow directly to the victim target. Through these metrics, we evaluate the SDN-based AI-driven IDS in counteracting malicious flows. In order to provide a comprehensive test, we evaluated the system through an online simulation of 300 s. Within the simulation time, 300 clients are connected to the SDN network, and half of them inject malicious traffic. In this simulation, malicious and benign flows from unseen entries in the CSE-CIC-IDS 2018 dataset are crafted and sent through the network, being classified by the IDS running on the SDN controller. More than a million traffic traces have been injected into the network, considering a balanced distribution among benign and malicious traces.

7.4.1 DNN-based IDS results

In **Figure 2(a)**, the results of the analysis of FPr and FNr on the injected network traffic flows are shown. More specifically, these results highlight the effectiveness of the model in distinguishing between malicious and benign traffic. Indeed, the DNN shows an extremely low value for FPr, almost close to zero, i.e., 0.0017. The same considerations can be made for the FNr, which is also negligible with a value equal to 0.0046. These results directly affect the remaining performance metrics: accuracy, precision, recall, and F1-score. The results concerning these metrics are summarized in **Table 5**. Additionally, these results are further

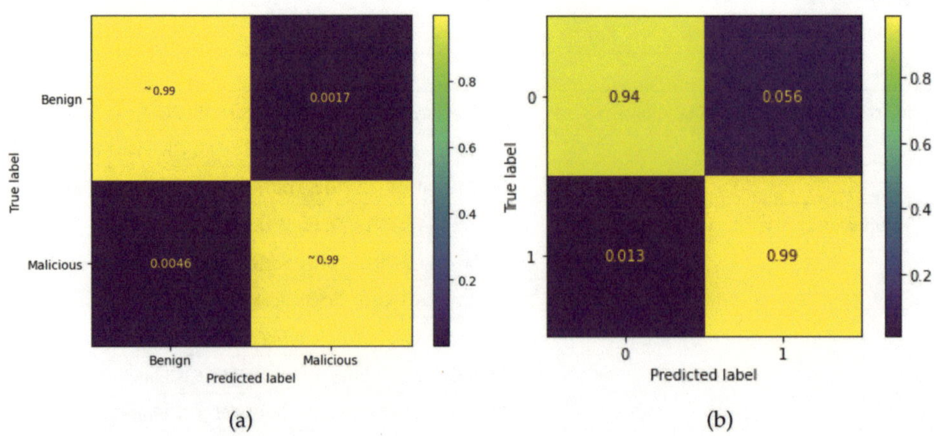

Figure 2.
Confusion matrix for the considered (a) DNN and (b) RF.

confirmed by the performance demonstrated by DNN during training and testing time. **Figure 3** depicts the accuracy and the loss of the DNN considered during training, comparing it with the validation test. These results are obtained during the training of the DNN over 5 epochs. The number of epochs is obtained, instead, through the use of the EarlyStopping technique, optimizing the number of epochs for the training and therefore avoiding long and time-wasting training procedures.

7.4.2 RF-based IDS results

Also for the RF-based IDS, the same experiment has been conducted to assess the two approaches under the same experimental conditions. **Table 6** shows the results of the performance metrics. While **Figure 2(b)** is the relevant confusion matrix. The RF-based IDS shows slightly worse performance compared to the DNN-based approach. However, the results can still be considered extremely valid and noteworthy in terms of security. In fact, RF-based IDS is capable of achieving low values for FPr and FNr while guaranteeing an accuracy of 94%. Finally, on the basis of the conducted experiments, it is worth noticing that the two approaches are capable of providing comparable results in terms of security and detection capabilities. These results are therefore crucial since they highlight the potential of the usage of both deep learning and machine learning techniques as valid alternatives to meet application-specific and network-relevant constraints and requirements.

Metric	Value
Accuracy	0.9527
F1-score	0.8985
Precision	0.8249
Recall	0.9865

Table 5.
Performance metrics for the RF-based IDS.

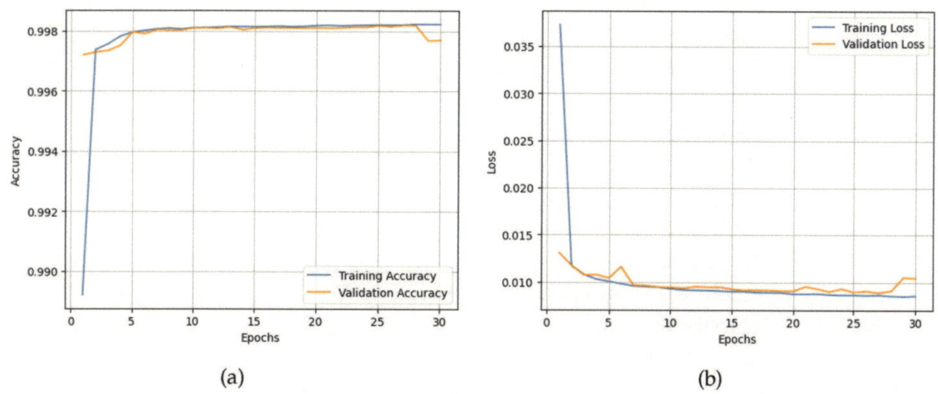

Figure 3.
DNN offline performance with (a) accuracy and (b) loss evaluations.

Metric	Value
Accuracy	0.99771
F1-score	0.99854
Precision	0.99877
Recall	0.99832

Table 6.
Performance metrics for the DNN-based IDS.

8. Conclusions

The growing development of telecommunication networks, coupled with the proliferation of connected devices, has led to increasingly complex challenges in cybersecurity. This work explores emerging technologies and their applications for intrusion detection in diverse network contexts, highlighting how the adoption of innovative IDS solutions is essential to counter evolving threats. The network programmability enabled by technologies such as SDN and NFV has been shown to enhance IDS capabilities, enabling more flexible and dynamic network security management, particularly in complex and highly mobile infrastructures such as IoTs, Mobile Ad-hoc NETworks (MANETs), Vehicular Ad-hoc NETworks (VANETs), Flying Ad-hoc NETworks (FANETs), and Wireless Sensor Networks (WSNs).

Acknowledgements

This work was partially supported by project SERICS (PE000 00014) under the MUR National Recovery and Resilience Plan funded by the European Union - NextGenerationEU.

Abbreviations

AI	artificial intelligence
ANN	artificial neural network
CNN	convolutional neural network
DDoS	distributed denial of service
DL	deep learning
DNN	deep neural network
DoS	Denial of Service
FL	fuzzy logic
IDS	intrusion detection system
KNN	K-nearest neighbors
ML	machine learning
NBI	northbound interface
NFV	network function virtualization
NIDS	network intrusion detection system
OVS	Open v-Switch
RF	random forest

SBI	southbound interface
SDN	software-defined networking
SVM	support vector machine

Author details

Mauro Tropea[1,2*†], Mattia Giovanni Spina[1,2†] and Floriano De Rango[1,2†]

1 DIMES Department, University of Calabria, Italy

2 CNIT – National Inter-University Consortium for Telecommunications, Italy

*Address all correspondence to: m.tropea@dimes.unical.it

†These authors contributed equally

References

[1] Vaid P, Bhadu SK, Vaid RM. Intrusion detection system in software defined network using machine learning approach-survey. In: 2021 6th International Conference on Communication and Electronics Systems (ICCES). Coimbatre, India: IEEE; 08-10 July 2021. pp. 803-807

[2] Spina MG, Tropea M, De Rango F. Mitigation of LLDP Topological Poisoning Attack in SDN Environments Using Mininet Emulator. In: Simultech. Rome, Italy; 12-14 July 2023. pp. 318-325

[3] Salatino F, Spina MG, Tropea M, De Rango F. Detecting DDoS Attacks Through AI driven SDN Intrusion Detection System. In: 2024 IEEE 21st Consumer Communications & Networking Conference (CCNC). Las Vegas, NV, USA: IEEE; 6-09 January 2024. pp. 990-993

[4] Nunes BAA, Mendonca M, Nguyen XN, Obraczka K, Turletti T. A survey of software-defined networking: Past, present, and future of programmable networks. IEEE Communications Surveys & Tutorials. 2014;**16**(3):1617-1634

[5] Kodali SK, Muntean CH. An investigation into deep learning based network intrusion detection system for iot systems. In: 2021 IEEE International Conference on Data Science and Computer Application (ICDSCA). Dalian, China: IEEE; 29-31 October, 2021. pp. 374-377

[6] Spina MG, Tropea M, De Rango F. SURA-LB: Software-defined IDS with UAV resource aware load-balancing in FANET disaster scenarios. Computer Communications. 2024;**223**:101-114

[7] Tropea M, Spina MG, De Rango F. Supporting dynamic ids deployment with load balancing strategy for sdn-enabled drones in emergency scenarios. In Proceedings of the Int'l ACM Conference on Modeling Analysis and Simulation of Wireless and Mobile Systems. Montreal, Canada; 30 October 2023 - 3 November 2023. pp. 297-300

[8] Zang M, Yan Y. Machine learning-based intrusion detection system for big data analytics in VANET. In: 2021 IEEE 93rd Vehicular Technology Conference (VTC2021-Spring). Helsinki, Finland: IEEE; 25-28 April 2021. pp. 1-5

[9] Farooq Y, Beenish H, Fahad M. Intrusion detection system in wireless sensor networks-A comprehensive survey. In: 2019 Second International Conference on Latest trends in Electrical Engineering and Computing Technologies (INTELLECT). Karachi, Pakistan: IEEE; 13-14 November 2019. pp. 1-6

[10] Masoudi R, Ghaffari A. Software defined networks: A survey. Journal of Network and Computer Applications. 2016;**67**:1-25

[11] Mahalingam M, Dutt D, Duda K, Agarwal P, Kreeger L, Sridhar, T, et al. Virtual extensible local area network (VXLAN): A framework for overlaying virtualized layer 2 networks over layer 3 networks (No. RFC7348). 2014

[12] Mijumbi R, Serrat J, Gorricho JL, Bouten N, De Turck F, Boutaba R. Network function virtualization: State-of-the-art and research challenges. IEEE Communications Surveys & Tutorials. 2015;**18**(1):236-262

[13] Bhardwaj A, Tyagi R, Sharma N, Khare A, Punia MS, Garg VK. Network

intrusion detection in software defined networking with self-organized constraint-based intelligent learning framework. Measurement: Sensors. 2022;**24**:100580

[14] Mustafa Z, Amin R, Aldabbas H, Ahmed N. Intrusion detection systems for software-defined networks: A comprehensive study on machine learning-based techniques. Cluster Computing. 2024;**27**:9635-9661

[15] Kengalahalli NV. Implementing lightweight intrusion detection systems based on network function virtualization. In: The Colloquium for Information System Security Education (CISSE). 2018

[16] Zhang N, Li H, Hu H, Park Y. Towards effective virtualization of intrusion detection systems. In: Proceedings of the ACM International Workshop on Security in Software Defined Networks & Network Function Virtualization. Scottsdale, Arizona, USA; 24 Mar 2017. pp. 47-50

[17] Chen X, Wu C, Liu X, Huang Q, Zhang D, Zhou H, et al. Empowering network security with programmable switches: A comprehensive survey. IEEE Communications Surveys & Tutorials. 2023;**25**(3):1653-1704

[18] Saeed R, Qureshi S, Farooq M, Zeeshan M. SDN/NFV enabled security for an enterprise network using commodity hardware. In: 2022 International Conference on Computing, Electronics & Communications Engineering (iCCECE). Southend, United Kingdom: IEEE; 17-18 August 2022. pp. 25-30

[19] Domínguez-Dorado M, Calle-Cancho J, Galeano-Brajones J, Rodríguez-Pérez FJ, Cortés-Polo D. Detection and mitigation of security threats using virtualized network functions in software-defined networks. Applied Sciences. 2023;**14**(1):374

[20] Lu C. Research on the technical application of artificial intelligence in network intrusion detection system. In: 2022 International Conference on Electronics and Devices, Computational Science (ICEDCS). Marseille, France: IEEE; 20-22 September 2022. pp. 109-112

[21] Vapnik V. The Nature of Statistical Learning Theory. Springer Science & Business Media; 2013

[22] Sowmya T, Anita EM. A comprehensive review of AI based intrusion detection system. Measurement: Sensors. 2023;**28**:100827

[23] Peng K, Leung VC, Zheng L, Wang S, Huang C, Lin T. Intrusion detection system based on decision tree over big data in fog environment. Wireless Communications and Mobile Computing. 2018;**2018**(1):4680867

[24] Htun PT, Khaing KT. Anomaly intrusion detection system using random forests and k-nearest neighbor. PRO. 2013;**41102**(4107):2377

[25] Patcha A, Park JM. An overview of anomaly detection techniques: Existing solutions and latest technological trends. Computer Networks. 2007;**51**(12):3448-3470

[26] Poojitha G, Kumar KN, Reddy PJ. Intrusion detection using artificial neural network. In: 2010 Second International Conference on Computing, Communication and Networking Technologies. Karur, India: IEEE; 29-31 July 2010. pp. 1-7

[27] Kumar G, Kumar K, Sachdeva M. The use of artificial intelligence based techniques for intrusion detection: A

review. Artificial Intelligence Review. 2010;**34**:369-387

[28] Shun J, Malki HA. Network intrusion detection system using neural networks. In: 2008 Fourth International Conference on Natural Computation. Vol. 5. Jinan, China: IEEE; 18-20 October 2008. pp. 242-246

[29] Fortuna C, Fortuna B, Mohorčič M. Anomaly detection in computer networks using linear SVMs. In: Proc. Conference on Data Mining and Data Warehouses. Ljubljana, Slovenia: SiKDD; 2007

[30] Tianfield H. Data mining based cyber-attack detection. System Simulation Technology. 2017;**13**(2):90-104

[31] Sabhnani M, Serpen G. Application of machine learning algorithms to KDD intrusion detection dataset within misuse detection context. In: MLMTA. Las Vegas, Nevada, USA; June 23 - 26 2003. pp. 209-215

[32] De Rango F, Guerrieri A, Raimondo P, Spezzano G. HED-FL: A hierarchical, energy efficient, and dynamic approach for edge federated learning. Pervasive and Mobile Computing. 2023;**92**:101804. DOI: 10.1016/j.pmcj.2023.101804

[33] Colosimo F, De Rango F. Dynamic gradient filtering in federated learning with byzantine failure robustness. Future Generation Computer Systems. 2024;**160**:784-797. DOI: 10.1016/j.future.2024.06.044

[34] cicflowmeter. Available from: https://pypi.org/project/cicflowmeter [Accessed: December 2024]

[35] Sharafaldin I, Lashkari AH, Ghorbani A. Toward generating a new intrusion detection dataset and intrusion traffic characterization. In: International Conference on Information Systems Security and Privacy. Funchal, Madeira, Portugal; 22-24 January 2018

[36] Tang TA, Mhamdi L, McLernon D, SAR Z, Ghogho M. Deep learning approach for network intrusion detection in software defined networking. In: 2016 International Conference on Wireless Networks and Mobile Communications (WINCOM). Fez, Morocco: IEEE; 26-29 October 2016. DOI: 10.1109/WINCOM.2016.7777224

[37] Fioravanti G, Spina MG, De Rango F. Entropy based DDOS detection in software defined networks. In: 2023 IEEE 20th Consumer Communications & Networking Conference (CCNC). Las Vegas, NV, USA: IEEE; 08-11 January 2023. pp. 636-639

Chapter 2

About Industrial Network Cybersecurity

Silvana Gamboa and Ricardo Mogro

Abstract

In this chapter a brief introduction to industrial automation and control systems (IACS) and industrial networks is provided, as well as their main differences with respect to information technology (IT) networks are identified. Next, cybersecurity issues in the industrial networks field and how this can influence the operation of IACS are presented. The most common vulnerabilities detected in industrial communications networks are also described. In addition, some of the current regulations in this field are presented, and the basic measures that must be applied to protect this type of network are suggested. Finally, a practical demonstration of vulnerabilities and cybersecurity rules application over a test IACS has been developed.

Keywords: vulnerability, cybersecurity, industrial automation and control system, industrial network, SCADA, programmable logic controller

1. Introduction

Until a couple of decades ago, industrial automation and control systems (IACS) and their industrial communication networks were seen as a complex and unattractive black box for cyberattacks. But this changed in 2010 with the event that many experts call the "World's First Digital Weapon Attack" [1], caused by the Stuxnet worm, whose victims were PLCs of the IACS of a nuclear power plant, with the apparent objective of interrupting its operation. This attack, among other things, showed how attractive IACS can be for cyberattackers, since they play a fundamental role in monitoring, protecting, and controlling critical sectors such as energy, manufacturing, water, or transportation.

Fourteen years after the first cyberattack on IACS, which put these systems in the crosshairs of experts, cybersecurity in industrial communication networks is on track and seeking to mature, but it still has to face old and new challenges. Among the old challenges, are the ever-present possibility of zero-day vulnerabilities in industrial automation and control devices or software, and even the reluctance to change of certain users. Among the new challenges, the current demands, such as Industry 4.0, which, among other things, have marked the current trend toward the convergence of IT and Operational Technology (OT) environments that has expanded the "attack surface of IACS," creating several edges that must be considered.

With this background, this document presents a brief summary of relevant aspects regarding the cybersecurity of IACS and their industrial communication networks, as well as a practical example to show the vulnerabilities of the IACS when its industrial network is integrated with an information network. In addition, it shows how the use of certain tools already available in industrial devices can strengthen the security of these systems.

2. Industrial automation and control system (IACS)

IACS is the system responsible for the automation of production tasks, as well as monitoring, control, protection, and security tasks of an industrial process with the aim of improving its operation. Since many devices are integrated into an IACS, a digital communication network, known as an industrial network, is responsible for enabling the exchange of information between such components that make up an IACS.

But IACS is not a new one in the industrial environment, as it has been present since the late 1700s when machinery was designed and developed for manufacturing. This system has evolved along with technological advances such as electronic computers and the Internet. Today, there has been great progress in digitalization and interconnectivity in industrial environments where industrial networks have gone from being isolated environments to becoming part of an organization's technological infrastructure, thanks to advances in information technology (IT), improving monitoring efficiency and its control and automation capacity.

However, this leads to the introduction of vulnerabilities and threats in the cyber field that did not exist before. These new threats to critical infrastructures imply catastrophic consequences such as the interruption of critical services, damage to expensive equipment, economic and human losses, and low credibility and reputation for the organization.

3. Industrial network cybersecurity issues

When talking about cybersecurity at IACSs, it is important to remember that the first time a cyber attack managed to damage the infrastructure of the "real world" was in January 2010 when the Stuxnet worm took control of the PLCs of 1000 machines that participated in the production of nuclear materials and gave them instructions to self-destruct [2].

As is well known, the objectives of cybersecurity are (1) *Confidentiality*, which aims to protect sensitive information from unauthorized access, (2) *Integrity*, which seeks to ensure that data and systems are not altered in an unauthorized manner, and (3) *Availability*, to guarantee that systems are operational and accessible when needed. In industrial environments, the main focus is on *availability*, since any interruption can have serious consequences, such as damage to equipment, risks to human safety, and economic losses.

3.1 Information network vs. industrial network

Although IT and OT are related, their goals and priorities are different. Understanding these differences is key to developing effective cybersecurity strategies in industrial environments; **Table 1** summarizes these differences.

Aspect	IT (Information Technology)	OT (Operational Technology)
Priority	Confidentiality and data integrity.	Availability and operational security.
Focus	Enterprise networks, servers, devices.	Physical equipment, SCADA systems, and PLCs.
Lifecycle	Frequent and rapid updates.	Equipment with long lifecycles.
Impact	Data loss or business process disruption.	Interruption of critical operations.

Table 1.
Comparison of IT (Information Technology) and OT (Operational Technology).

3.2 Actual vulnerability on industrial communication networks

The hacking process of an industrial network is not far from the process applied to business networks, so there is a starting point to know how this can be executed on IACS. But, at the same time, it is important to take into account that the industrial network has its representative characteristics, such as its need to be a deterministic network, as well as the need to have specialized devices, protocols, and interfaces, to which is added that patching or reconfiguring in order to minimize its vulnerability is not simple.

4. The cybersecurity risks in industrial networks

It is well known that industrial automation and control systems lack security in their design because they were largely designed before sound cybersecurity principles were established. Therefore, this section seeks to summarize the most representative attacks and vulnerabilities, as well as, applicable standards in industrial automation systems.

4.1 Applicable standards

The regulations used in the development of this document and their validity until the date of publication are described below:

ANSI/ISA 62443-4-2 (2018) - Security for Industrial Automation and Control Systems: Technical Security Requirements for IACS Components.

A set of guidelines for carrying out security risk assessments in industrial automation and control systems (IACS) is presented, and technical security requirements for their components are specified.

ISO 31000 (2018) - Risk management – Guidelines.

Principles and guidelines are provided for risk management in organizations of any type and size and are applicable to any type of risk.

ISO/IEC 27001 (2022) - Information security, cybersecurity and privacy protection – Information security management systems – Requirements.

Requirements are specified for the implementation, maintenance, and continuous improvement of information security management systems (ISMS).

NIST SP 800-50r1 (2023) -Building an Information Technology Security Awareness and Training Program.

It covers cybersecurity training and awareness, providing guidelines for developing, implementing, and maintaining cybersecurity programs in organizations. It includes 17 controls, grouped into 5 categories focused on the identification, evaluation, and management of information security risks.

NIST SP 800-61r2 (2012) - Computer Security Incident Handling Guide.

A guide to managing computer security incidents is described, providing guidelines for the selection and implementation of security controls.

NIST SP 800-82r3 (2023) - Guide to Industrial Control Systems (ICS) Security.

Guidance is provided on the security of industrial control systems (ICS), including SCADA and other critical systems, detailing guidelines for risk management, risk identification and assessment, implementing security controls, and monitoring and improving the security program.

NIST SP 800-94 (2007) - Guide to Intrusion Detection and Prevention.

Details about intrusion detection systems (IDS) and intrusion prevention systems (IPS) and guidelines for their implementation.

NIST SP 800-184 (2016) - Guide for Cybersecurity Event Recovery.

Comprehensive guidance is provided to improve organizations' preparedness and ability to respond to and recover from cybersecurity incidents.

UNE-EN IEC 62443-3-3 (2020) - Security for Industrial Automation and Control Systems: System Security Requirements and Security Levels.

Security requirements for industrial automation and control systems are presented, focusing on system security and secure design. A set of guidelines for the implementation of an information security management system (ISMS) in industrial control systems (ICS) is described.

4.2 Cyberattack categorization

It begins with a categorization of the most common cyber attacks and their effects on SCADA systems [3], which are summarized in **Table 2**.

4.3 Vulnerabilities identification

Vulnerabilities can be introduced into the industrial environment due to incomplete, inappropriate, or even non-existent security policies. System vulnerabilities can

Attacks	Description
Rootkits	A rootkit is a type of malware designed to hide detection processes and provide the attacker access at the highest level of the system. It starts undetectable processes and deceives malware detection mechanisms.
Buffer overflow	Occurs due to the absence of any boundary-checking mechanism. The attacker introduces more data than the buffer can hold, allowing overflow into adjacent memory, altering program behavior, and modifying its functionality. Servers controlling PLCs and RTUs are susceptible to this type of attack.
Code injection	The attacker gains access to a critical process in the system and inserts instructions or commands into data that are later executed.
Physical attacks on SCADA subsystems	SCADA systems, often covering large areas and sometimes located in remote sites, are vulnerable to physical attacks on subsystems. Attackers may gain physical access to subsystems, enabling attacks. Access control is, therefore, one of the primary security challenges.
Resource exhaustion	The attacker sends updates faster than the SCADA system's data acquisition server can process. While the attack does not take control of the system, it degrades its functionality.
Denial of Service attack (DoS)	The attacker sends commands, typically remotely, to limit resources required by SCADA subsystems, leaving them unresponsive to legitimate requests.

Table 2.
Most common cyberattacks and their effects on industrial network of SCADA systems.

occur at the hardware, firmware, and software levels and can be design flaws, development flaws, or poor equipment maintenance. Below are some of the most common vulnerabilities that can occur in an IACS [4], which have been classified according to the following categories: (1) IACS architecture and design, (2) Configuration and maintenance, (3) Communication network configuration, and (4) Physical and predisposing conditions, which are summarized from **Tables 3-6**. It is important to

Vulnerability	Description
Inadequate incorporation of security in architecture and design	Incorporating security into architecture and design starts with a designated budget and schedule. It should address user identification and authorization, access control mechanisms, network topology, and system configuration and integrity mechanisms.
Control networks used for uncontrolled traffic	Having both controlled and uncontrolled traffic on a single network can present challenges in meeting traffic control requirements.
Inadequate management of architectural changes	Network infrastructure often evolves due to operational and commercial requirements without considering potential security impacts. This can inadvertently introduce security breaches into the infrastructure. Security must be incorporated into change management for all operational devices.
Inadequate collection of event data logs	Without adequate data collection, it may be impossible to determine the cause of security incidents, potentially leading to undetected breaches or damage. Continuous monitoring is essential for ensuring security.

Table 3.
Vulnerabilities related to the IACS architecture and design.

Vulnerability	Description
Hardware, firmware, and software are not under asset management	Not knowing device models, their locations, or versions results in a poor defensive posture. There must be an accurate inventory of assets in the environment, along with procedures for managing additions, removals, and modifications, including asset inventory management.
Hardware, firmware, and software are not under configuration management	Lack of knowledge about patch management leads to an ineffective defensive posture. A process must be implemented to control modifications of hardware, firmware, and software with proper documentation to prevent improper changes.
Inadequate security change testing	Modifications to hardware, firmware, and software without prior testing could compromise the normal functioning of devices. Procedures must be in place to test and document changes.
Misconfigurations	Poorly configured systems may have open ports or unnecessary protocols, creating vulnerabilities and posing a greater risk to the system.
Critical configurations are neither backed up nor stored	Documented procedures must exist to restore device configurations in case of accidental or malicious changes initiated by an adversary.
Use of default vendor passwords	Default passwords provided by vendors are often easy to guess, increasing system vulnerability.
Inadequate access controls	Access controls must ensure that privileges align with the way the organization assigns responsibilities to personnel.
Malware protection not installed or outdated	Malware protection software must be kept up to date. When outdated, it leaves the system exposed to malware threats.
Denial of Service (DoS)	The software may be vulnerable to DoS attacks, preventing access to system resources or causing delays in operations and functions.

Table 4.
Vulnerabilities related to the configuration and maintenance.

Vulnerability	Description
Not using data flow controls	Data flow controls should be implemented based on the characteristics of the data to restrict information allowed between systems.
Misconfigured or non-existent firewalls	Misconfigured firewalls can allow unnecessary data to pass between networks, enabling attacks and malware to spread across networks, including control and corporate networks.
Deficient authentication of users, data, or devices	Many protocols lack authentication, making it possible to falsify data or devices, such as sensors and user identities.
Inadequate data protection between wireless clients and access points	Data between wireless clients and access points should be protected with strong encryption to prevent unauthorized access by adversaries.

Table 5.
Vulnerabilities related to the communication network configuration.

Vulnerability	Description
Unauthorized physical access to equipment	Physical access to equipment must be restricted solely to authorized personnel. Otherwise, it may lead to data and hardware theft, equipment damage or destruction, process alterations, or unauthorized changes to the functional environment.
Lack of backup power supply	If critical assets lose power, it may create an unsafe situation, causing undesired default configurations. If program data is stored in volatile memory, the process may not restart without adequate backup.
Unsecured physical ports	Unsecured PS/2 and USB ports can allow unauthorized connections of USB drives or keyloggers.
Unauthorized physical access to sensors or endpoint devices	If devices are configured on a field bus, unauthorized physical access to the sensor network can enable manipulation of control parameters, granting full physical access to the entire circuit.
Unauthorized wireless access to sensors or endpoint devices	If devices allow wireless configuration via Bluetooth, Wi-Fi, WirelessHART, etc., wireless access must be configured or disabled under secure protection to prevent unauthorized hardware modifications or alterations to sensors and endpoint devices.

Table 6.
Vulnerabilities related to the physical and predisposing conditions.

highlight that some of the most common vulnerabilities are present, requiring a more in-depth analysis of each process and its corresponding IACS.

5. Some applicable cybersecurity rules for industrial networks

To select the most appropriate treatment, a balance is raised between the benefits achieved against the costs, effort, or disadvantages of implementation [5]. The controls necessary to implement the information security risk treatment must be determined; each organization is able to design controls if necessary [6]. These controls can be grouped into the following categories [7]: (1) Organizational controls, (2) Physical controls, and (3) Technological controls. The technological controls are described in **Table 7** in this document.

Control	Description
Network segmentation and isolation	Implemented physically using network switches or logically using virtual local area network (VLAN) configurations.
Privileged access rights	The allocation and use of privileged access rights must be appropriately restricted and managed.
Access restriction to information	Access to information and related assets must be limited according to the specific access control policy established.
Identification and authentication of human users	Field devices must be capable of identifying and authenticating all human users through passwords, tokens, biometrics, or physical keys.
Wireless access management	Network devices supporting wireless access management must be capable of identifying and authenticating all users involved in communication.
Password-based authentication strength	Configurable password security should be enforced, including minimum length, character variety, or expiration time.
Failed login attempts	A configurable limit of consecutive invalid access attempts must be enforced, denying access for a specific period or until an administrator unlocks it.
System use notification	When providing access to human users or HMIs, a system use notification message must be displayed before authentication.
Authorization compliance	After verifying a user's identity, the control system must also ensure that the requested operation complies with security policies and procedures.
Wireless usage control	Devices and applications using wireless networks must include network admission control and implement different access limitations for wireless and wired devices.
Session lock	If the component provides a human user interface, it must protect against subsequent access by initiating a session lock after a configurable period of inactivity.
Concurrent session control	The number of simultaneous sessions per interface for any user must be limited.
Communication integrity	The network infrastructure must be designed to minimize physical/environmental effects, and components must verify the authenticity of received information during communication.
Source code access	Read and write access to source code, development tools, and software libraries must be adequately managed.
Malware protection	Implemented and supported through appropriate user awareness provided by the control system, service, or third-party applications.
Technical vulnerability management	Information about technical vulnerabilities of systems in use must be obtained, exposure to such vulnerabilities assessed, and necessary measures taken.
Configuration management	Hardware, software, services, and network configurations must be documented, monitored, and reviewed.
Input validation	Components must validate the syntax of input data, including out-of-range values, invalid characters, missing or incomplete data, buffer overflow, and manipulated information.
Deterministic output	Components must provide the ability to configure outputs to a predefined state if normal operation cannot be maintained.
Control system backup	Updated backups must be available for recovery from failures or incorrect control system configurations, including protection mechanisms and a list of maintained backups.

Control	Description
Control system recovery and reconstitution	Components are reinstalled and configured with established settings, the latest backup data is loaded, and the system is brought to a secure state after an interruption or failure.
Minimum functionality	Components must be capable of restricting the use of unnecessary functions, ports, protocols, and services.
Error handling	Error messages must provide useful information without revealing potentially harmful details.
Update support	Embedded devices must support patching and updates without affecting the essential functions of high-availability systems.
Boot process integrity	Embedded devices must verify the integrity of firmware, software, and configuration data required for boot processes.
Information deletion	Information stored in information systems, devices, or any other storage medium must be erased when no longer required.
Data masking	Must be used according to the organization's specific access control policy and related business and legal requirements.
Data leakage prevention	Measures must be implemented to prevent data leaks in systems, networks, and any devices handling, storing, or transmitting sensitive information.
Backup of information, software, and systems	Backups must be maintained and periodically tested according to the agreed specific backup policy.
Information processing facility redundancy	Information processing facilities must have sufficient redundancy to meet availability requirements.
Logging activities	Logs of activities, exceptions, failures, and other relevant events must be stored, protected, and analyzed.
Monitoring activities	Networks, systems, and applications must be monitored for anomalous behavior, and appropriate actions must be taken to evaluate potential cybersecurity incidents.
Software installation on operating systems	Procedures and measures must be established to effectively manage software installation on operating systems.
Network security	Networks and devices must be secured, managed, and controlled to protect information in systems and applications.
Network service security	Security mechanisms, service levels, and requirements for network services must be identified, implemented, and managed.
Cryptography usage	Rules for the effective use of cryptography, including key management, must be defined and implemented.

Table 7.
Controls for industrial networks.

6. Network vulnerability testing and application of protection guidelines

6.1 Implemented industrial network

For validating the proposed guidelines, a test IACS is implemented in the laboratory, the same one shown in **Figure 1**. The test system includes the 3 lower levels of the CIM model: (1) Field level 1, (2) Control level 2, and (3) Supervision level 3. The validation is carried out at levels 2 and 3, which are implemented as described in the following sections.

6.1.1 Control level and controller network

The control level is made up of a network of 4 PLCs connected via an Ethernet network, three of which act as RTUs and the other one acts as an MTU. The 4 controllers exchange data via a Modbus TCP network, for which the MTU has been configured as a Modbus client and the RTUs as Modbus servers. Each RTU is in charge of controlling a tank, while the client is in charge of centralizing the information from the RTUs, thus facilitating the exchange of data between the control level and the supervision level, communication that is also based on Modbus TCP.

A Modicon M580 PLC from Schneider is used as an MTU, and it is configured as a Modbus client for the remaining PLCs. On the other hand, this controller will function as a gateway between the controller network and the supervision network, for which Modbus TCP will also be used, but in this case, the MTU will function as a Modbus server for the DASMBTCP application in order to upload the data to the supervision level. Since the tests contemplate the modification of the Modbus registers of the MTU, these registers and their addresses are presented in **Table 8**.

Three Allen Bradley ML-1400 PLCs are configured as RTUs in the controller network. The three RTUs are programmed with the same liquid level control function for each tank, and the same Modbus map is used, the same one shown in **Table 9**.

6.1.2 Supervisory level and supervision network

The supervision level is made up of a network of 3 PCs with Windows operating systems where the industrial software applications are executed and which are integrated through a wireless network. The implemented stations are of two types: (1) operating station through an HMI, and (2) two engineering stations with programming and configuration software for the PLCs. As can be seen in **Figure 1**, the supervision network is made up of three stations, which are detailed below:

Operating station: PC with Windows Server 2008 R2 operating system, on which the HMI implemented in Wonderware Intouch and the DASMBTCP application are run.

Engineering station 1: PC with Windows 10 operating system with Unity Pro-XL software for programming the Modicon M580 PLC.

Engineering station 2: PC with Windows 10 operating system with RSLogix 500 Pro software for programming ML-1400 PLCs.

Variable name	Variable type	Address
Sensor 1	Holding register	%MW100
Sensor 2	Holding register	%MW102
Sensor 3	Holding register	%MW104
Setpoint 1	Holding register	%MW106
Setpoint 2	Holding register	%MW108
Setpoint 3	Holding register	%MW110
Valve 1	Holding register	%MW112
Valve 2	Holding register	%MW114
Valve 3	Holding register	%MW116

Table 8.
Modbus map for MTU.

Variable name	Variable type	Address
Valve command	Digital output	O:0/0
Level sensor	Analog input	I:1.0
Scaled level sensor	Holding register	N12:0
Setpoint level	Holding register	N12:1
Valve status	Holding register	N12:2

Table 9.
Modbus map for RTUs.

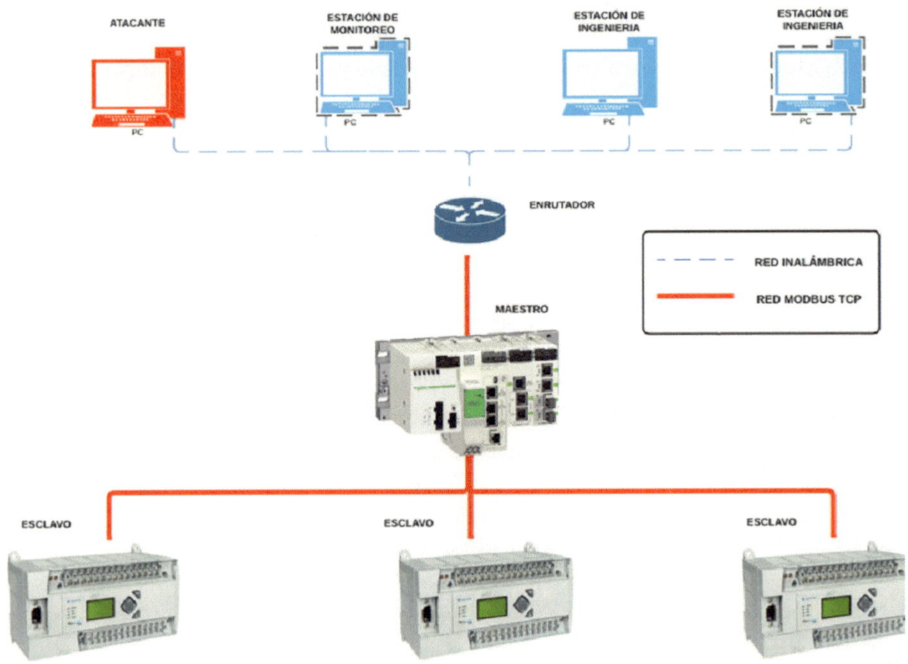

Figure 1.
Implemented industrial network for vulnerability testing.

6.2 Industrial network attack testing

The Kali Linux operating system is used to perform penetration testing on the test system, as well as the Metasploit framework exploit repository for security testing. For this purpose, a fourth PC running Kali Linux is integrated into the monitoring network and connected via the monitoring wireless network. The steps executed as part of the attack procedure are: (1) Reconnaissance, (2) Scanning, (3) Enumeration, and finally (4) Disruption; the execution of these steps will be described in the following sections.

6.2.1 Recognition

In this case, it is considered that passive reconnaissance was performed, and the attacker (e.g., an insider) collects information about this type of IACS, identifying the type of industrial communication protocol and the network address without directly interacting with the system.

6.2.2 Scanning

With the information obtained in the recognition stage, we proceed to perform scanning tests through *Nmap* of the Kali Linux tool in order to identify open logical processes and ports. Part of the execution of this test is shown in **Figure 2**.

6.2.3 Enumerating

Knowing that logical port 502 is open, the modbus_banner_grabbing exploit was executed, which will provide information such as the manufacturer and model of the device's CPU. This can be seen in **Figure 3** for the case of the PLC that acts as MTU.

Once the MTU CPU has been recognized, the Modbus registers reading test is carried out, which is executed through the Metasploit tool using the *ModbusClient* exploit. After the exploit is executed, the current values of the target registers are returned. The read registers are shown in **Figure 4**, and their values correspond to the process values collected by the MTU from the 3 RTUs which are displayed in the HMI shown in **Figure 5**.

6.2.4 Interruption

Finally, in order to compromise the system's operation, writing tests are carried out on the MTU registers, for which the *WRITE_REGISTERS* command was used. The configuration used to write the MTU registers one by one is shown in **Figure 6**. In this test, the values collected from the RTUs are overwritten, with 120 for the level setpoint, 30 for the measurement value, and the status of the valves, which now appear as off. This can also be seen in **Figure 7**, which corresponds to the values displayed on the HMI.

6.3 Application of security guidelines

The guidelines applied are organized under the criteria briefly described below.

Human User Identification and Authentication: Field devices must be able to identify and authenticate all human users at all interfaces capable of human access through the use of passwords, tokens, biometrics, or a physical key.

Information Access Control: Policies for managing physical and logical access to information and related assets must be defined and implemented in accordance with security requirements.

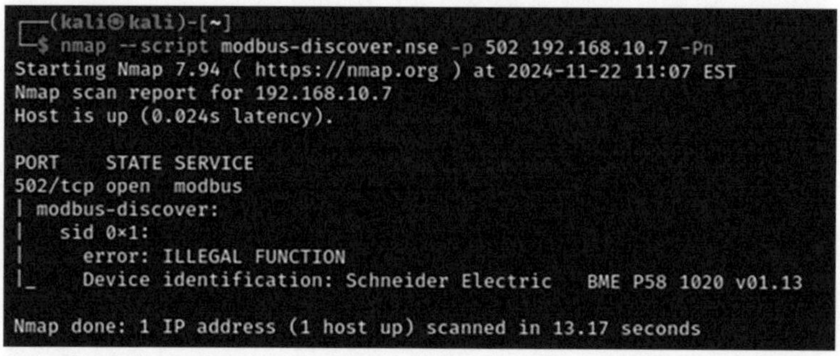

```
┌──(kali㉿kali)-[~]
└─$ nmap --script modbus-discover.nse -p 502 192.168.10.7 -Pn
Starting Nmap 7.94 ( https://nmap.org ) at 2024-11-22 11:07 EST
Nmap scan report for 192.168.10.7
Host is up (0.024s latency).

PORT    STATE SERVICE
502/tcp open  modbus
| modbus-discover:
|   sid 0x1:
|     error: ILLEGAL FUNCTION
|_    Device identification: Schneider Electric   BME P58 1020 v01.13

Nmap done: 1 IP address (1 host up) scanned in 13.17 seconds
```

Figure 2.
Nmap command execution for port 502 scanning.

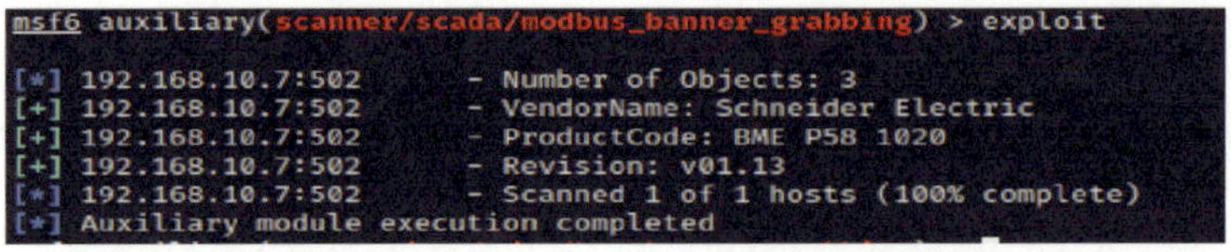

Figure 3.
Manufacturer and model device obtained using modbus_banner_grabbing exploit.

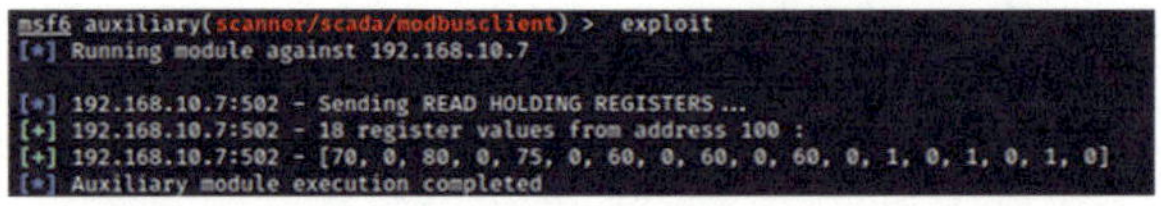

Figure 4.
MTU register values obtained using ModbusClient *exploit.*

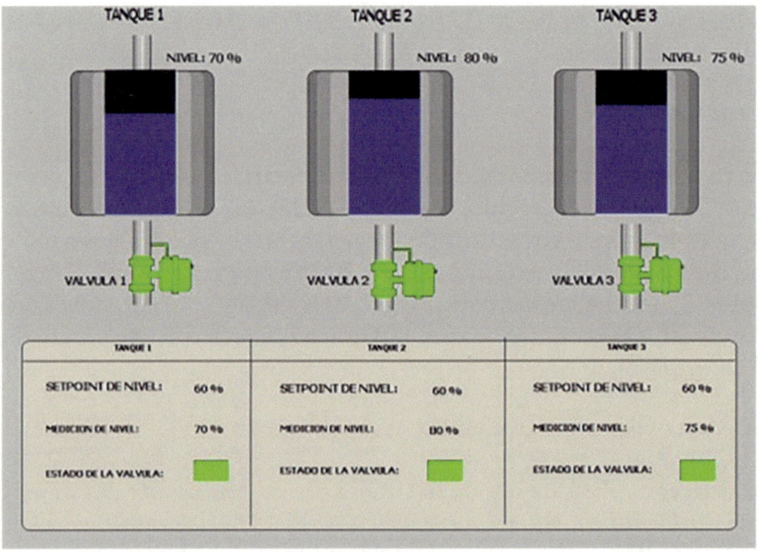

Figure 5.
Process values displayed on HMI in operating station.

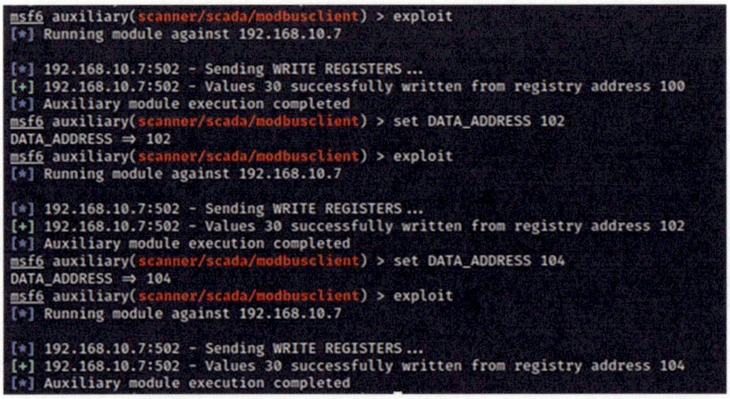

Figure 6.
MTU register values overwritten using ModbusClient *exploit.*

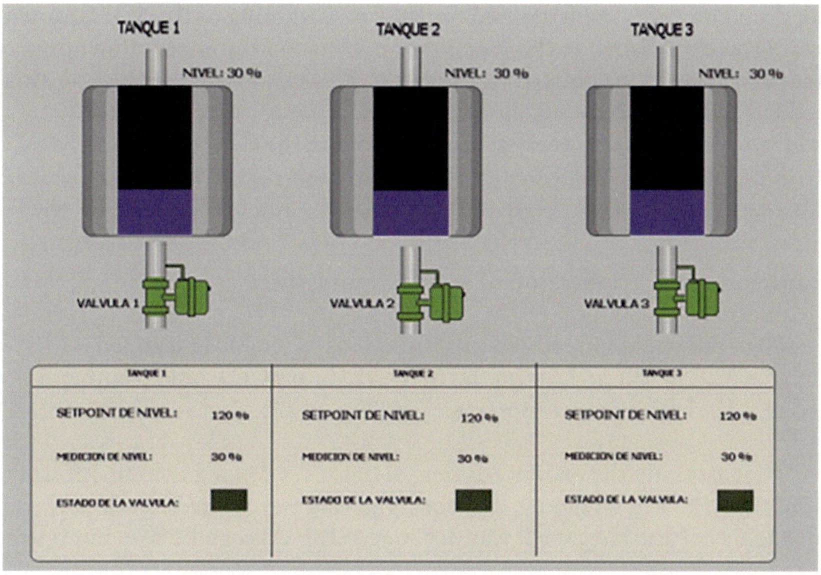

Figure 7.
Overwritten values displayed on HMI in operating station.

Minimum Functionality: Components must be able to specifically restrict the use of unnecessary functions, ports, protocols, and services. Devices must be thoroughly tested before being deployed in the OT network.

6.3.1 Human user identification and authentication

As part of the identification and authentication, password-based login is implemented, both for connecting to the wireless supervision network and for accessing the computers on this network.

6.3.2 Information access control and minimum functionality

As part of the access control, a "User Verification Window" was activated to identify the operator prior to using the HMI to enter the HMI of the operating station. As can be seen on the left of **Figure 8**, it is necessary to correctly enter the user name and password to enable the HMI option; this can be seen on the right of **Figure 8**. The guideline also establishes the use of the option to return to the user verification window at the end of the session so that a new login can be made through the use of credentials.

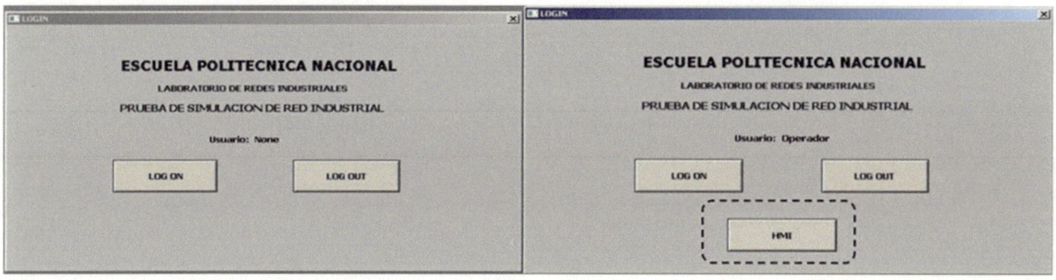

Figure 8.
User verification window in operating station.

Also, protection was implemented for the programming of the MTU, for which a password was established in the "Sections" option and the encryption option was activated. With these measures, the possibility of programming is blocked; this can be observed in **Figure 9**, where a padlock is shown in the security section.

In addition, an access control list is configured in the CPU of the MTU and the RTUs to limit the access of stations or PCs that are not part of the supervision network; this can be observed in **Figure 10** for the MTU and in **Figure 11** for the RTUs.

6.4 Evaluation of the application of security guidelines

To validate the implemented security functions, port 502 is scanned with *Nmap*. Although the PLC is still present on the network through the ping command, it is recorded that the logical port is not open (see **Figure 12**), that is, access control is achieved.

Also, when running the exploit *Modbus_Banner_Grabbing* to obtain information about the CPU and its model, it is observed that the connection through port 502 is not achieved and the attack was not successful; this can be seen in **Figure 13**.

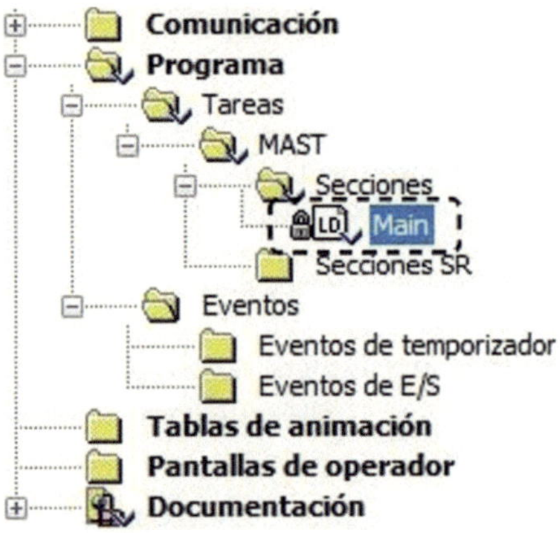

Figure 9.
Configuration of MTU programming protection.

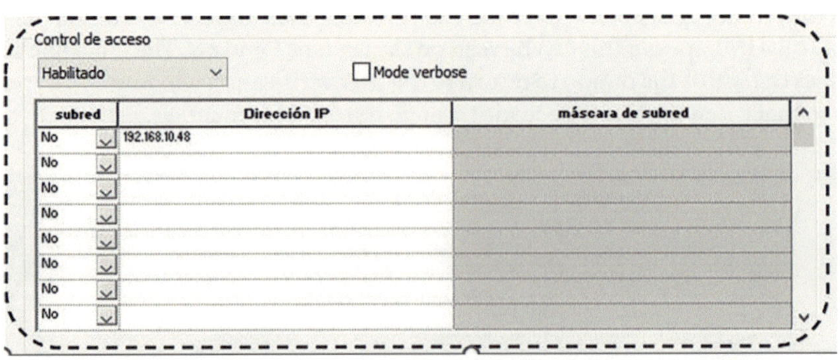

Figure 10.
Configuring access control list on MTU.

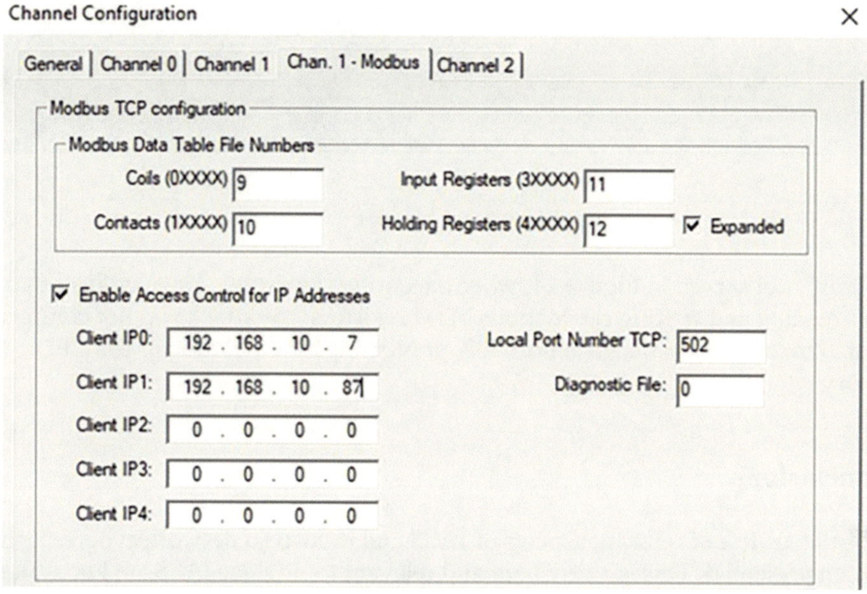

Figure 11.
Configuring access control list on RTUs.

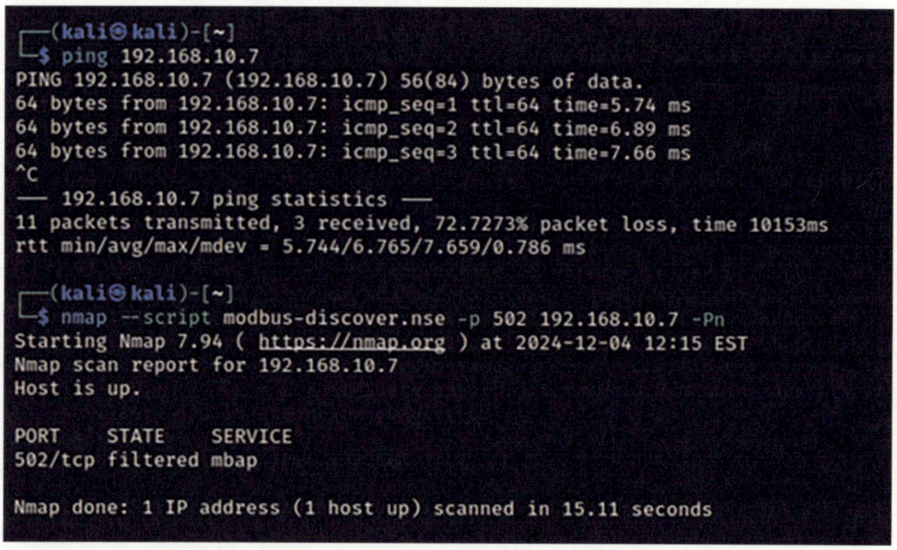

Figure 12.
Nmap command execution for port 502 scanning after security guidelines application.

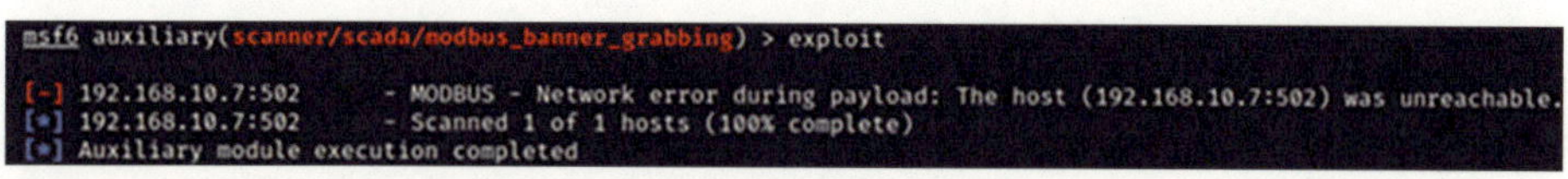

Figure 13.
Attempt to read manufacturer and model device after security guidelines application.

Figure 14.
Attempt to read MTU register after security guidelines application.

Similarly, as observed in **Figure 14**, when executing the exploit *ModbusClient* that allows reading and writing the Modbus MTU registers, the attack was not completed by not allowing access to logical port 502, preventing manipulation of the CPU memory.

7. Conclusions

A brief review of relevant aspects of IACS and industrial network cybersecurity has been presented. This is a pertinent and relevant topic since IACS are key systems for the correct functioning of critical infrastructures such as water, energy, manufacturing, and transportation. IACS is facing an important challenge such as the current proposal of the Interconnected Industry, or Industry 4.0, which is leading to the convergence of OT environments with IT but which at the same time is strongly compromising the security of these systems.

Nomenclature

HMI	human machine interface
IACS	industrial automation and control system
PLC	programmable logic controller
MTU	master terminal unit
RTU	remote terminal unit
IT	information technology
OT	operational technology
CIM	computer integrated manufacturing
SCADA	supervisory control and data acquisition

DOI: http://dx.doi.org/10.5772/intechopen.1009083

Author details

Silvana Gamboa*† and Ricardo Mogro†
Escuela Politécnica Nacional, Quito, Ecuador

*Address all correspondence to: silvana.gamboa@epn.edu.ec

†These authors contributed equally.

References

[1] Hemsley K, Fisher R. History of Industrial Control System Cyber Incidents. 2nd rev. ed. Idaho Falls: Idaho National Laboratory; 2018. 33 p

[2] BBC News. The Virus That Took Control of a Thousand Machines and Ordered them to Self-Destruct (in Spanish). El Virus Que tomó Control de Mil máquinas y les ordenó Autodestruirse. 2015 [Online]. Available from: https://www.bbc.com/mundo/noticias/2015/10/151007_iwonder_finde_tecnologia_virus_stuxnet [Accessed: January 03, 2025]

[3] Ortega J. Cybersecurity. In: Practical Manual (in Spanish), Cyberseguridad. 1st ed. Paraninfo: Manual Práctico; 2021

[4] Morales J, Avellán N, Lectong J, Zambrano I. Proceso de Ciberseguridad: Guía Metodológica para su implementación. Revista Ibérica de Sistemas y Tecnologías de la Información. 2020;**E29**:41-50

[5] Ballestero F. La ciberseguridad en tiempos difíciles ¿Nos ocupamos de ella o nos preocupamos por ella? Vol. 3122. Madrid-España: Boletín Económico de ICE; 2020. DOI: 10.32796/bice.2020.3122.6993

[6] Patricia R, Villacís C. Ciberseguridad y Ciberdefensa: Perspectiva de la situación actual en el Ecuador. Revista Tecnológica Ciencia y Educación Edwards Deming. 2022;**6**:50-62 [Online]. Available from: https://revista-edwardsdeming.com/index.php/eshttps://orcid.org0000-0002-7210-2642

[7] Ciberdelincuencia EJ. Aproximación criminológica de los delitos en la red. Revista La Razón Histórica. 2019;**44**:153-173

Chapter 3

Perspective Chapter: Intrusion Detection Systems in Cloud Environment

Waleed Almuseelem

Abstract

This chapter covers surveys on intrusion detection systems in cloud environments, such as Suricata, OSSEC, Bro (Zeek), and Snort, to monitor an Amazon VPC's traffic to demonstrate the Intrusion Detection System (IDS) tools' effectiveness in countering network attacks in the cloud environment. We test the systems using practical experiments on them using Amazon VPC's. For additional enhancement, we study the ability to use artificial intelligence tools with IDS to take advantage of features from these IDS tools to arrive at high-performance systems that will be influenced to improve cloud security and data privacy in the cloud environment and make a mechanism to protect cloud users and their data from intruders' threats. Practical experiments reveal that OSSEC recorded more alarms than Snort and Suricata within 3 hours. The use of AI with Amazon CloudWatch allows real-time metrics from IDS tools such as Suricata, Snort, and Zeek to be monitored. Potential challenges of using AI in IDSs include latency in data processing and query execution that limit real-time application and the need for careful planning (with large-scale log data).

Keywords: intrusion detection system, cloud computing, data security, privacy, artificial intelligence

1. Introduction

Cybersecurity has gained much attention globally following the introduction of cloud computing [1]. Cloud computing is associated with numerous benefits, including providing customers with self-service (on demand), high-speed resilience, extensive and constant access to network and data, and resource-related pooling. However, IT resource and infrastructure dumping by companies in the cloud environment is a common occurrence that elevates the risk of cybersecurity attacks, including phishing, data abuse, hijacking, breaches, and inadequacy of diligence [2]. These risks are aggravated by the distributed and open nature of cloud computing, which has led to the uprise of intrusion detection systems (IDSs) [3, 4]. Numerous IDSs are implemented in the cloud environment; hence, it is necessary to assess their efficacy before implementing them.

Intending to guide cybersecurity professionals in choosing an IDS, Chapter 1 focuses on the various IDS systems, such as Bro, Suricata, Snort, and OSSEC, that can be applied in the cloud environment. To do this, an outline of what IDSs and cloud environments will be provided. The application of IDS in the cloud environment will also be explored by analyzing various surveys of IDSs to explore what has been identified in terms of their usability, advantages, disadvantages, and critical success factors. Besides, IDSs will be assessed in terms of the extent to which AI can be integrated into them to enhance security.

2. Meaning of an IDS

Different organizations and individuals use varying terminologies to define an IDS. It is regarded as a cyber IDS by the Department of Energy [5]. It defines it as a network-based cybersecurity technology that detects vulnerabilities that might affect a computer or network system. IDS is a countermeasure against threats that occur in the cloud environment. The IDS aids in identifying any anomalies in the cloud environment by creating an opportunity for analyzing patterns in all activities and traffic [2]. Overall, an IDS is viewed as security software used to monitor the devices and traffic on a network for any potential activities that appear to be violating existing security policies, are suspicious, or are malicious. **Figure 1** indicates a simple architecture of an IDS.

2.1 Types of IDS

There are two types of IDS based on the system involved: network and host IDSs.

2.1.1 Network IDS (NIDS)

The IDS involves analyzing network packets through anomaly approaches to detect any incidence of malicious traffic or activities [2]. According to Efe and Abaci

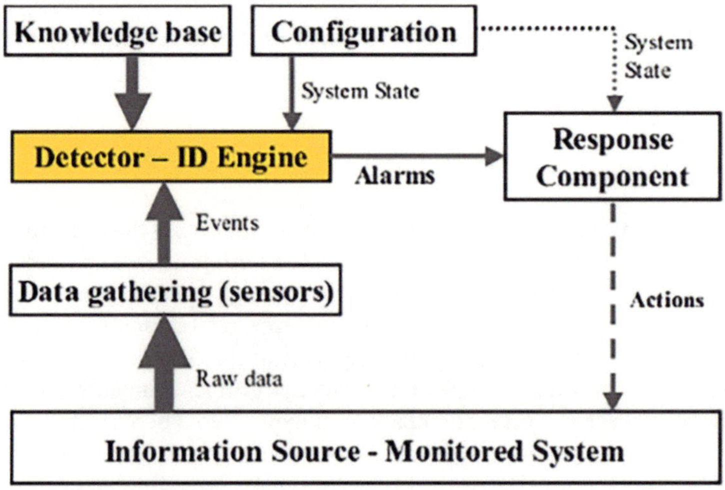

Figure 1.
Architecture of IDSs. Note. Source. Adapted from Ref. Khaliq ([6], p. 1).

[7] and Ahmad et al. [8], NIDS facilitates the monitoring of traffic between devices on a network. In the NIDS approach, network traffic is monitored using sensors, with doubtful packets being captured and assessed to ascertain whether they are malicious; if yes, they are reported to a system administrator or dropped if identified as non-malicious [9].

2.1.2 Host IDS (HIDS)

HIDS is run on individual devices on a network [7]. The IDS involves monitoring and analyzing hosts' behavior, kernels, and systems to reveal potential changes. It also includes reviewing a host's system logs against implemented host controls to uncover any anomalies in the traffic patterns [2]. A HIDS examines a host system's audit trails, gathering any activity patterns and associated behaviors [9].

IDS categorization by detection type includes two approaches: signature and anomaly-based detection. Khraisat et al. [10] illustrate a comparison between SIDS and AIDS in **Figure 2**.

2.1.3 Signature-based detection (SIDS)

SIDS/Misuse-based IDS are used to compare network activities using signatures stored in respective databases. Examples of analyzed signatures include text strings, byte codes [9], IP addresses, and network packets [6]. If a SID matches a signature to known attacks in the databases, the involved activity is immediately categorized as an attack. Therefore, they raise the alarm to the system administrator [9]. However, SIDS is disadvantageous in the case they fail to detect an attack with a signature that is not known in their databases, especially zero-day ones) [9]. In addition, any fault in the detection model will decrease SIDS' efficiency because there is a risk of revealing false results.

2.1.4 Anomaly-based detection systems (AIDS)

AIDS/Profile-oriented IDSs create profiles representing the normal activities on host devices, and behaviors that deviate from them are viewed as attacks. A network or system administrator is notified of the attacks' existence [9]. An AIDS enables a network administrator to identify new attacks because they do not rely on those with signatures registered on a database as in SIDs [7].

		Advantages	Disadvantages
Detection methods	SIDS	• Very effective in identifying intrusions with minimum false alarms (FA). • Promptly identifies the intrusions. • Superior for detecting the known attacks. • Simple design	• Needs to be updated frequently with a new signature. • SIDS is designed to detect attacks for known signatures. When a previous intrusion has been altered slightly to a new variant, then the system would be unable to identify this new deviation of the similar attack. • Unable to detect the zero-day attack. • Not suitable for detecting multi-step attacks. • Little understanding of the insight of the attacks
	AIDS	• Could be used to detect new attacks. • Could be used to create intrusion signature	• AIDS cannot handle encrypted packets, so the attack can stay undetected and can present a threat. • High false positive alarms. • Hard to build a normal profile for a very dynamic computer system. • Unclassified alerts. • Needs initial training.

Figure 2.
A comparison between SIDS and AIDS. Note. Source. Adapted from Ref. Khraisat et al. ([10], p. 4).

3. Cloud environments

According to Tissir et al. [1], the cloud environment includes a system where computing resources are stored in one location and distributed to customers without interactions. Various actors on the cloud facilitate the success of the ecosystem. Some of these actors are cloud-related consumers, auditors, brokers, and providers [11], and their specific roles are shown in **Table 1**.

A cloud service provider is responsible for customer data security [12]. The three cloud computing deployment models are discussed below and illustrated in **Figure 3**.

- Private cloud deployment model: Deployment and management are in a single company [14]. Islam et al. [12] define the private cloud model as suitable for large organizations that need higher levels of customization, control, and security. It is hosted in an organization's or a third party's data center.

- Public cloud deployment model: A third-party service provider gives customers a data storage solution that does not require them to manage their network systems [13]. This infers that customers do not manage the network system [14], and the best example is Microsoft Azure [12].

- Hybrid: It combines the technologies and approaches of the above systems [14].

- Community cloud deployment model: This deployment model involves many companies sharing computing infrastructure and resources [14].

Cloud service providers identify and implement security measures to ensure that data are well protected within the infrastructure under each deployment model [14]. A service provider implements measures in cloud computing to secure the infrastructure while a customer handles user access controls and application and data protection [13].

Intrusion detection is pertinent in the cloud environment because of the associated threats at the software level. The large number of networks in the cloud environment has aggravated the high risk of attacks that commonly occur and need to be addressed by the cloud provider and the customers. Khan [15] explains that various attacks often occur on network systems. The first is malware, which is malicious software that hackers

Cloud actors no.	Cloud actor's name	Cloud actor's role
1	Cloud provider	Allocates and manages the resources on the cloud. They also provide cloud computing services to individuals interested in them.
2	Cloud consumer	An individual, firm, or group of companies interested in obtaining the services that cloud provider(s) sell.
3	Cloud broker	An entity that negotiates a cloud provider's and consumer's relationship.
4	Cloud carrier	I am the network provider who acts as the mediator between a provider and consumer of cloud services.
5	Cloud auditor	It is a specialist focused on auditing cloud computing services to ascertain that they have the best performance and are secure.

Table 1.
Cloud environment actors.

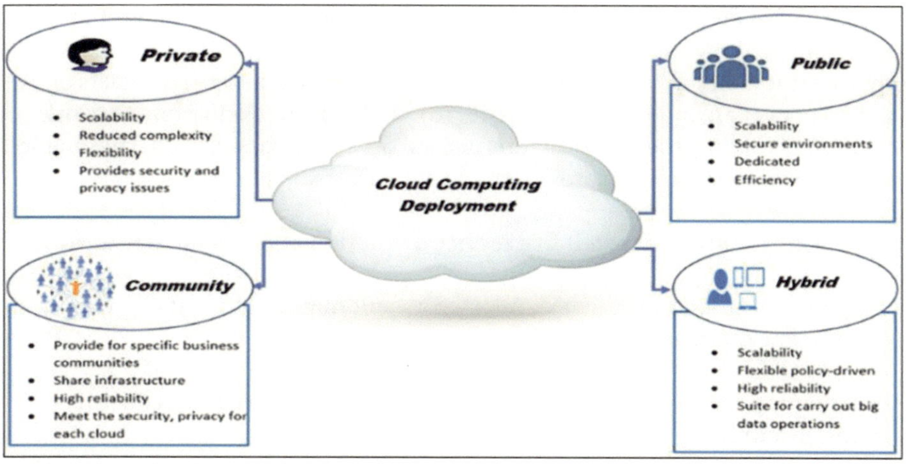

Figure 3.
Cloud deployment models. Note. Source. Ref. Ang'udi ([13], p. 158).

create to obtain unauthorized access to computer systems [15]. A malware attack leads to numerous concerns with software whose aim is to disrupt all system operations or hamper data integrity on a network. The attack thus leverages cloud system vulnerabilities, which shows the need to identify ways of mitigating them [16].

Malware attacks in cloud computing are cyberattacks that use malicious applications or software to compromise cloud resources and infrastructure. The goal of these attacks can be to steal data, disrupt operations, or cause chaos. Malware attacks can occur in numerous ways, including:

i. *Exploiting vulnerabilities*: Attackers can exploit vulnerabilities in the cloud infrastructure, systems, or applications.

ii. *Exploiting live migration*: Attackers can exploit the process of live migration to steal data or install malware on target machines.

There are various examples of malware; one is viruses, which are self-replicating to modify programs and integrate them with bad codes. Trojans can disguise themselves as legitimate programs, making them difficult to detect. Examples of signs of existing malware include unprecedented decreases in disk-related space, slowness, and extreme downtimes [15].

Phishing might also occur in the cloud environment, where a user might be tricked into providing their security logins or financial information through accessing fraudulent sites or links [15]. The attack occurs when malicious actors create legitimate-looking messages that tempt the receiver to click on a link or enter personal information. Phishing emails may contain malware-embedded links masquerading as legal links or links that direct the user to valid-looking websites and deceive them into entering their login information [15]. Phishers' tactics are constantly evolving to evade established security measures, posing a significant problem. Phishing attackers frequently exploit new vulnerabilities and attack methods [17]. Phishers collect encryption keys to gain unauthorized access to cloud accounts. Internal attacks can involve hacked employee accounts. Mobile device usage and Bring Your Own Device (BYOD) rules have led to an increase in phishing attacks targeting mobile users [17].

A distributed denial of service (DDoS) entails attacks on the systems of an organization, making them unusable by legitimate users [15]. In a DDoS, an attacker overpowers the cloud network with large traffic; hence, the authorized users of the system do not get an opportunity to use it [16]. A DDoS attack disrupts network functions by flooding a server with internet traffic. DDoS assaults can have major implications for cloud service providers and consumers, including:

- A DDoS assault might result in a service disruption or complete shutdown.
- Impaired customer experience: A DDoS assault might significantly affect the customer experience.
- Economic unsustainable: A DDoS attack can generate absolute economic unpredictability.

The malicious traffic originates from a range of IP addresses, many of which are part of a botnet, making the attack more difficult to fight against [15]. Addressing the DDoS attacks might be challenging because the attackers might use numerous approaches to initiate them on one victim [2]. This reveals the need for an artificial intelligence (AI)-based system because they have learning algorithms that make it easier to detect DDoS attacks [8, 18, 19].

In a man-in-the-middle attack, a malicious individual might gain access to a secure communication and modify it by gaining access to databases or any leaked data on the internet [15]. It is basically a cyberattack where a criminal inserts themselves between two parties in a communication channel to steal data. It can occur through

- Eavesdropping: The attacker listens in on the conversation between the two parties.
- Impersonation: The attackers are impersonating a party in a communication line.
- Spoofing: The attacker spoofs an entire communications system to scrape data.
- Session-related hijacks: Attackers might access a session cookies session cookie and use it to impersonate the user.

Man-in-the-middle attacks involve the theft of sensitive data, which the attacker can then use this information for identity theft, unapproved fund transfers, or other malicious purposes [15]. To help prevent MitM attacks, you can detect malware using IDSs, have strong encryptions, enable multifactor authentication, and avoid using open or poorly secured public networks. A man-in-the-middle attack might occur if there is no encryption on the communication channels between a customer and the databases that store their data on the cloud [2].

In SQL injection, malicious code might be injected into networks, thus allowing malicious individuals to gain unauthorized access to data. An SQL injection (SQLi) attack is a cyber threat that occurs when an attacker exploits vulnerabilities in an application's code to enter a database [15]. SQL is might lead to various losses, including:

a. A data breach: Attackers can get their hands-on sensitive company data, customer lists, or financial records.

b. Data corruption: Attackers can tamper with existing data, modify transactions, or destroy all server data.

c. Loss of system control: Attackers can gain root access to a machine, giving them complete control.

Ransomware might also occur, whereby files might be hacked or an entire system taken over by malicious individuals who demand payment to return access to authorized users [15]. Ransomware attacks are whereby attackers gain access to a cloud storage account, identify target data, and encrypt it. They then create a ransom note and provide contact information for negotiating the ransom. Cloud storage accounts are a primary target for ransomware attacks, including those from Amazon Web Services (AWS), Azure, and Google. Attackers may use sophisticated tactics, such as disabling key material in S3 buckets, to make the encrypted data inaccessible. Ransomware attacks can cost organizations millions of dollars. The attackers can exploit vulnerabilities in systems, networks, software, and humans. Attackers may use phishing scams to trick users into installing malware. They may also use brute force or credential-stuffing attacks to log into systems as legitimate users [15].

4. IDS challenges on cloud deployment models

See **Table 2**.

Cloud detection model	Challenge	Solution
Private cloud	Resource constraints	Implementing security measures in the cloud model might be challenging because it requires numerous skilled employees and professionals to effectively implement the relevant systems. Outsourcing of such activities is also costly to the organization because they need continuous detection and prevention systems,
	High cost	Organizations have to assess the return on investment of security systems. This might be a challenging task, especially if the result of the return on investment is significantly low.
Public cloud	Compliance challenges	It is challenging to address them because there are no specific guidelines for addressing the issues.

Table 2.
Security challenges in cloud deployment models.

5. Artificial intelligence (AI)

AI is focused on using a machine to perform a task similar to that of a human with a similar intelligence level. It has many fields, including information technology, statistics, neuroscience, and philosophical aspects. AI applications are software programs that use AI techniques to perform tasks from simple to complex. These frameworks include:

5.1 Data analytics

Data analytics is the collection of information with the goal of generating insights. Data scientists primarily handle high-level analysis, although the most recent data analytics systems include capabilities like natural language processing queries and automated insights that allow business users to delve deeper into information. It is a discipline that employs tools and techniques to examine and analyze data in real-time or near-real-time to discover hidden patterns, correlations, and trends. The goal is predictive and prescriptive analysis, which uses advanced methodologies to generate accurate, dynamic, and forward-looking forecasts and suggestions. Related business intelligence (BI) features enable you to collect up-to-date data from your organization, show it in simple formats like tables and graphs, and disseminate.

5.2 Machine learning (ML)

MLs are systems that are focused on learning the data they use to make decisions. In supervised learning, algorithms are trained using clearly labeled datasets [20]. The unsupervised machine allows computers to learn to detect complicated processes and patterns without the need for close, ongoing human guidance. Unsupervised machine learning is the process of training on data without labels or a specific, defined outcome.

Cloud-based systems require significant and effective security measures because their distributed nature makes them prone to attacks from fraudulent individuals Tayyebi and Bhilare [21]. This reveals the essence of intrusion detection activities because they aid in preventing and implementing measures for mitigating attacks on cloud networks and data. Intrusion detection software has gained prevalence among cyber security professionals, cloud service providers, and cloud computing customers in their quest for mitigating attacks on data and distributed network systems. Examples of IDS software that have been adopted and investigated by Syamsuddin and Barukab [22, 23] include Suricata, Snort, Bro, OSSEC, and Falco. Tayyebi and Bhilare [21] revealed that these IDS software are open-source. They are preferred over commercial IDS, which are perceived to be highly costly and require a lot of resources, which might not be affordable to most companies. The open-source IDS provides security similar to commercial IDS but is free and only requires the acquisition of a license to use it. In this chapter, modern open-source IDS systems are evaluated based on their working behavior and outcomes in the cloud environment. Their implementation in practical environments is surveyed, and outcomes from the surveys are presented in image form, followed by a relevant discussion analyzing it. The IDS systems are also analyzed based on their ability to use AI-based on the findings of conducted experiments and research.

6. Overview of literature on tests in IDSs in the cloud

Snort refers to an open-source IDS that Martin Roesch created in 1998. Its major advantage is that it can enable the performance of real-time traffic and packet analysis [21]. Bros uses anomaly and signature-based approaches to monitor the traffic in a network for suspicious activities passively. On the other hand, Suricata is a signature-based IDS that uses a pre-developed set of rules for monitoring the traffic in a network and reporting threats [24].

The first surveyed experiment was intrusion detection using Snort, Suricata, and Bro to detect DDoS attacks on a simulated cloud environment. Eight servers were used in the experiment for the computer nodes, with each having a virtual machine. The cloud platform that was used was OpenStack Mitaka, which had ten virtual machines (see **Figure 4**). An online web server that detects intrusions, Snort, Bro, or Suricata, to detect all traffic on the cloud server network.

A total of 9000 packets were recorded from the analysis of DDoS attacks. Snort was able to block 900 packets from the attacks, while Suricata only dropped 450 (5%) and Bro 720 packets. Snort is single-threaded, a disadvantage that was noticed during the analysis because a total of 1970 packets were identified in the initial 15 minutes, but more of them were rejected 30 minutes later. In contrast, Bro revealed 2000 DDoS packets in the initial 15 minutes (see **Figure 5**). Overall, Mirza and Kumar [24] showed that Suricata was found to be similar to Snort in DDoS attack detection despite losing communication early. Snort is, however, suitable for IDS in small networks [24].

Suricata has also been tested in comparison with Snort and found that the IDS yields better outcomes with a small amount of data, unlike Snort [25]. Idrus et al. [26] obtained a virtual private server where they installed the Suricata IDS software. The server had four tools. The first is the Nmap software, whose purpose was scanning the software for scanning for attacks to identify any ports on the server. A Brute force-based software was also in the server to prevent the forced logins that an attacker might be trying to use to log into the cloud system. It also had the DDoS software to assess similar attacks on the network. Analysis of the proposed system led to the findings shown in **Figure 6**.

Another surveyed IDS on the cloud environment was one conducted using the OSSEC and Snort software. The proposed system used anomaly and signature-oriented approaches and assessed how programs are executed, as well as network, processor, and memory-related usage metrics by the virtual machine in detecting any intrusions.

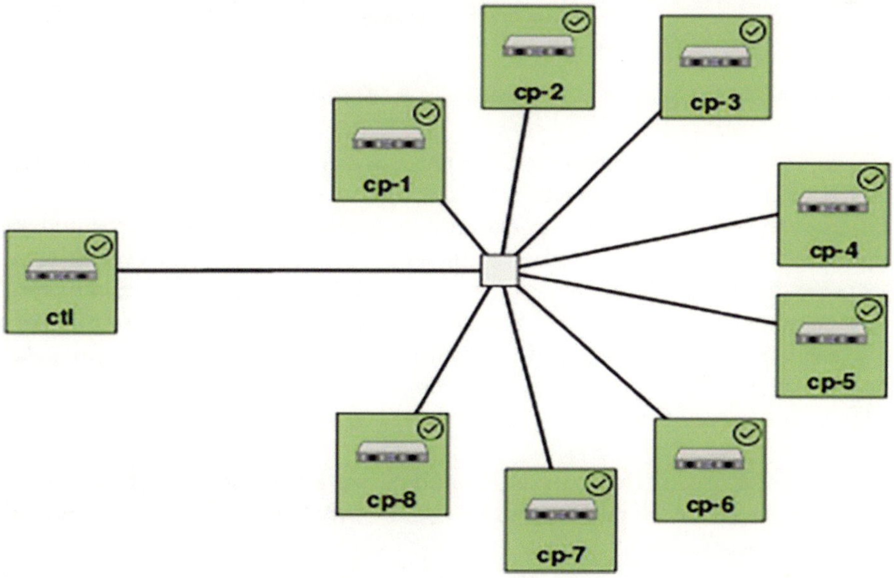

Figure 4.
Cloud software administrative and computer nodes.

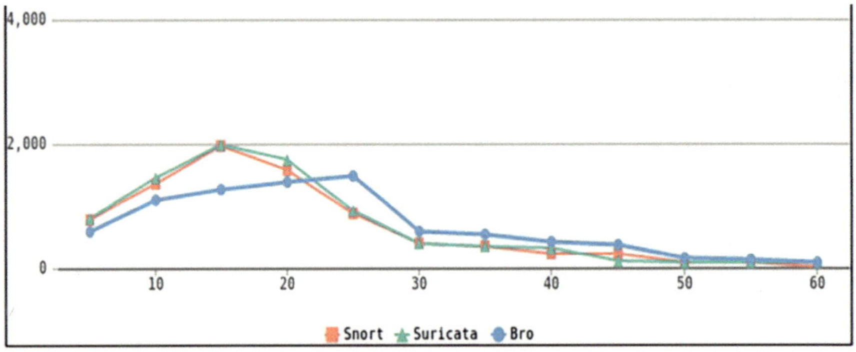

Figure 5.
Comparison of number of DDoS packets reported during the analysis.

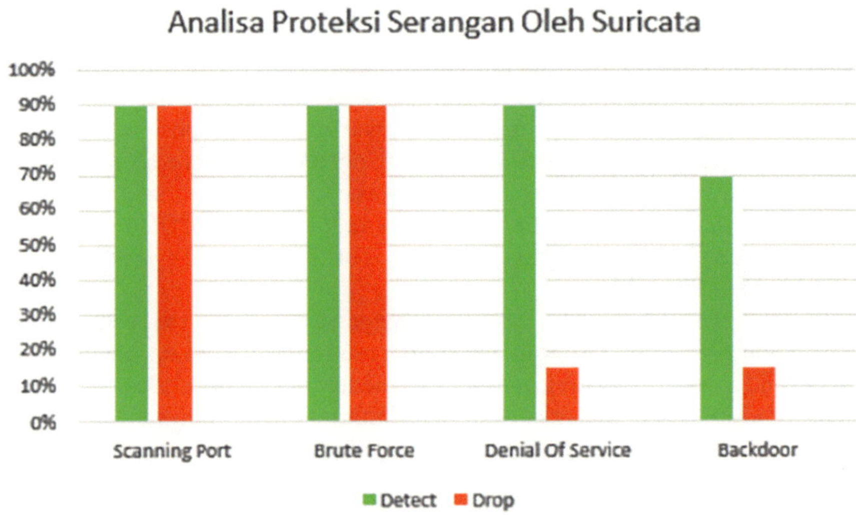

Figure 6.
The outcome of the Suricata-based IDS. Note. Adapted from Ref. Idrus et al. ([26], p. 149).

The survey revealed that the prediction of intrusions using Snort and OSSEC has a high accuracy of 97.1, 94.1% detection rate, and 0.2% false alarm rates [27].

Based on the surveys of previous experiments, it was found that Snort could detect more attacks on a cloud network, unlike Bro and Suricata. However, Snort and Suricata are slightly similar in terms of their accuracy and detection rates. The results of previous experiments also reveal that creating an IDS that combines more than one software enhances the accuracy and detection rates and lowers the risk of false alarms in the assessment of intrusions on a cloud network. The major proposition that can be made from the survey of practical IDSs on the cloud environment are as follows:

- Snort can be used in the analysis of cloud network intrusion detections because it can flag down a lot of packets that do not align with the behavior of users on the systems.
- Use Suricata when scanning for DDoS, brute force, and backdoor attacks on a system.

- Combine many types of open-source software, such as OSSEC, Suricata, Bro, and Snort, in the analysis of intrusions on a network system. This will allow a network administrator to leverage the benefits of each system. The benefits of the systems exceed the disadvantages associated with each and are thus masked by the advantages of other IDS software.

The findings from previous practical experiments are tested using hands-on experiments. These experiments are conducted using similar IDS tools that are explored in the studies outlined above. Specifically, the tested IDS include Zeek, Suricata, OSSEC, and Snort. However, these reviewed literature are based on experiments from other scholars, hence it is pertinent to conduct them to test whether there are similar findings in intrusions tested recently. They are tested on the Amazon VPC (cloud environment). The results of the experiments and steps taken to attain them are indicated in the subsection below.

7. Experiments on IDS application in the cloud

This practical guide used IDS tools (Suricata, OSSEC, Bro (Zeek), or Snort) to monitor an Amazon VPC's traffic to demonstrate the IDS tools' effectiveness in countering network attacks. The guide involves steps to deploy the IDS tools, as highlighted in **Figure 7** below.

Zeek, Suricata, OSSEC, and Snort IDS tools were installed on an Amazon Elastic Compute Cloud (Amazon EC2) instance. The instance for each IDS tool was used as an Amazon VPC traffic mirroring target. This approach of IDS tools deployment to AWS helped demonstrate their use as an intrusion detection and security monitoring tool inside cloud environments.

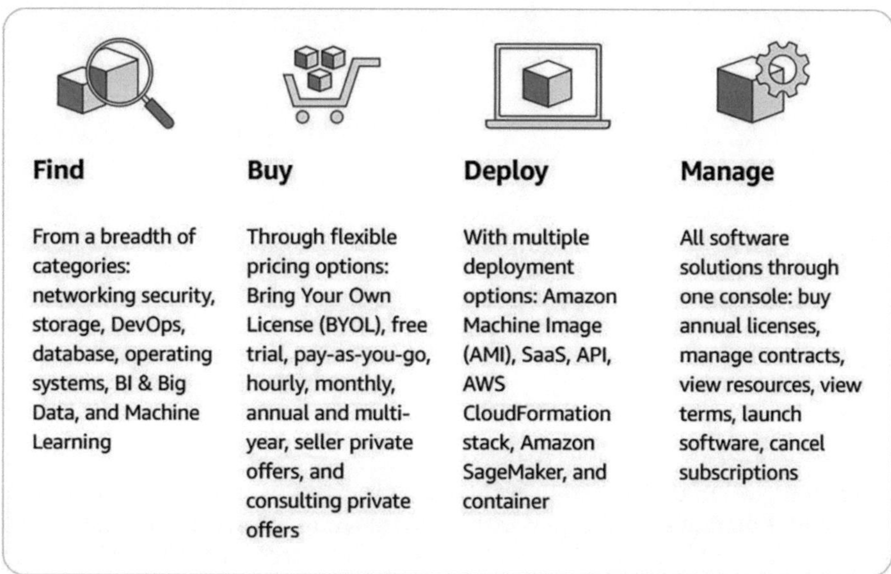

Figure 7.
IDS tools deploying steps overview.

Bro (Zeek)

Step 1

An EC2 instance from AWS was launched, as illustrated in **Figure 8** below.

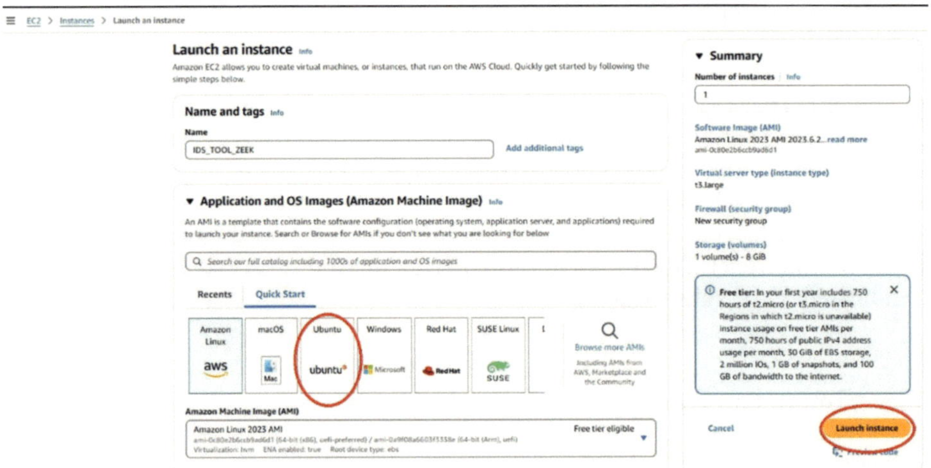

Figure 8.
Launch of an EC2 instance with Ubuntu as the OS.

Step 2

The EC2 instance connect was used to install Zeek (**Figure 9**).

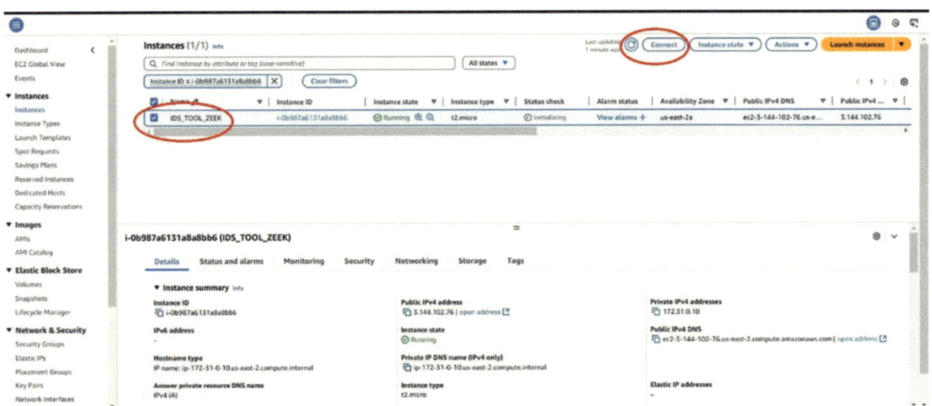

Figure 9.
EC2 connection.

Step 3

After connection to the instance, the following code was used to install Zeek 6.0 to the EC2 instance. (**echo** 'deb http://download.opensuse.org/repositories/security:/zeek/xUbuntu_22.04/ /' |sudotee/etc/apt/sources.list.d/security:zeek.list

curl -fsSL https://download.opensuse.org/repositories/security:zeek/xUbuntu_22.04/Release.key | gpg --dearmor | sudo tee /etc./apt/trusted.gpg.d/security_zeek.gpg > /dev/null.

sudo apt update **sudo** apt install zeek-6.0) (**Figure 10**).

Figure 10.
Installation of Zeek to EC2 instance.

Step 4

No configuration was selected to proceed with default Zeek configurations (**Figure 11**).

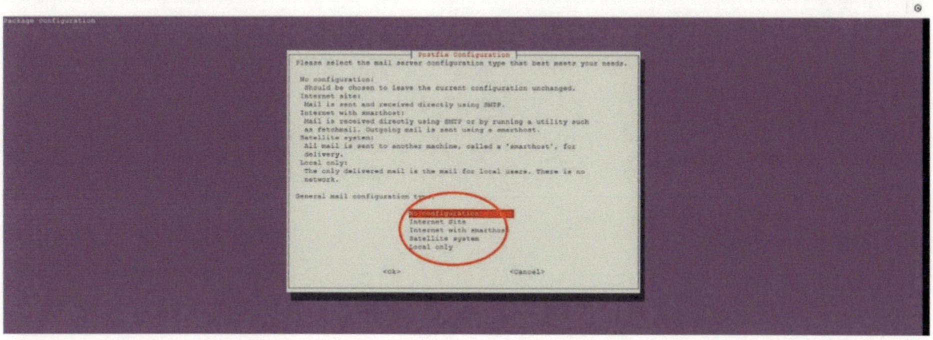

Figure 11.
Zeek configuration.

Step 5

A traffic mirror target was created by navigating to the VPC section (**Figure 12**).

A traffic filter was created with the following inbound rule (**Figure 13**).

As illustrated in **Figure 14** below, a traffic mirror session was created using the traffic mirror target and filter created in the above steps with the following inbound rule.

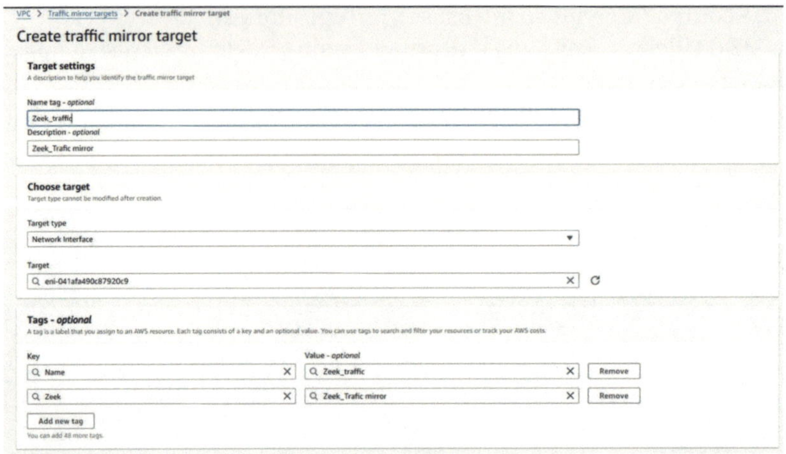

Figure 12.
Traffic mirror creation.

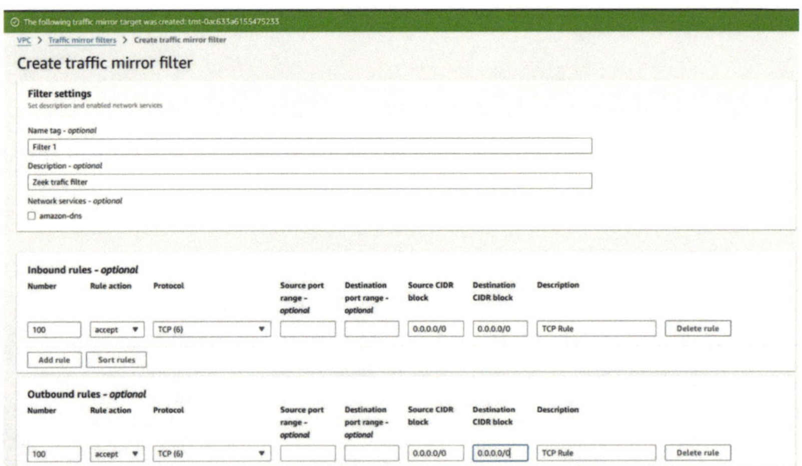

Figure 13.
Traffic filter creation.

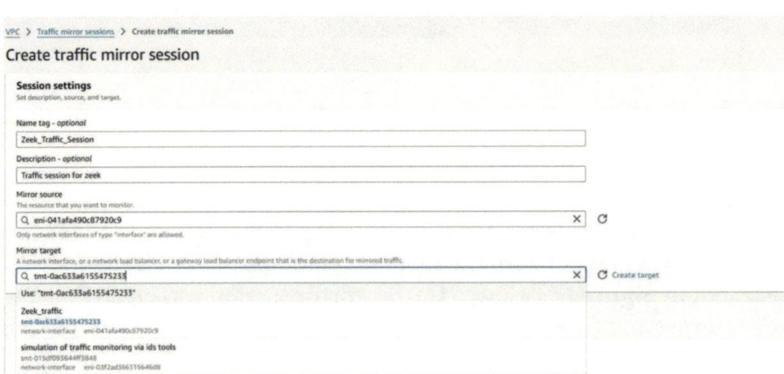

Figure 14.
Creation of traffic mirror session.

Suricata

Step 1

AWS Marketplace was used to locate the IDS tool to deploy Suricata with Amazon Virtual Private Cloud (Amazon VPC) Traffic Mirroring. The next step was to launch the subscription as an EC2 instance (**Figure 15**).

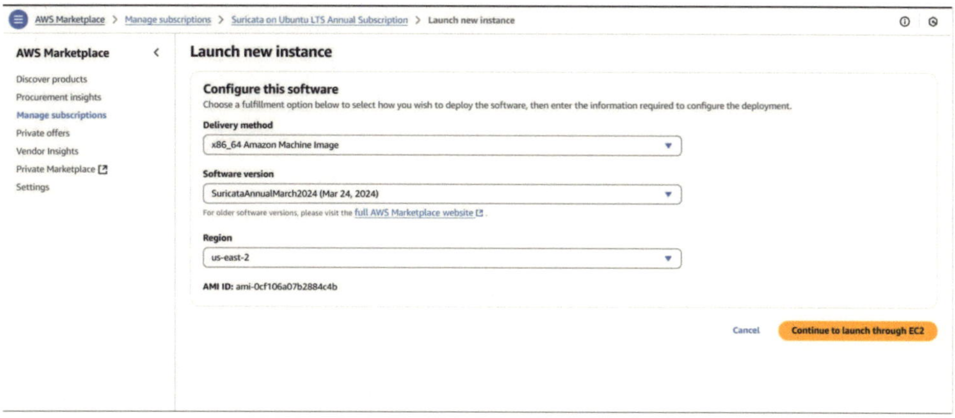

Figure 15.
Suricita launched as an EC2 instance.

Step 2

After launching the IDS tool, a network traffic simulation was created using mirror traffic (**Figure 16**).

A target filter and session were also created (**Figure 17**).

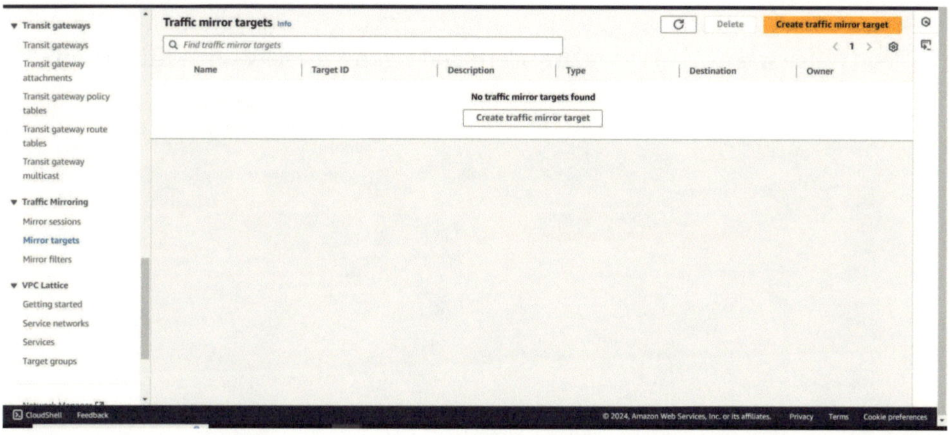

Figure 16.
Creation of mirror traffic target.

Step 3

CloudWatch was used to create alarms (**Figure 18**).

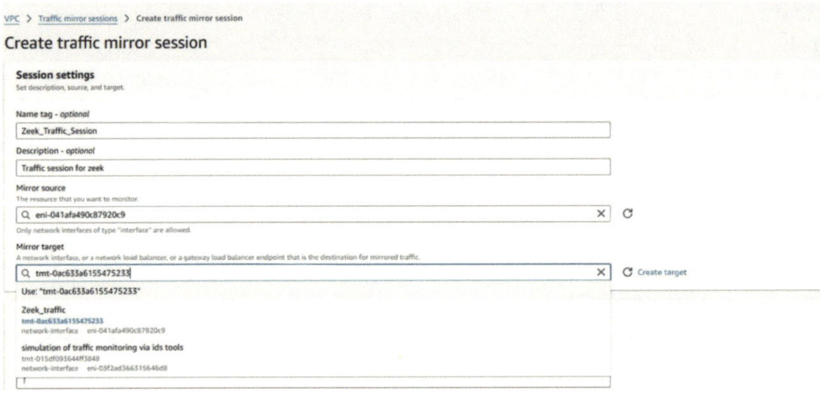

Figure 17.
Traffic session creation.

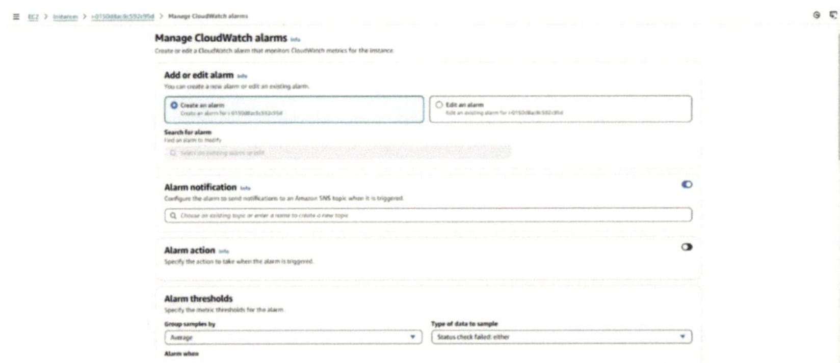

Figure 18.
Alarm creation via CloudWatch.

Step 4

CloudWatch was used to view alarm alerts and logs for the network traffic (**Figure 19**).

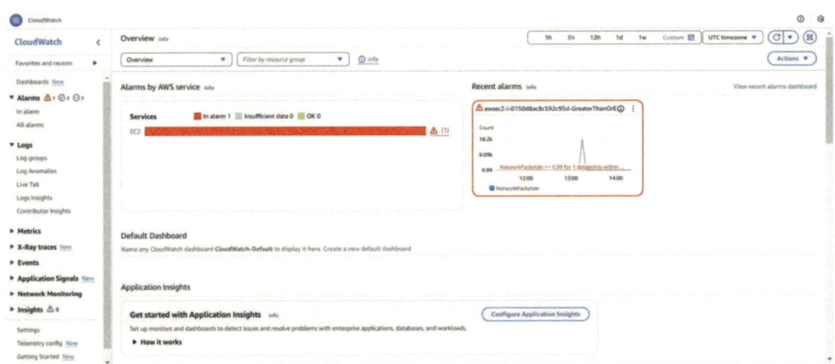

Figure 19.
CloudWatch's in-alarm state.

OSSEC

Step 1

An EC2 instance was launched to deploy OSSEC (**Figure 20**), as illustrated in **Figure 21** below.

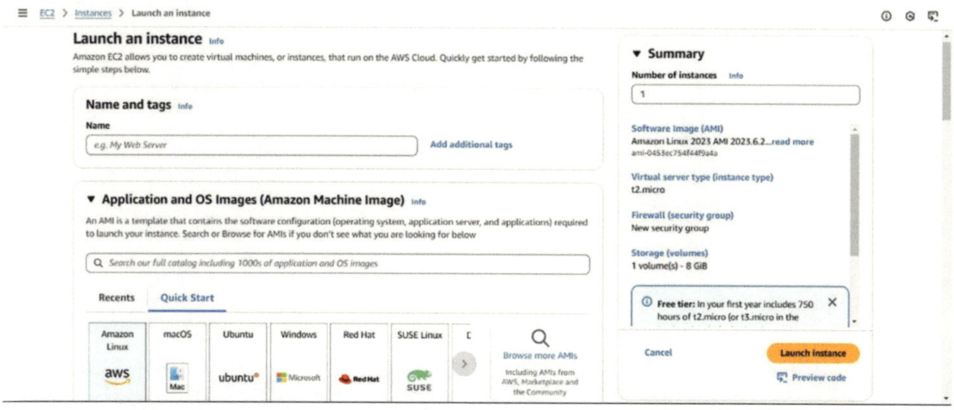

Figure 20.
EC2 instance launch.

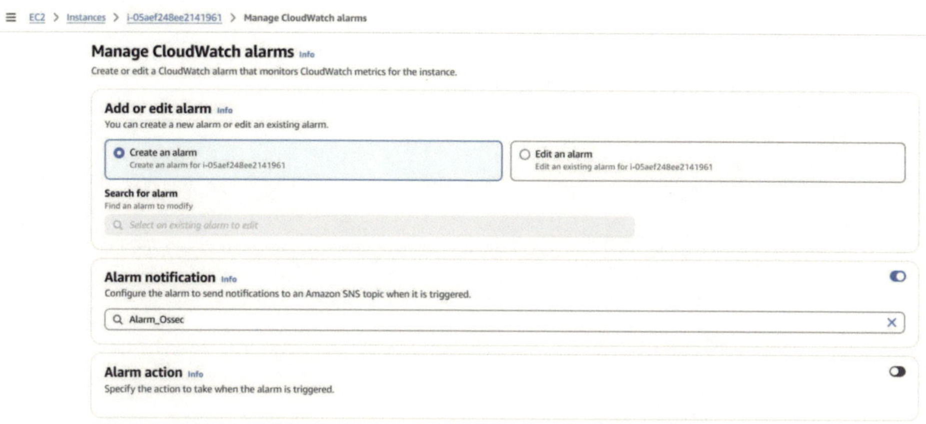

Figure 21.
Alarm creation via CloudWatch.

Step 2

EC2 Instance connect was used to establish a connection with the server (**Figure 22**).

Step 3

The following code "sudo apt-get install build-essential make zlib1g-dev libpcre2-dev libevent-dev libssl-dev sudo apt-get install build-essential zlib1g-dev" was used to install OSSEC's to the EC2 instance (**Figure 23**).

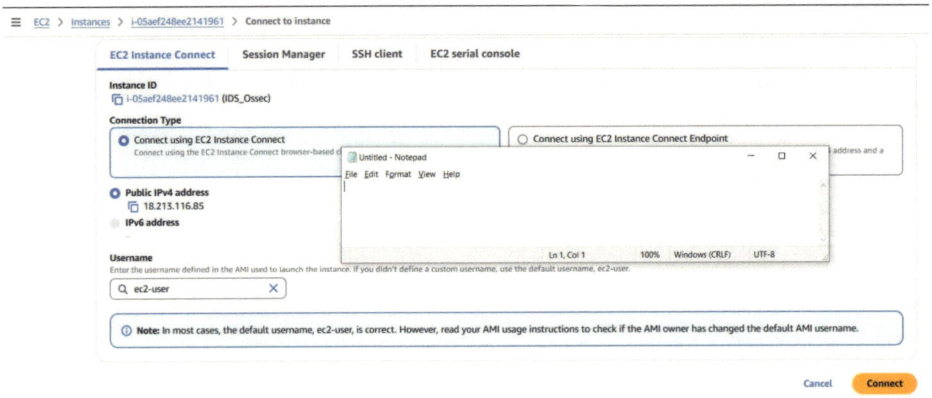

Figure 22.
Connection to instance.

Figure 23.
Installation code.

Step 4

A mirror session for OSSEC was created using a mirror filter and mirror target (**Figure 24**), as illustrated in **Figure 25** below.

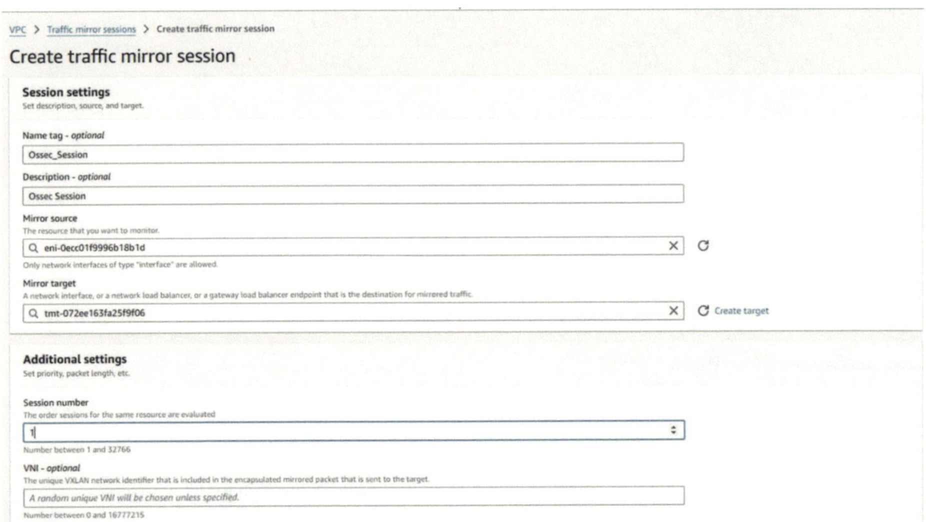

Figure 24.
Mirror session creation.

Step 5

An alarm was created *via* AWS CloudWatch to create alerts.
AWS CloudWatch was used to view the status of alarms and logs created (**Figure 26**).

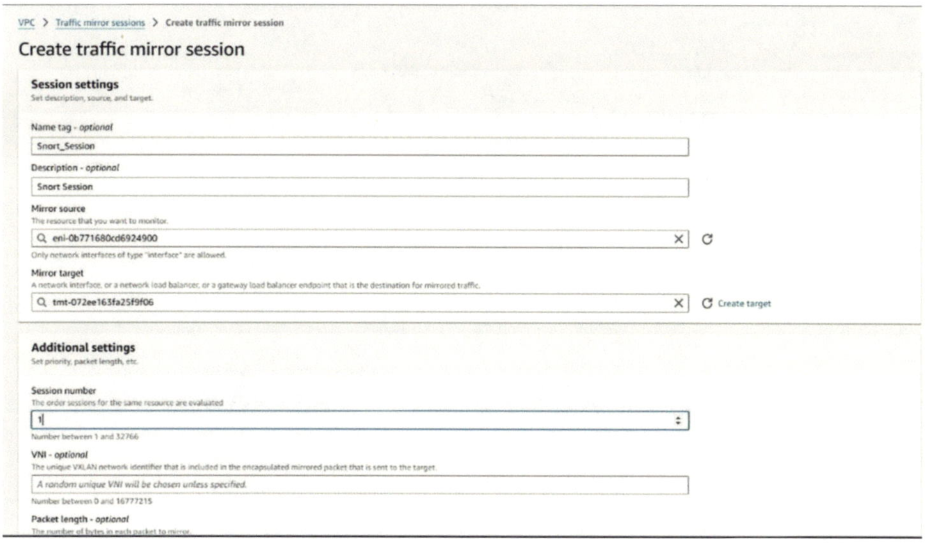

Figure 25.
Traffic mirror creation.

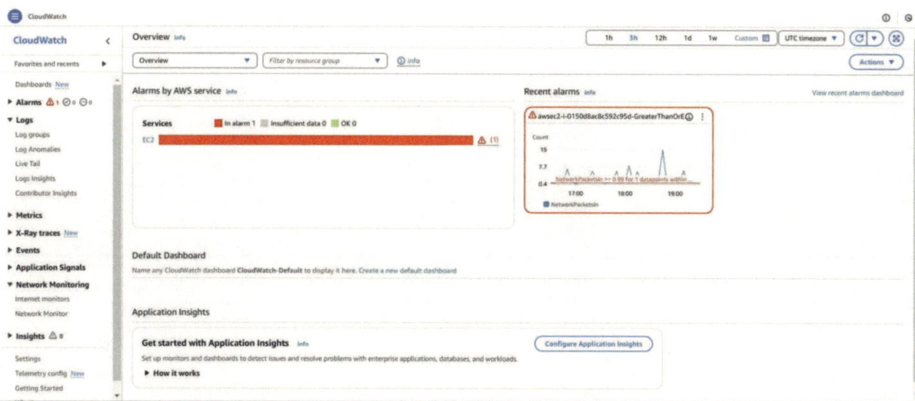

Figure 26.
In alarm state.

Snort

Step 1

To deploy Snort in AWS, AWS Marketplace was used to subscribe to the IDS tool, then launched as an EC2 instance (**Figure 27**).

Step 2

Navigating to the VPC to simulate intrusions, as shown in Step 1 above, created a traffic mirror session. The left navigation panel was used to select mirror Targets, as highlighted in the **Figure 25** below.

Step 3

The running EC2 instance (Snort) was selected. The tab "Status and alarms" available at the bottom of the page was selected as highlighted by the **Figure 28** below.

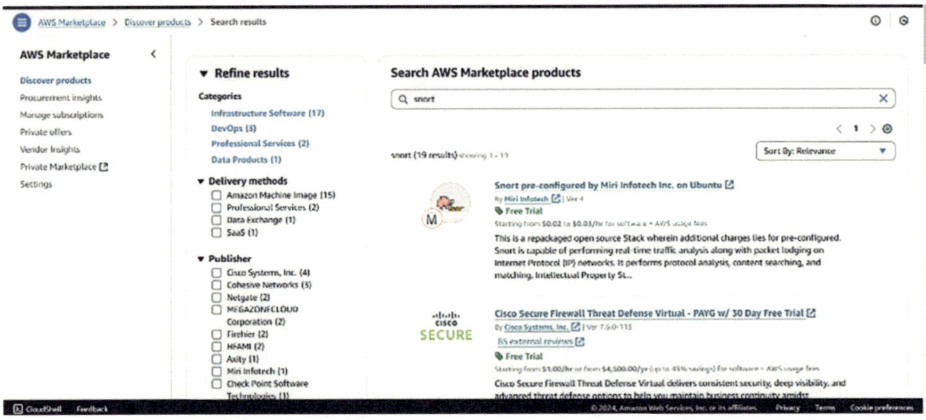

Figure 27.
Snort identification in AWS MarketPlace.

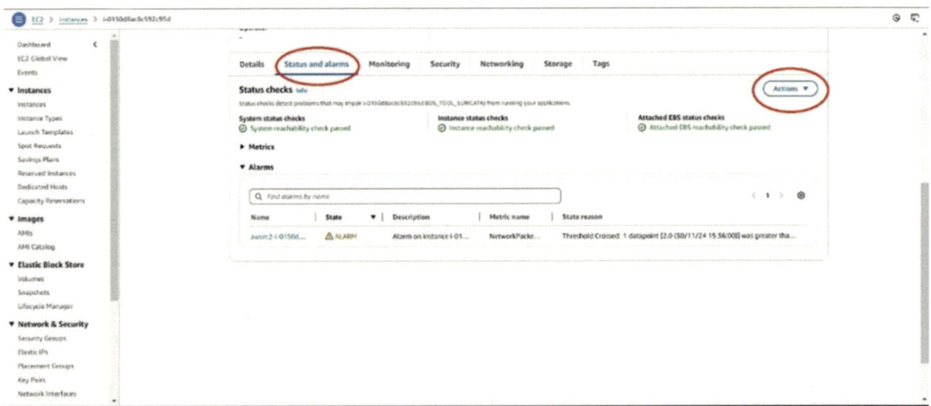

Figure 28.
Alarm creation.

Step 4

CloudWatch was used to view the state of created alarms. The **Figure 29** below shows the alarm state *via* a red color bar. A green bar indicates an "Okay" state of the network traffic.

7.1 Analysis of results

7.1.1 Experiment concepts overview

Traffic Mirroring was used to copy network traffic from an elastic network interface of type interface and then send the traffic to out-of-band security and monitoring appliances for threat monitoring [28]. The traffic mirroring concepts involve the network interface to monitor, which is the Ec2 instance with the installed IDS tool in this experiment. Traffic filters set rules that define the traffic that is mirrored. This experiment allowed all inbound traffic. A traffic target helped establish the destination for mirrored traffic. A mirror session was established to create a relationship between a source, a filter, and a target.

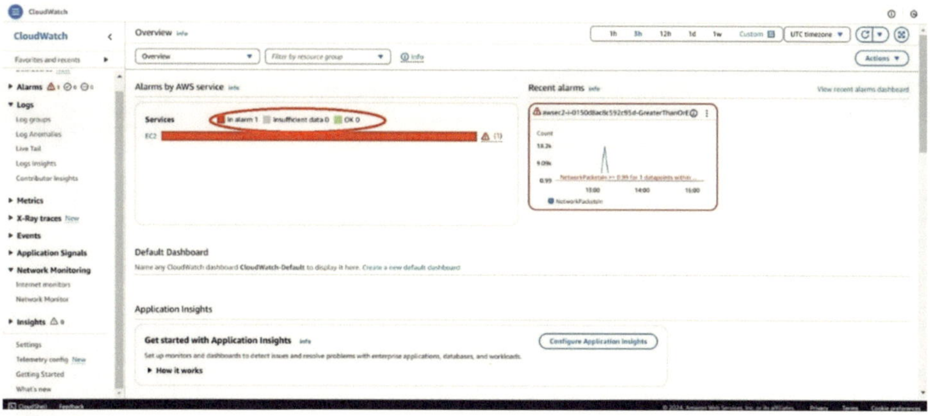

Figure 29.
Alarm view via CloudWatch.

An EC2 instance was created to mirror inbound TCP traffic on the instance and send the traffic to the instances that have Zeek, Suricata, OSSEC, and Snort software installed. Amazon CloudWatch was used to monitor the mirrored traffic based on EC2 instances with IDS tools. The metrics used for the mirror traffic involved NetworkMirrorIn, NetworkMirrorOut, NetworkPacketsMirrorIn, and NetworkPacketsMirrorOut. Alarms were established *via* AWS CloudWatch to help create alerts *via* dashboard or send notifications to authorized users *via* mail or text [28].

Step 1

AWS CloudWatch was used to centralize and analyze the logs and metrics generated by IDS tools. Instances (Zeek, Snort, Suricata, and OSSEC) were created in the previous section (**Figure 30**).

Step 2

Metrics for the IDS tools were selected to help with analysis (**Figure 31**).

Step 3

AWS CloudWatch was used to create a dashboard that visualizes the IDS tools' metrics analysis (**Figure 32**).

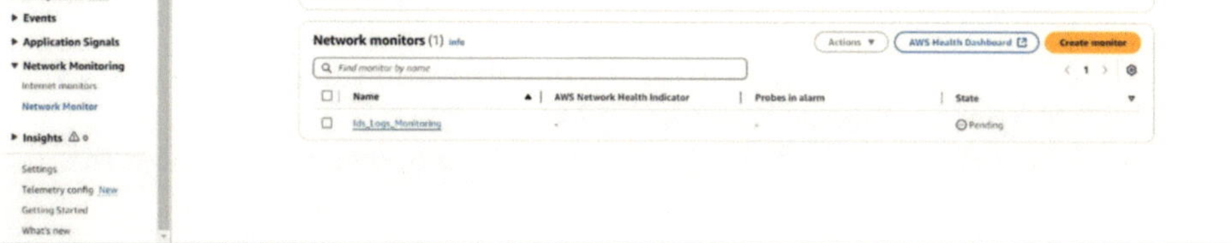

Figure 30.
Centralized monitoring creation via CloudWatch.

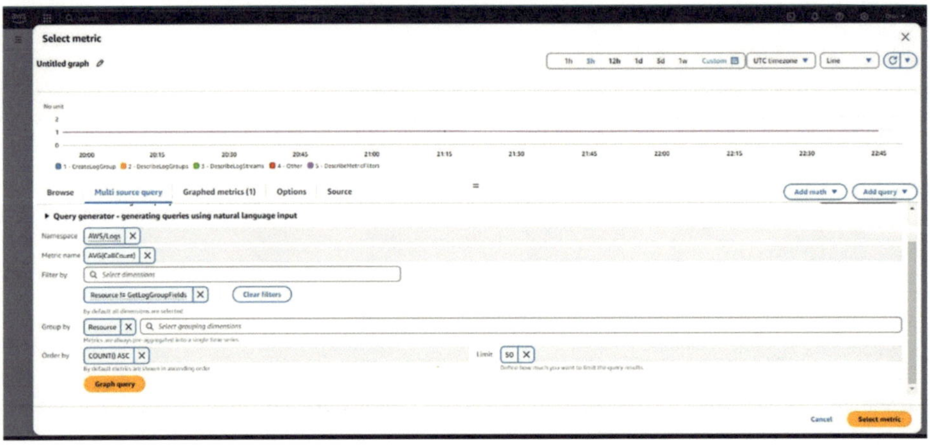

Figure 31.
Metrics selection.

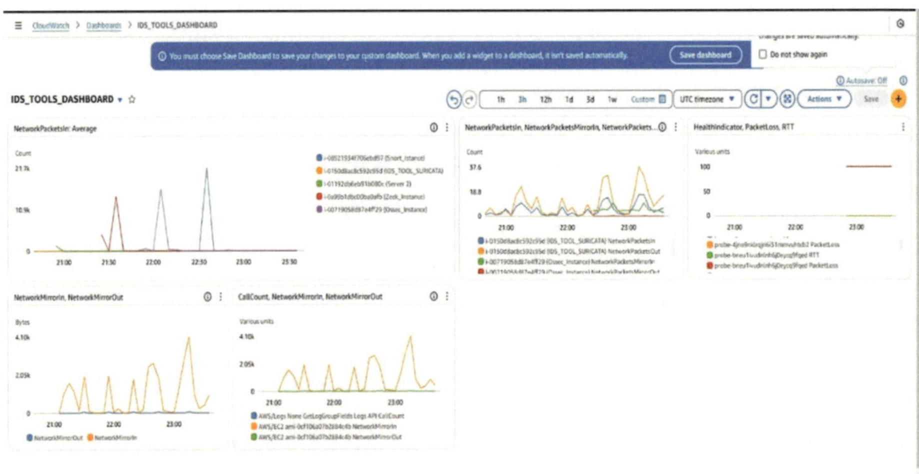

Figure 32.
AWS CloudWatch dashboard.

7.1.2 AI integration practical experiment

Step 1

Amazon Athena was used with AmazonCloudWatch to analyze IDS tools metrics (**Figure 33**).

Step 2

Athena enabled alarm creation with an email notification alert based on AWS CloudWatch metrics configurations (**Figure 34**).

The analysis of the outputs of the IDSs in the AWS cloud system revealed the following:

i. Suricata – 0.99 network packet for a data point identified within a span of 3 hours. Only one alarm within this period, with a high count of 18.2.

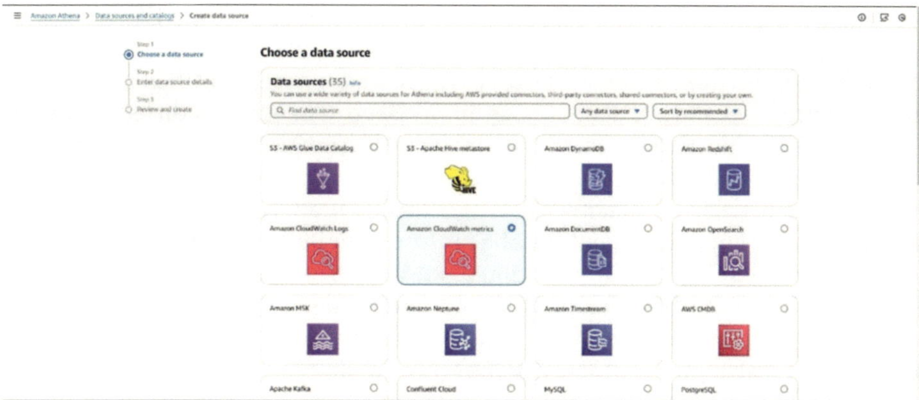

Figure 33.
Amazon athena.

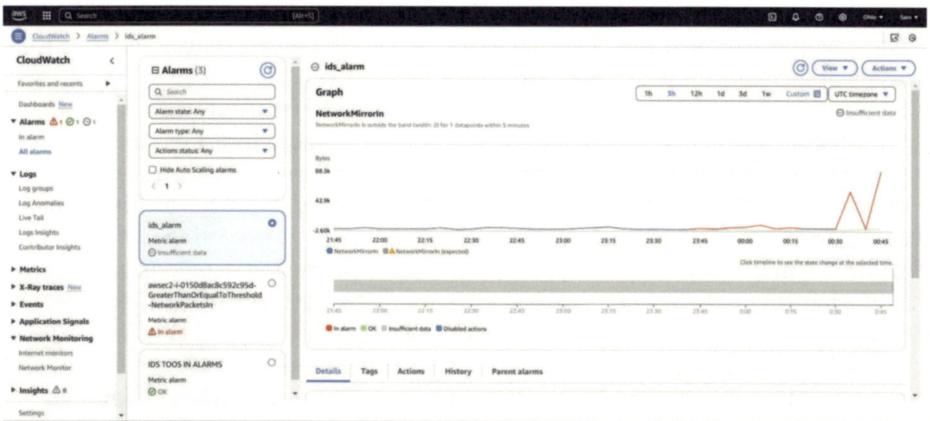

Figure 34.
Alarm, alerts, and graph creation via amazon athena and CloudWatch.

ii. OSSEC – 7 alarms within a span of 3 hours, with the highest having a count of 15. It recorded 0.99 network packets for a data point identified in a period similar to Suricata.

iii. Snort – 0.99 network packet for a data point identified within 3 hours. It had one alarm within the period, with a high count of 18.2, similar to Suricata.

8. Analysis of the potential of including AI in intrusion detection systems

8.1 Overview of literature on AI use in IDSs in the cloud

Artificial Intelligence (AI) has also gained traction in intrusion detection as technology continues to be advanced [29]. Examples of intelligence systems are machine and deep learning. According to Poornima et al. [30], machine learning is the best and most practical field of AI that can enhance the efficacy of intrusion detection activities. However, numerous studies have overwhelmingly shown that other AI approaches, including deep learning and federal learning, can effectively strengthen intrusion detection efficacy [18, 19, 31, 32].

Similarly, approximately 80% of proposed IDSs have been identified as using deep learning approaches and are perceived as more effective in learning different features independently, unlike those created with machine learning systems [8]). Deep learning approaches are adopted more in IDS; however, they require more resources or data to be used in decision-making activities during the analysis processes [19, 20]. A machine learning approach might thus be preferred for its use of fewer resources than deep learning-based IDSs in the detection of known threats and attacks. However, it might not facilitate the detection of unknown ones. Federal learning IDS is suitable for firms that prefer to withhold their data for security purposes because it allows for the training of distributed datasets with less information sharing [18].

The concept of AI technologies used in intrusion detection activities in the cloud environment has been investigated by numerous scholars. A summary of these studies is illustrated in **Table 3**. This book chapter posits the argument that AI has enhanced the efficacy of IDS systems on the cloud. The argument is based on the results of numerous studies that have shown the significance of AI algorithms in the success of IDS activities. For instance, Sowmya and Anita [32] revealed that AI enhances the accuracy of intrusion detection systems.

Singh et al. [29] used the CICIDS2017 dataset to explore the efficacy of the hybrid cockroach swarm-intelligent integrated and boosted random forest use in detecting attacks and preventing the loss of data in a cloud environment. Their test of the IDS approach on a Python platform revealed that the proposed approach yielded a higher accuracy, predictability, F1 score, and precision in intrusion detection in the cloud [29]. For instance, the proposed approach had a 96% intrusion detection accuracy, while the logistic regression approach's result was 73%, the K-nearest neighbor was 78%, and the support vector machine was 83%. Hence, a revamped IDS with many AI technologies and algorithms is more likely to yield better accuracy, precision, and efficiency in detecting attacks in the cloud environment, unlike when single algorithms are implemented [29].

An IDS whose infrastructure has the support vector machine, a machine learning algorithm, has a high accuracy in predicting attacks in a cloud environment. Alheeti et al. [34] also revealed the high accuracy of a support vector machine-based IDS in a cloud environment. An IDS that uses the support vector machine in detecting behaviors on a cloud system had a 99.92% accuracy rate. This shows that the support vector machine-based IDS counters the low true positive rates, high false positive findings, and low accuracy results associated with most programs or systems used to detect intrusions [34]. Ibrahim and Bhaya [33] used the NSL-KDD and UNSW-NB15 datasets, support vector machine, and GridSearch to test anomalies on a software-defined network cloud system. The accuracy of the detection of all attack types on both data sets was high [33].

Rathore and Sahu [39] explored how machine learning and neural networks can be used to detect threats to a cloud without overloading or overworking its resources. Their analysis revealed that feature selection in the proposed IDS approach enhanced the accuracy of detection of anomalies in the cloud environment. It was also revealed that the traits that are selected during feature selection influence the execution time of IDS programs [39]. Saeed et al. [38] used the CICIDS2019 data set to explore the accuracy of a random forest-based IDS in detecting attacks in a cloud environment in comparison to other AI models. Their random forest architecture-based IDS has

Author	Software and artificial intelligence type	Algorithms	Metrics when choosing AI technologies	Results in the cloud environment
Singh [29]	Neural networks	Random Forests, J48 classifiers, Random Trees, Bayesian Network, and Naive Bayes.	TPR; Accuracy; Execution Time; FPR; % of Incorrect Categorization; Precision and Recall	Random forest trees were found to learn and perform better in attack detection than all the other algorithms.
Ibrahim and Bhaya [33]	Software-Defined Networks Machine learning	Support vector machine	Accuracy, F-measure, sensitivity, and precision	99.8% intrusion attack detection rate. There has been positive progress in the detection of all attacks on networks in software-defined networks-based cloud environments.
Alheeti et al. [34]	Machine learning	Support vector machine	Accuracy, predictability, recall, and precision	The system was suitable for intrusion detection on the cloud because it leads to high accuracy.
Attou et al. [35]	Machine learning	Random forest	Accuracy, recall, and precision	Random forest leads to higher intrusion detection accuracy than the support vector machine and decision trees.
Elmasry et al. [36]	Deep learning	Deep Neural Networks (DNN), Long Short-Term Memory Recurrent Neural Networks (LSTM-RNN), and Deep Belief Networks (DBN)	Detection rate False alarm rate	The detection rates for the experimented data sets were high for all models under the tested cloud-based IDS. The system also had a low false alarm rate.
Al-Ghuwairi et al. [37]	Machine learning	Facebook prophet model Feature selection	Training, prediction, and cross-validation times	Decreased training (85%), prediction (15%), and cross-validation times (97%).
Nazeema et al. [36]	Machine learning framework.	Light Gradient Boosting Machine (LGBM)	Accuracy, F1, recall, and precision	LGBM yielded more accurate and precise detection results, unlike the random forest.
Saeed et al. [38]	Machine learning	Random forest	Accuracy, F1, recall, and precision	The IDS using random forest had a higher accuracy than the decision tree classifier, naïve Baye classifier, and logistic regression AI models.

Author	Software and artificial intelligence type	Algorithms	Metrics when choosing AI technologies	Results in the cloud environment
Rathore and Sahu [39]	Machine learning	Random Forest, Bayes Net, Random Tree, Naive Bayes, and J48 classifiers	False positive rate, execution time, accuracy, recall, precision, and the percentage of incorrectly classified	Available resources can be leveraged to conduct intrusion detection without placing excessive pressure on a cloud server by using the neural network IDS approach.
Singh et al. [40]	Machine learning	Hybrid cockroach swarm-intelligent integrated and boosted random forest	Accuracy, F1, recall, and precision	Unlike current approaches that do not use AI, 97% precision, 94% recall, 96% accuracy, and 95% F1 score in the model's IDS.
Bakro et al. [41]	Machine learning Deep learning	Crow search algorithm	Accuracy, F1, recall, and precision	The Crow search algorithm and machine and deep learning used in IDSs enhance detection rates and reduce false alarms.
Garg et al. [42]	Optimization	Artificial bee colony algorithm	Detection, accuracy, and false alarm	The intrusion detection model was more effective than the support vector machine and machine learning-based intrusion detection systems.
Vibhute and Nakum [43]	Deep learning	deep Convolutional Neural Network (CNN) model Random forest	Accuracy, F1, recall, and precision	The CNN-based IDS had a 97.07% testing accuracy with a 2.93% error rate.

Table 3.
Artificial Intelligence Technology Implementation in Cloud Computing.

a 99.99% accuracy, unlike the other AI-based architectures. This shows that the architecture is suitable for detecting anomalies in a network system on the cloud [38]. Nazeema et al. [44] tested a Light Gradient Boosting Machine (LGBM) in a cloud environment. The LGBM model had a 94% accuracy, unlike that of decision trees (83%), logistic regression (88%), and random forest (87%). Its precision was also higher (94%) than that recorded in random forests (79%), decision trees (74%, and logistic regression (91%).

Machine and deep learning architectures can be combined in an IDS system in cloud environments. Bakro et al. [41] integrated the crow search algorithm and AI frameworks, deep and machine learning, and tested its accuracy, recall, and F1 score in the cloud using the following datasets, Kyoto, CSE-CIC-IDS-2018, and NSL-KDD. False alarm rates and accuracy of attack detections were more efficient in the IDS processes for the three datasets. The false alarm rate in the NSL-KDD data ranged from 0.00 to 0.02, 0.00 to 2.00 in the Kyoto data, and 0.00 for all types of attacks for the

CSE-CIC-IDS-2018. The system's accuracy in the detection of attacks in the NSL-KDD set ranged from 99.99 to 99.98; in Kyoto, the accuracy of intrusion detection ranged from 99.48 to 99.83, and 100 for all attack types in CSE-CIC-IDS-2018 [41].

Vibhute and Nakum [43] explored the accuracy, precision, and recall of a Deep CNN as a tool for testing intrusions on networks. The test results revealed that the CNN-based IDS was effective in intrusion detection on the cloud system. This was evident in the test results, which showed an accuracy rate of 97.07, 98.11% precision, 96.93% recall, and an F-1 score of 97.51%. The dimensionality of data needs to be lowered, and the best features for an IDS need to be chosen using the random forest approach to attain the highest success rate of intrusion detection when using the CNN-based IDS system [43].

According to Elmasry et al. [36], an improved CIDS that can be tested using numerous deep learning algorithms can effectively resolve the inaccuracy that is associated with cloud-based IDS. The scholars tested the system using the NSL-KDD and CICIDS2017 datasets. The results were evident in the detection and false alarm rates. The detection rates in the NSL-KDD data using the PSO algorithm were 92.22% for the DNN, 95.36% for LSTM-RNN, 98.8% for DBN, and 99.3% for Ensemble. Subsequently, the false alarm rates were 2.4% for the DNN, 1.66% for LSTM-RNN, 1.55% for DBN, and 1.17% for Ensemble. The results of the detection rates were higher, and false alarm rates were lower in the Double PSO algorithm under the NSL-KDD dataset. The detection rates were 96.38% for the DNN, 98.18% for LSTM-RNN, 99.81% for DBN, and 99.9% for Ensemble. Reported false alarm rates in the Double PSO algorithm were 0.51% for the DNN, 0.39% for LSTM-RNN, 0.23% for DBN, and 0.16% for Ensemble [36]. Attou and colleagues revealed that their proposed cloud-based IDS had 98.3% accuracy, 96.3% precision, and 100% recall. According to the scholars who tested their system on an Internet of Things (IoT) bot, the random forest is a classifier that can effectively enhance the accuracy of intrusion detection systems [35].

Al-Ghuwairi et al. [37] also proposed a cloud-based IDS that uses machine learning frameworks and models. The prediction model in the proposed system was based on *feature selection, and its overall efficiency was assessed using the Facebook Prophet framework*. Their results revealed it had low errors, which led to higher forecast accuracy. The training time of the cloud-based IDS was also lowered to 1 s from 7.37 s, while the prediction period was lowered to 2.05 s from 2.39 s. The time to perform cross-validation was also reduced from 21 to 907.8 s. Memory consumption was also lowered because IDS activities were identified to take less time, thus mitigating the high resource usage associated with such systems [37].

The improved accuracy of cloud inclusion systems was also evaluated by Garg et al. [42]. The proposed En-ABC algorithm was found to perform better. In the NSL-KDD data set, the detection rate of the proposed system was higher (97.59%) than 82.88% in the FCM, 85.52% in the SVM, 95.17% in the ML-IDS, and 92.74% in the MS-ADA. The prediction accuracy was also higher for the proposed En-ABC system (97.62), unlike the 86.35% in FCM, 90.17% in SVM, 95.75% in ML-IDS, and 95.83% in the MS-ADA. In the NAB data set, the accuracy was 98.92% in the En-ABC system, 97.40% for the MS-ADA, 95.41% for the ML-IDS, 86.52% for the SVM, and 87.07% for the FCM [42].

Overall, the various tests of cloud IDSs that have been tested by numerous scholars are presented. A summary of the surveyed experimental studies is indicated in **Table 3** below. According to the analysis, it is evident that IDS that adopt machine learning models have higher accuracy, precision, and detection rates and low false alarm rates, unlike those that do not use artificial intelligence algorithms. AI thus appears to be the solution to the challenges associated with IDSs on the cloud. However, it is pertinent to acknowledge the potential difficulties associated with implementing AI-based IDSs, considering the high cost of such technologies and the absence of clear regulations regarding the systems.

Further analysis of the work of Vadhil [45] also revealed that open-source IDS software can adopt AI algorithms and technologies that enhance their accuracy and reduce false alarm rates [45]. OSSEC has also been found to successfully detect intrusions when using a Naïve Bayes AI algorithm, leading to a 69% accuracy [45].

The findings from previous literature are analyzed based on the cloud system and IDS tools used during the hands-on experiments. These experiments were conducted using Zeek, Suricata, OSSEC, and Snort and tested on the Amazon VPC (cloud environment). The reviewed literature supported the benefit of AI used in IDS, and the application of the tools used in the hands-on experiments is outlined in the subsection below.

8.2 Analysis of AI integration in the conducted hands-on (experiments)

The integration of artificial intelligence (AI) into Intrusion Detection Systems (IDS) has the potential to transform cybersecurity in cloud environments by enhancing the accuracy, efficiency, and scalability of detection mechanisms. By combining AI tools such as Amazon Athena with monitoring solutions like Amazon CloudWatch, organizations can leverage advanced capabilities for analyzing IDS performance metrics and improving threat detection processes [46].

Amazon Athena is a serverless query tool that enables in-depth analysis of IDS log data stored in Amazon S3. Leveraging Athena's SQL querying capabilities, security teams can extract actionable insights regarding alert trends, detection rule effectiveness, and false positives. This facilitates a more informed approach to intrusion detection. Athena's ability to handle big data makes it particularly suitable for environments with high traffic and extensive logging requirements. While primarily designed for batch analysis, its functionality can be expanded by integrating it with real-time streaming tools to enable prompt threat detection and response.

AI enhances IDS by automating the monitoring and analysis of key performance metrics. With Amazon CloudWatch, real-time metrics from IDS tools such as Suricata, Snort, and Zeek can be monitored, allowing administrators to set up threshold-based alarms for potential anomalies. AI-powered solutions significantly reduce the manual effort required for routine monitoring by automating the detection of subtle patterns that may indicate advanced or emerging threats. This is especially crucial in addressing advanced persistent threats (APTs) that traditional systems might overlook.

Moreover, integrating AI with IDS systems facilitates the development of proactive security measures. For instance, Amazon CloudWatch metrics analyzed using Athena can help create dynamic dashboards, detailed reports, and real-time alerts. This allows organizations to adjust their IDS configurations based on data-driven insights, improving their overall detection and response capabilities. Furthermore, AI-driven anomaly detection models, such as those developed with Amazon SageMaker, can identify deviations in system behavior, providing a higher degree of accuracy compared to rule-based systems.

Despite these advantages, implementing AI in IDS presents challenges. For example, latency in data processing and query execution, particularly with tools like

Athena, may limit real-time application. Additionally, integrating and configuring AI tools with IDS requires careful planning, especially for managing large-scale log data stored in Amazon S3, which may result in significant retention costs. Defining meaningful alarm thresholds is critical to minimize false positives and ensure alerts are actionable.

The potential of AI in IDS is further enhanced by combining it with real-time response capabilities. For instance, integrating Amazon CloudWatch with AWS Lambda can automate responses to detected threats, reducing response times and effectively mitigating risks. Additionally, preprocessing log data using AWS Glue can optimize its structure for efficient querying, which lowers costs and improves analysis speed.

In summary, incorporating AI into IDS offers significant potential for enhancing intrusion detection capabilities. By leveraging tools such as Amazon Athena, CloudWatch, and SageMaker, organizations can achieve improved accuracy, operational efficiency, and scalability in their IDS systems. While challenges exist in the implementation process, these can be addressed through thoughtful integration strategies, making AI a transformative addition to modern intrusion detection systems.

9. Conclusion

The concept of privacy and data security is significant in cloud computing, considering the potential risk of access by attackers, which proves the need to understand the best IDS systems. Intrusion Detection Systems (IDS), including Snort, Suricata, Bro/Zeek, and OSSEC, have demonstrated considerable efficacy in mitigating network-based attacks within cloud environments. Each of these tools possesses distinct features that render them suitable for specific scenarios, and their deployment in experimental settings showcases robust capabilities for detecting and responding to security threats. For instance, AWS Traffic Mirroring has enabled these IDS tools to analyze inbound network traffic, providing insightful data regarding their efficiency in real-world applications. Metrics such as NetworkMirrorIn, NetworkMirrorOut, and packet traffic counts were monitored utilizing Amazon CloudWatch, which empowers administrators to configure alarms and receive real-time alerts regarding potential security incidents.

The experiments conducted within this study underscore the transformative potential of AI in IDS, particularly in cloud environments. Incorporating AI-driven models, such as machine learning algorithms developed in Amazon SageMaker, significantly enhances the capacity of IDS tools to detect advanced persistent threats (APTs) and adapt to the ever-evolving nature of contemporary cyberattacks. Integrating AI with IDS systems facilitates the development of automated responses to identified threats. These are associated with challenges, such as computational overhead associated with real-time data analysis and the necessity for meticulous configuration to efficiently manage large-scale log data. Although traditional IDS tools remain integral to cybersecurity strategies, their effectiveness is substantially amplified when integrated with AI technologies. By reducing false alarms and enhancing recall rates, AI-based IDS systems present a compelling solution for organizations aiming to improve the accuracy and reliability of their security infrastructures.

Author details

Waleed Almuseelem
Faculty of Computing and Information Technology (FCIT), University of Tabuk, Saudi Arabia

*Address all correspondence to: waleedalmuseelem@ut.edu.sa

References

[1] Tissir N, El Kafhali S, Aboutabit N. Cybersecurity management in cloud computing: Semantic literature review and conceptual framework proposal. Journal of Reliable Intelligent Environments. 2020;**7**:69-84. DOI: 10.1007/s40860-020-00115-0

[2] Dawood M, Tu S, Xiao C, Alasmary H, Waqas M, Rehman SU. Cyberattacks and security of cloud computing: A complete guideline. Symmetry. 2023;**15**(11):1-33. DOI: 10.3390/sym15111981

[3] Rana P et al. Intrusion detection systems in cloud computing paradigm: Analysis and overview. Complexity. 2022;**2022**:1-14. DOI: 10.1155/2022/3999039

[4] National Institute of Standards and Technology, Security Best Practices for the Electronic Transmission Of Election Materials for UOCAVA voters NISTIR 7711. 2011. Available from: https://nvlpubs.nist.gov/nistpubs/Legacy/IR/nistir7711.pdf

[5] U.S. Department of Energy. Intrusion Detection System (IDS). Washinton DC: U.S. Department of Energy; 2023. Available from: https://www.directives.doe.gov/terms_definitions/intrusion-detection-system-ids

[6] Khaliq S. Intrusion detection survey: A survey and taxonomy. Information Systems. 2020:1-6. DOI: 10.20944/preprints202006.0065.v1

[7] Efe A, Abaci İN. Comparison of the host-based intrusion detection systems and network-based intrusion detection systems. Celal Bayar Üniversitesi Fen Bilimleri Dergisi. 2022;**18**(1):1-11. DOI: 10.18466/cbayarfbe.832533

[8] Ahmad Z, Shahid Khan A, Wai Shiang C, Abdullah J, Ahmad F. Network intrusion detection system: A systematic study of machine learning and deep learning approaches. Transactions on Emerging Telecommunications Technologies. 2021;**32**(1):1-29. DOI: 10.1002/ett.4150

[9] Satilmiş H, Akleylek S, Tok ZY. A systematic literature review on host-based intrusion detection systems. IEEE Access. 2024;**9**:1-31. DOI: 10.1109/access.2024.3367004

[10] Khraisat A, Gondal I, Vamplew P, Kamruzzaman J. Survey of intrusion detection systems: Techniques, datasets, and challenges. Cybersecurity. 2019;**2**(1):1-22. DOI: 10.1186/s42400-019-0038-7

[11] Mell P, Grance T. The NIST Definition of Cloud Computing Recommendations of the National Institute of Standards and Technology. National Institute of Standards and Technology. 2011;**53**:1-7. DOI: 10.6028/NIST.SP.800-145

[12] Islam R et al. The future of cloud computing: Benefits and challenges. International Journal of Communications, Network and System Sciences. 2023;**16**(4):53-65. DOI: 10.4236/ijcns.2023.164004

[13] Angudi JJ. Security challenges in cloud computing: A comprehensive analysis. World Journal of Advanced Engineering Technology and Sciences. 2023;**10**(2):155-181. DOI: 10.30574/wjaets.2023.10.2.0304

[14] Chang V et al. A survey on intrusion detection systems for fog and cloud computing. Future Internet.

2022;**14**(3):1-27. DOI: 10.3390/fi14030089

[15] Khan MM. Developing AI-powered intrusion detection system for cloud infrastructure. Journal of Artificial Intelligence, Machine Learning and Data Science. 2024;**2**(1):1074-1080. DOI: 10.51219/jaimld/mohammed-mustafa-khan/255

[16] Ahmadi S. Systematic literature review on cloud computing security: Threats and mitigation strategies. International Journal of Information Security. 2024;**15**(2):148-167. DOI: 10.4236/jis.2024.152010

[17] Attuluri S, Ramesh M, Budaraju RR, Kumar S, Swain J, Kurmi J. Original research article defending against phishing attacks in cloud computing using digital watermarking. Journal of Autonomous Intelligence. 2024;**7**(5):1-13. DOI: 10.32629/jai.v7i5.1061

[18] Muneer S, Farooq U, Athar A, Raza MA, Ghazal TM, Sakib S. A critical review of artificial intelligence-based approaches in intrusion detection: A comprehensive analysis. Journal of Engineering. 2024;**2024**:1-16. DOI: 10.1155/2024/3909173

[19] Vanin P et al. A study of network intrusion detection systems using artificial intelligence/machine learning. Applied Sciences. 2022;**12**(22):1-27. DOI: 10.3390/app122211752

[20] Sarker IH. Deep learning: A comprehensive overview on techniques, taxonomy, applications and research directions. SN Computer Science. 2021;**2**(6):1-20. DOI: 10.1007/s42979-021-00815-1

[21] Tayyebi Y, Bhilare DS. A comparative study of open source network based intrusion detection systems. International Journal of Computer Science and Information Technologies. 2018;**9**(2):23-26. Available from: https://www.ijcsit.com/docs/Volume%209/vol9issue2/ijcsit2018090201.pdf

[22] Syamsuddin I, Barukab OM. SUKRY: Suricata IDS with enhanced kNN algorithm on raspberry Pi for classifying IoT botnet attacks. Electronics. 2022;**11**(5):1-18. DOI: 10.3390/electronics11050737

[23] Gusrianda MF, Fajrizal F, Guntoro GG. Monitoring on solid foundation servers using Suricata through telegram bot notifications. CommniTech: Journal of Computational Intelligence and Informatics. 2024;**1**(1):38-48. Available from: https://journal.unilak.ac.id/index.php/CommniTech/article/view/21380

[24] Mirza AU, Kumar A. Big data analytics for intrusion detection in cloud based systems: A performance analysis. International Journal of Research in Engineering and Applied Sciences (IJREAS). 2022;**12**(9):27-32. Availablefrom: https://euroasiapub.org/wp-content/uploads/IJREAS1Sep22-Agha.pdf

[25] Asad H, Adhikari S, Gashi I. A perspective–retrospective analysis of diversity in signature-based open-source network intrusion detection systems. International Journal of Information Security. 2024;**23**:1331-1346. DOI: 10.1007/s10207-023-00794-9

[26] Idrus A, Sugiyanta L, Nugraheni M, Subhiyanto. Design and implementation of Sucirata-based instrusion detection system as a network security system cloud computers. International Journal of Information & Technology. 2023;**7**(2):144-160. Available from: https://ijistech.org/ijistech/index.php/ijistech/article/viewFile/310/309

[27] Ibraheem IO. Hybrid Intrusion Detection System in Cloud Computing Environment. Nigeria: Al-Hikmah University; 2022. Available from: https://www.academia.edu/116705151/Hybrid_Intrusion_Detection_System_in_Cloud_Computing_Environment

[28] AWS. Work with Open-Source Tools for Traffic Mirroring. 2024. Available from: https://docs.aws.amazon.com/vpc/latest/mirroring/tm-example-open-source.html

[29] Singh N. Artificial intelligence-based intrusion detection system for cloud computing. International Journal for Research in Applied Science and Engineering Technology. 2024;**12**(3):701-709. DOI: 10.22214/ijraset.2024.58920

[30] Poornima G, Sakkari DS, Pallavi R. Artificial intelligence for intrusion detection systems. In: Swarnkar M, Rajput SS, editors. Intrusion Detection System Using Artificial Intelligence. Florida: CRC Press; 2023. pp. 2-33

[31] Andresini G, Appice A, Mauro ND, Loglisci C, Malerba D. Multi-channel deep feature learning for intrusion detection. IEEE Access. 2020;**8**:53346-53359. DOI: 10.1109/access.2020.2980937

[32] Sowmya T, Anita EAM. A comprehensive review of AI based intrusion detection system. Measurement: Sensors. 2023;**28**:1-13. DOI: 10.1016/j.measen.2023.100827

[33] Ibrahim OJ, Bhaya WS. Intrusion detection system for cloud based software-defined networks. Journal of Physics: Conference Series. 2021;**1804**(1):1-15. DOI: 10.1088/1742-6596/1804/1/012007

[34] Alheeti A, Azawii A, Alzahrani NA, Imran NA, Al-Dosary ND. Cloud intrusion detection system based on SVM. International Journal of Interactive Mobile Technologies (iJIM). 2023;**17**(11):101-114. DOI: 10.3991/ijim.v17i11.39063

[35] Attou H, Guezzaz A, Benkirane S, Azrour M, Farhaoui Y. Cloud-based intrusion detection approach using machine learning techniques. Big Data Mining and Analytics. 2023;**6**(3):311-320. DOI: 10.26599/bdma.2022.9020038

[36] Elmasry W, Akbulut A, Zaim AH. A design of an integrated cloud-based intrusion detection system with third party cloud service. Open Computer Science. 2021;**11**(1):365-379. DOI: 10.1515/comp-2020-0214

[37] Al-Ghuwairi A-R, Sharrab Y, Al-Fraihat D, AlElaimat M, Alsarhan A, Algarni A. Intrusion detection in cloud computing based on time series anomalies utilizing machine learning. Journal of Cloud Computing. 2023;**12**(1):1-17. DOI: 10.1186/s13677-023-00491-x

[38] Saeed MS, Saurabh R, Bhasme SB, Nazarov AN. Machine learning based intrusion detection system in cloud environment. In: 2022 VIII International Conference on Information Technology and Nanotechnology (ITNT). Vol. 20. Samara: Russian Federation; 2022. pp. 1-6. DOI: 10.1109/itnt55410.2022.9848611

[39] Rathore A, Sahu T. AI-based intrusion detection system in cloud computing. International Journal of Emerging Technologies and Innovative Research. 2024;**11**:45-51. DOI: 10.55524/csistw.2024.12.1.8

[40] Singh N, Singh A, Chakravarty A, Ramalingam K. Artificial intelligent based intrusion detection system for safe cloud information retention.

Multidisciplinary Science Journal. 2024;**6**:1-8. DOI: 10.31893/multiscience.2024ss0308

[41] Bakro M et al. Efficient intrusion detection system in the cloud using fusion feature selection approaches and an ensemble classifier. Electronics. 2023;**12**(11):1-27. DOI: 10.3390/electronics12112427

[42] Garg S et al. En-ABC: An ensemble artificial bee colony based anomaly detection scheme for cloud environment. Journal of Parallel and Distributed Computing. 2020;**135**:219-233. DOI: 10.1016/j.jpdc.2019.09.013

[43] Vibhute AD, Nakum V. Deep learning-based network anomaly detection and classification in an imbalanced cloud environment. Procedia Computer Science. 2024;**232**:1636-1645. DOI: 10.1016/j.procs.2024.01.161

[44] Nazeema RA, Kouser S, Hasen SM, Babikar N, Boush AMS. An improved explainable artificial intelligence for intrusion detection system in cloud environment. International Journal of Intelligent Systems and Applications in Engineering. 2024;**12**(3):352-360. Available from: https://ijisae.org/index.php/IJISAE/article/view/5258

[45] Vadhil FA, Nanne MF, Salihi ML. Importance of machine learning techniques to improve the open source intrusion detection systems. Indonesian Journal of Electrical Engineering and Informatics (IJEEI). 2021;**9**(3):774-783. DOI: 10.52549/ijeei.v9i3.3219

[46] Balajee RM, Jayanthi Kannan MK. Intrusion detection on AWS cloud through hybrid deep learning algorithm. Electronics. 2023;**12**(6):1-21. DOI: 10.3390/electronics12061423

Section 2

Emerging Threats and Innovative Detection Approaches

Chapter 4

Advancements in Vehicle Intrusion Detection Systems: Enhancing Cybersecurity in Intelligent Transportation

Mahdi Sahlabadi, Md Rezanur Islam,
Munkhdelgerekh Batzorig and Kangbin Yim

Abstract

Advancements in in-vehicle Intrusion Detection Systems (IDS) are critical to addressing cybersecurity challenges in modern intelligent transportation. This chapter explores vulnerabilities inherent in Controller Area Network (CAN) protocols, such as DoS, spoofing, and replay attacks, and their impacts on vehicular systems. By analyzing the LISA Vehicle Dataset collected through innovative techniques like gateway-based methods and custom testbeds as injection tools, the study provides insights into abnormal behaviors and attack patterns. It evaluates IDS approaches, including rule-based and machine learning-based systems, highlighting the strengths of deep learning models like RNNs and CNNs for robust anomaly detection. Feature selection and optimized chunking methodologies, such as mutual information analysis, are discussed to enhance IDS efficiency while reducing computational demands. The chapter also emphasizes real-world simulation using synchronized CAN datasets and testbeds, contributing to the development of scalable, real-time IDS frameworks for secure and reliable vehicular communication.

Keywords: vehicle intrusion detection systems (IDS), controller area network (CAN) security, in-vehicle network (IVN) vulnerabilities, deep learning for anomaly detection, feature selection and chunking in IDS

1. Introduction

This chapter delves into the advancements in Vehicle Intrusion Detection Systems (IDS), addressing the critical need for enhanced cybersecurity in intelligent transportation systems. It builds on practical research conducted in the LISA laboratory, incorporating findings from real-world testbeds, including Connected and Autonomous Vehicles (CAV) and Vehicle-to-Everything (V2X) systems. The chapter begins with the foundational Vehicles Dataset, detailing data collection processes, environments, and the characteristics of the collected datasets, which form the basis for understanding IDS development. It then transitions into an exploration of In-Vehicle Network (IVN) Vulnerabilities, highlighting risks within automotive networks and presenting practical solutions such as simulation environments and V2X data frameworks. Finally, the chapter focuses on Data Analysis and Feature Selection, discussing methodologies for analyzing data, identifying critical features, and building robust intrusion detection models using advanced machine learning techniques. Together, these sections provide a cohesive narrative, blending theoretical insights with practical experimentation to offer actionable solutions for mitigating cyber threats in modern vehicular networks, ensuring their safety and reliability in an increasingly connected and autonomous era.

2. Vehicles dataset

Modern vehicles use various communication protocols, such as FlexRay, Media Oriented Systems Transport (MOST), Local Interconnect Network (LIN), and automotive Ethernet (100BASE-T1). However, the Controller Area Network (CAN) message protocol is the most widely used because of its cost-effectiveness and efficient data transfer. Despite its advantages, the CAN protocol lacks robust security features, which can lead to severe risks, including damage to the vehicle and potential harm to human life. To address these vulnerabilities, vehicles require security systems, such as IDS [1].

The LISA Vehicle Dataset for Intrusion Detection is a collection of CAN message datasets gathered from actual vehicles while they are in motion. During the data collection, attack messages were intentionally injected into the vehicle's internal network. A specialized tool was used to collect the resulting dataset, creating an attack dataset for analysis on Volkswagen GOLF (2014), KIA SOUL (2015), BMW 118d (2015), KIA SOUL Booster (2019), Tesla Model 3 (2020), Genesis G80 (2022), as shown in **Figure 1**.

2.1 Dataset collection

2.1.1 Collection environment

The OBD-II port, or onboard diagnostics, is typically used to collect CAN messages. It monitors and controls a vehicle's operation. Initially, it was used to improve

Figure 1.
Test vehicles used in the study: Volkswagen GOLF (2014), KIA SOUL (2015), BMW 118d (2015), KIA SOUL Booster (2019), Tesla Model 3 (2020), and Genesis G80 (2022).

the efficiency of vehicle maintenance. However, due to security concerns related to using the OBD-II port, newer vehicles have limited data transfer and installed filters on the port. The other method we found for collecting IVN data is the gateway-based EDA (Gateway ECU Direct Approach) method [2]. The IVN gateway is connected to all vehicle networks to maintain the vehicle system. In this method, we first locate the gateway position based on the manufacturer's guidelines, as shown in **Figure 2**. We then compared data collection from the OBD-II port and the gateway-based collection method. As shown in **Figure 3**, we can see that the gateway-based method collects an average of 4340 messages per millisecond. The OBD-II port collects an average of only 50 messages per millisecond [3].

We developed our own collection and injection tools for CAN messages using APIs provided by PEAK and VECTOR collection tools. This allowed us to collect and analyze various CAN message data, providing a wealth of information.

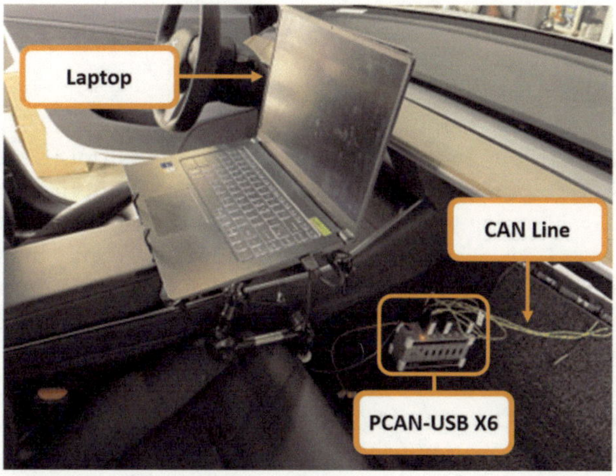

Figure 2.
Illustration of the data collection method via the ICU.

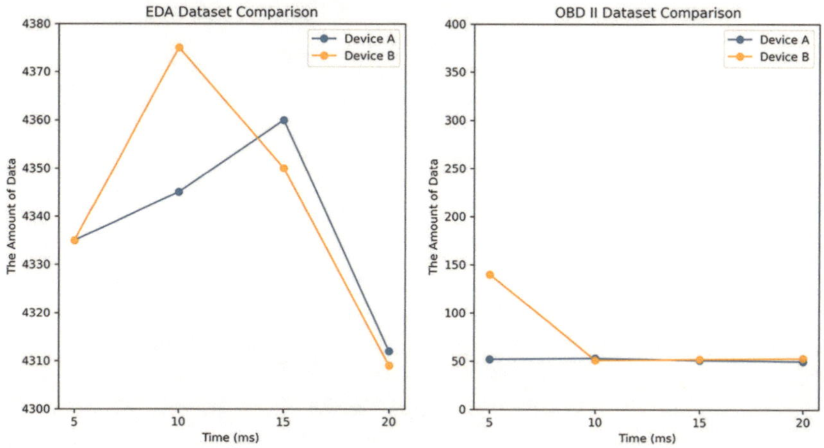

Figure 3.
Data collection difference between ICU and BOD-II.

2.1.2 Data collection scenario

Establishing an accurate scenario for dataset collection is crucial, as it is just as important as building the collection environment. Data analysis could lead to accurate results if the dataset needs to be corrected. If such accurate results are used in machine learning or deep learning models, it could result in misdetection, making it easier to evaluate the model. Therefore, it is essential to collect the dataset from the beginning. We begin by configuring the dataset collection settings within the vehicle. Once the environment is set up, we revert the vehicle to its original state before the driver unlocks the door, and after that, we begin the data collection. During the collection, we have an attack scenario for each attack based on its specification. The data collection process continues until the driver shuts down the engine, exits the vehicle, locks it, and takes the smart key with them [4]. **Figure 4** demonstrates the Stages of the vehicle state: Stage 0 (Original state before it is unlocked), Stage 1 (Before the engine is started), Stage 2 (After the engine is started), Stage 3 (After the engine is shut down), Stage 4 (After the vehicle is locked).

2.1.3 Dataset description

In a vehicle, as shown in **Figure 5**, there are typically multiple CAN networks. Each of these networks is responsible for different functions within the vehicle's electronic control unit (ECU), allowing various systems within the vehicle to communicate. For example, the Chassis CAN (C-CAN) network communicates at a high speed of 500 Mbit/s and controls systems such as the Transmission Control Unit (TCU) and Anti-lock Braking System (ABS). The Body CAN (B-CAN) network controls systems unrelated to the vehicle's power components, such as the Body Control Module (BCM), Smart Key Module, and Power Window. The Multimedia CAN (M-CAN) network operates slower than 100 Mbit/s and controls in-vehicle multimedia systems such as Audio, Video, Navigation (AVN) systems and instrument panels.

The Diagnosis CAN (D-CAN) network is used for vehicle diagnostics, while the Powertrain CAN (P-CAN) network controls the vehicle's power transmission system. These different CAN networks work together to ensure that various systems within

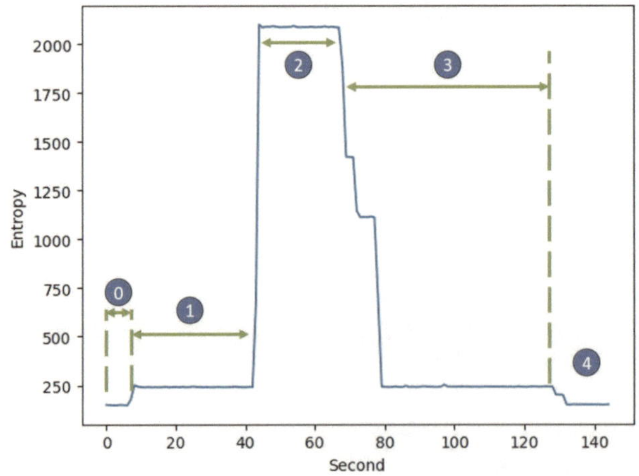

Figure 4.
Event triggered data scenario.

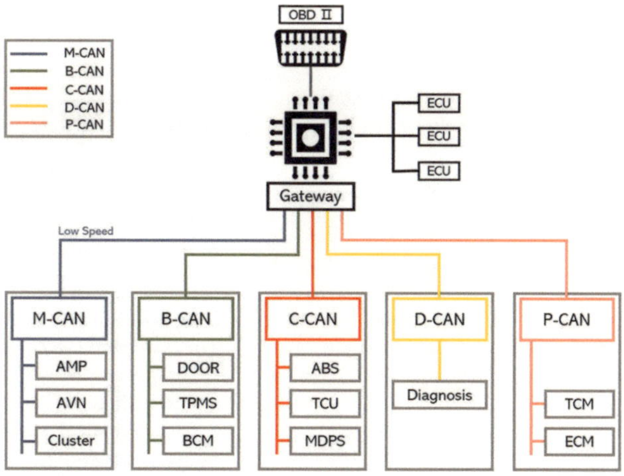

Figure 5.
IVN structure.

the vehicle can operate smoothly and efficiently. A vehicle's gateway is a system that plays a critical role in safely transmitting data between different CAN networks. When designing distributed CAN networks, it is essential to centralize information collection on vehicle networks. This makes expanding high-speed networks such as CAN-FD (CAN-Flexible D), Ethernet, and FlexRay easier. Additionally, these gateways can route different CAN channels flexibly based on traffic and environmental conditions. This allows for the transmission of signals between CAN domains and the ability to check the entire vehicle or devices for abnormal operation.

Our data collection contains columns such as "Time_offset_ms," "Type," "CAN_ID," "DLC," "Data Field," and "Label." The CAN FD dataset may include additional columns specific to the CAN FD protocol that are not found in other datasets. A detailed explanation of these columns is provided in **Table 1**, while an example of the collected dataset is shown in **Figure 6**.

2.2 CAN message details

See **Table 1**.

3. In-vehicle network vulnerabilities

In-vehicle networks (IVNs) rely on the Controller Area Network (CAN) protocol as the backbone for communication between Electronic Control Units (ECUs) [5]. CAN operates without built-in security mechanisms, making it vulnerable to a range of cyber-attacks [6]. The protocol transmits messages in a broadcast manner, allowing all ECUs to receive every message on the network [6]. However, ECUs process messages based on the priority of their identifiers (IDs), which determines the sequence of handling. This lack of authentication and encryption in CAN communication opens the door to various attack vectors, such as Denial of Service (DoS), Fuzzing, Replay, Spoofing, Malfunction, and Impersonation, which exploit the broadcast nature of the network [2, 7, 8]. Additionally, ECU-specific attacks like Suspension, Fabrication, and Masquerading can manipulate or disrupt the functionality of targeted ECUs [9].

Field name	Description	Application and value
Message Number	The message number indicates the order in which messages were collected by the collection tool.	Provides the exact order of each CAN message. Values start from 1 and continue until the collection tool stops recording.
Time Offset	Displays the timestamp of each message occurrence, measured in milliseconds.	Provides precise timing of CAN message collection. Values start from 0 and continue in float format until the collection tool stops.
Type	Identifies different message categories and explains their functions and usage.	Categorizes and filters messages based on type. Common values include: • 0x00: Standard Frame (11-bit identifier, Rx). • 0x01: Remote-Transfer-Request Frame. • 0x02: Extended Frame (29-bit identifier). • 0x04: FD frame (CiA Specs). • 0x08: FD bit rate switch. • 0x10: FD error state indicator. • 0x40: Error frame. • 0x80: PCAN status message.
CAN ID	Serves as an identifier for each ECU and determines priority when multiple messages are received simultaneously.	Messages can be filtered and categorized using hexadecimal CAN IDs. Confidential information links CAN ID to ECU.
Data Length Code (DLC)	Indicates the size of the data field in bytes.	Represents the number of bytes in the payload (0–8). Helps in understanding message content.
Data Bytes	Hold the information transmitted by the ECU. Can contain up to 8 bytes depending on DLC.	Analyze signals packaged in the payload: • Constants (unchanging values). • Multi-Values (changing bits, e.g., door status). • Counters (cyclic counters for transmitted messages). • Check Codes (CRC for error prevention). • Physical Values (real-world values). Bytes are represented as hexadecimal (00 to FF). NaN values are replaced with −1.

Table 1.
Detailed description of CAN message fields.

Addressing these vulnerabilities is critical to ensuring the security and reliability of IVNs, especially in connected and autonomous vehicle systems.

3.1 Denial of service (DoS) attack

- *Definition*: A DoS attack involves flooding the CAN bus with high-priority messages, monopolizing bus access, and preventing legitimate ECUs from communicating.

	No	Time_Offset	Type	ID	Data_Length	One	Two	Three	Four	Five	Six	Seven	Eight
0	1)	0.000	0	0545	8	C8	15	00	88	31	00	31	00
1	2)	0.244	0	0370	8	FF	20	00	80	FF	00	00	28
2	3)	0.484	0	043F	8	00	40	60	FF	61	F4	09	00
3	4)	0.726	0	0440	8	FF	A0	00	00	FF	F0	09	00
4	5)	0.966	0	04F2	8	A0	00	C0	38	00	00	00	FF
...	...	...	...	...	...	...	...	...	...	...	...	...	...
2872257	2872258)	1410654.449	0	043F	8	00	40	60	FF	72	10	0A	00
2872258	2872259)	1410654.681	0	0350	8	15	2B	65	5E	68	20	00	4D
2872259	2872260)	1410654.923	0	0370	8	FF	20	00	80	FF	00	00	A0
2872260	2872261)	1410655.161	0	0153	8	00	80	10	FF	00	FF	10	9E
2872261	2872262)	1410655.393	0	0220	8	E9	33	FD	03	0C	30	06	10

Figure 6.
CAN dataset examples.

- *Impact on CAN*: This disrupts normal operations by overwhelming the bus, leading to delays or complete loss of communication.

- *Example*: An attacker floods the bus with high-priority messages such as 0x100, causing critical ECU messages like brake or airbag signals to be delayed or dropped.

3.2 Fuzzing attack

- *Definition*: Random or malformed CAN frames are injected into the network, using a range of low- to high-priority IDs with varying payloads, to exploit undefined behaviors or crash ECUs.

- *Impact on CAN*: Can cause unpredictable ECU behavior, crashes, or trigger unintended actions in the vehicle.

- *Example*: An attacker sends random frames with varying priorities, e.g., ID: 0x050, Payload: [0xFF, 0xAA, 0x00, 0xEE] and ID: 0x200, Payload: [0x01, 0x02, 0x03, 0x04], to identify vulnerabilities in specific ECUs such as the engine or infotainment system.

3.3 Replay attack

- *Definition*: Captured CAN frames are retransmitted to mimic legitimate ECU communication, leading to repeated or unauthorized actions.

- *Impact on CAN*: Allows an attacker to replicate previous actions, such as unlocking doors or disabling alarms.

- *Example*: An attacker captures and replays a frame ID: 0x250, Payload: [0x01, 0x00, 0x01, 0xFF] used for door unlocking, causing the doors to unlock repeatedly.

3.4 Malfunction attack

- *Definition*: A malfunction attack targets specific CAN IDs extracted from the network and manipulates the associated data fields. By injecting crafted messages with altered payloads or values, the attacker induces abnormal behavior in the vehicle's ECUs.

- *Impact on CAN*: This type of attack disrupts normal vehicle operation by causing unintended actions, such as incorrect sensor readings or unexpected system responses.

- *Example*: An attacker manipulates the data field of a CAN message, such as ID: 0x153, by setting certain bytes to [0x00, 0x00, 0x00, 0x00], resulting in repeated beeping sounds in the vehicle. Similarly, modifying the third byte of ID: 0x43F causes the headlights to blink and the engine/emissions warning light to activate.

3.5 Impersonation attack

- *Definition*: An impersonation attack occurs when an attacker disables a legitimate ECU and replaces it with a malicious node that mimics the behavior of the original ECU. The impersonating node sends spoofed frames or responds to remote frames to appear as the legitimate ECU.

- *Impact on CAN*: This attack compromises the authenticity and integrity of messages, allowing the attacker to override legitimate commands without disrupting overall network availability.

- *Example*: An attacker disables the legitimate steering ECU and replaces it with a malicious node. The impersonating node sends spoofed frames, such as ID: 0x110, Payload: [0x01, 0x02, 0x03, 0x04], causing unintended changes in the vehicle's steering direction.

3.6 Spoofing attack

- *Definition*: Similar to impersonation, spoofing injects fake frames with valid-looking IDs to mislead ECUs about their origin.

- *Impact on CAN*: Deceives ECUs into executing unauthorized actions or sending false responses.

- *Example*: A spoofed frame ID: 0x400, Payload: [0xAA, 0xBB, 0xCC, 0xDD] tricks the vehicle into thinking the engine temperature is normal when it is overheating.

3.7 Suspension attack

- *Definition*: Frames are manipulated to stop a specific ECU from communicating by using higher-priority messages.

- *Impact on CAN*: Disables the targeted ECU's functionality, potentially affecting critical vehicle systems.
- *Example*: Continuous injection of high-priority frames such as ID: 0x050 prevents the airbag ECU (ID: 0x120) from transmitting safety-critical messages.

3.8 Fabrication attack

- *Definition*: A fabrication attack occurs when an attacker uses a compromised ECU to inject entirely fake messages into the CAN network. These forged messages typically mimic legitimate ones but include maliciously altered payloads.
- *Impact on CAN*: Misleads ECUs by introducing conflicting or non-existent data, potentially causing safety-critical malfunctions or erratic behavior in the vehicle.
- *Example*: An attacker compromises ECU A to inject fake speedometer messages with ID: 0x500, Payload: [0x00, 0x01, 0x00, 0xFF] at a higher frequency than the legitimate transmitter, ECU B. This causes receiving ECUs to predominantly process the attacker's fabricated messages, leading to false speed readings on the dashboard.

3.9 Masquerading attack

- *Definition*: A masquerading attack combines suspension and impersonation, where the attacker disables a legitimate ECU and injects messages at the original frequency from a compromised ECU, mimicking the legitimate one.
- *Impact on CAN*: Bypasses protection mechanisms by maintaining the expected timing of messages, deceiving receiving ECUs into treating the forged messages as authentic.
- *Example*: An attacker uses ECU A to inject forged RPM messages with ID: 0x600 and malicious payloads, while suspending ECU B (the legitimate sender). This prevents contradictions in timing or signal patterns, causing the dashboard to display false RPM values.

The impacts of various attacks on the Controller Area Network (CAN) manifest as anomalies in the ID sequence, payload sequence, and time gap of transmitted messages. Attacks such as Denial of Service (DoS) and Suspension disrupt the ID sequence by overwhelming the bus with high-priority frames, thereby preventing legitimate messages from being processed. Replay, Impersonation, and Masquerading attacks manipulate the payload sequence by injecting previously captured, spoofed, or maliciously crafted data to mimic legitimate ECUs and execute unauthorized actions. Fuzzing attacks corrupt the payload by injecting random or malformed frames across a range of low to high-priority IDs, while Malfunction attacks specifically target CAN IDs to alter data fields, inducing abnormal ECU behavior. Fabrication attacks introduce entirely fake messages that mislead ECUs into processing non-existent or harmful commands. Additionally, attacks such as DoS and Replay significantly alter the time gap between consecutive frames, either by flooding the network with excessive messages or delaying the transmission of legitimate ones. These disruptions in ID sequencing, payload integrity, and timing underscore the necessity of robust IDS to effectively identify and mitigate malicious activities in CAN networks, ensuring the security and reliability of in-vehicle communications.

3.9.1 Simulation in loop

The quality of an attack dataset significantly influences the effectiveness of an IDS. However, collecting attack data from a real vehicle involves substantial safety risks, particularly when the vehicle is in motion. To address these challenges, we developed a controlled testbed environment utilizing components from real vehicles, as illustrated in **Figure 7**. This setup enables safe and controlled data collection while effectively simulating various vehicle states.

3.9.1.1 Testbed configuration

The testbed is constructed using actual vehicle parts, following detailed circuit diagrams and manuals. These components are interconnected to create a functional simulation of a vehicle's communication system, providing a safe platform for attack dataset generation. By following these manuals and circuit schematics, we assemble and configure the testbed to replicate the vehicle's environment, ensuring the accuracy and reliability of the collected data. To simulate the vehicle, we need to inject the dataset that is collected from the vehicle into the testbed. In order to simulate the environment when the dataset is collected, the video is also recorded as well. To synchronize those CAN messages and videos, the first injection should be in the testbed. The injection tool is built in Python using the PCAN library, which is supported by the peak system. At the same time, the video should be played at the same time with the injection tool. All those tasks are handled by a thread since the thread is the method through which two different tasks run at the same time. CAN message datasets are inherently influenced by the vehicle's model and manufacturer. Different vehicle types exhibit unique CAN message characteristics, requiring tailored datasets for each type. To address this, we built separate testbeds for each vehicle model and manufacturer in our collection. This enables us to simulate various vehicles accurately and inject attack messages during the simulation to generate a diverse range of attack datasets. To simulate real vehicle conditions, we utilize data collected

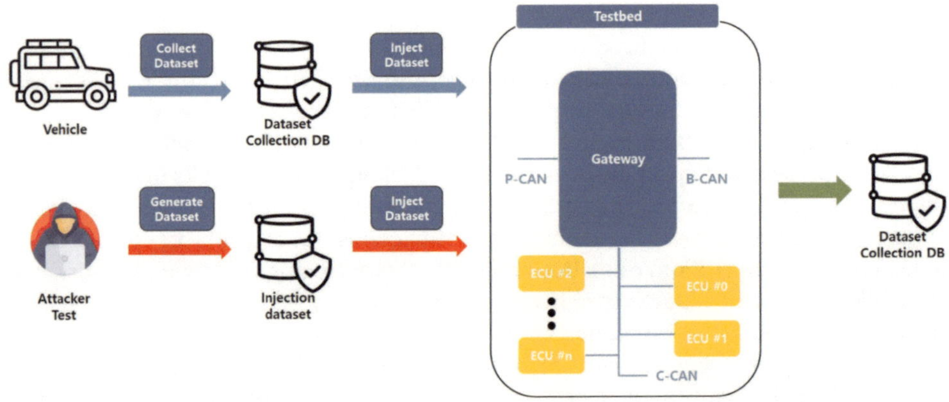

Figure 7.
Data collection overview.

from actual vehicles and replicate these conditions within the testbed. Each testbed corresponds to a specific vehicle type, ensuring that we capture the necessary variation in-vehicle data. CAN message dataset generation is different based on vehicle model and manufacture. However, we need different types of vehicle datasets. In order to do that, we have built different vehicle types of testbeds. For simulation purposes, the laboratory has a total of six different testbeds from six different vehicles, which are KIA SOUL, KIA SOUL BOOSTER, Genesis G80, etc., as shown in **Figure 8**. Each testbed corresponds to a specific vehicle type, ensuring that we capture the necessary variation in-vehicle data. Additionally, to recreate the environmental context, a synchronized video recording from the data collection process is also incorporated. This synchronized playback ensures accurate simulation of real-world conditions. The CAN message dataset is injected into the testbed using a custom Python-based injection tool. This tool is built using the PCAN library, a reliable framework provided by Peak Systems [6]. The injection replicates the exact sequence and timing of the original CAN messages, ensuring fidelity in simulation. Simultaneously, the recorded video is played back alongside the injection process. This synchronization is crucial to provide a comprehensive understanding of the vehicle's operational state during the original data collection. Multithreading is employed to manage the concurrent execution of CAN message injection and video playback. This approach ensures that both tasks run simultaneously and are synchronized effectively. Threads enable efficient handling of these independent yet interrelated processes, maintaining consistency throughout the simulation.

3.9.2 V2X data

LISA aims to develop a system capable of collecting and transmitting real-time vehicle data (**Figure 9**), including sensor (e.g., LiDAR) and in-vehicle network (IVN) data, to a cloud server using wireless communication technologies such as LTE-V2X and DSRC. Two approaches were explored: the first involves using an LTE-enabled Road-Side Unit (RSU) to collect and transmit data to the cloud, while the second involves injecting sensor data into custom V2X messages transmitted via DSRC and received by an RSU for cloud upload. Challenges include hardware limitations of On-Board Units (OBUs) that lack C-V2X capabilities, outdated SDKs, and incomplete

Figure 8.
Various testbeds.

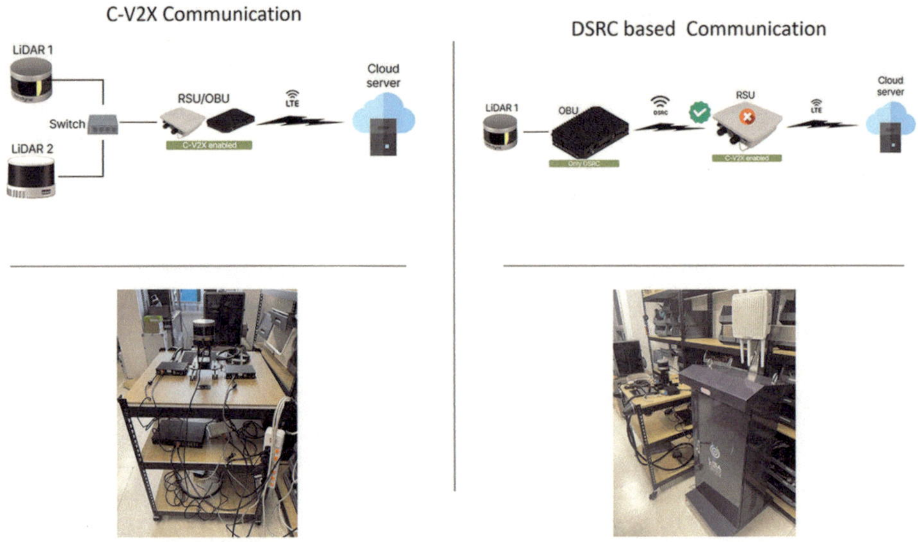

Figure 9.
V2X collection environment.

product documentation from Commsignia. The LISA overcame these hurdles by modifying existing software, cross-compiling binaries for the ARMv7 architecture, and dynamically linking libraries extracted from the devices.

In the first approach, an intermediary switch connects LiDAR sensors to the RSU, which uses an LTE connection to send data to a cloud server. A second approach utilizes OBUs to create custom V2X messages with sensor data. These messages are sent through DSRC to an RSU, which forwards them to the cloud. The team successfully injected sensor data into V2X messages using modified software and verified data transmission through packet analyzers. However, the issue of extracting sensor data at the RSU for cloud transmission remains unresolved. The project also includes developing methods to sniff WSM packets directly from DSRC antennas and enhancing LTE connectivity by integrating new hardware or using alternative LTE-enabled devices.

Future developments focus on refining data collection and synchronization for high-performance cloud processing. The team plans to explore server frameworks such as Flask or asyncio, real-time data processing tools like Apache Kafka, and database solutions like MySQL or MongoDB for data storage and retrieval. Solutions to address current limitations, such as obfuscated packet capture apps and hardware constraints, are also under consideration. These efforts aim to create a robust, scalable system for real-time vehicular data analysis and integration into intelligent transportation systems.

4. Data analysis and feature selection

4.1 Data analysis

Intrusion detection in CAN networks can be approached through various methods, primarily rule-based systems and machine learning-based models [2]. Both approaches rely heavily on extensive data analysis to ensure effectiveness. Rule-based methods require thorough analysis to define precise rules that can identify abnormal behaviors, while machine learning-based systems depend on detailed feature extraction and accurate data labeling to train models capable of distinguishing between normal and attack scenarios. This foundational data analysis is critical for identifying patterns, establishing baselines, and enabling robust detection mechanisms, making it a vital step in developing any reliable intrusion detection system.

In analyzing CAN data to distinguish between normal and attack scenarios, several key factors highlight the impact of malicious activities. Under normal conditions, the data generation frequency for specific vehicles remains consistent [10], determined by the manufacturer's ECU functionalities. For specific CAN IDs, there is a well-defined time gap interval in which these IDs generate messages or share status updates with other ECUs, maintaining system integrity [11]. However, during an attack, this frequency becomes irregular, and the time gap intervals for specific CAN IDs deviate from their expected ranges [2]. Additionally, sequential patterns in CAN IDs, which reflect the interactions between ECUs, are disrupted when an attack is initiated, breaking the order crucial for functionality. Furthermore, the payload, containing four types of information as specified by the CAN DBC [12], shows significant anomalies in its distribution during an attack, further indicating system compromise. These disruptions across frequency, time gaps, sequential patterns, and payload distribution collectively provide clear indicators of malicious activities within the CAN network.

Data analysis for CAN networks often relies on platforms such as Python and Pandas, which are widely utilized in existing studies for their efficiency and flexibility [11]. To effectively analyze CAN data, which is represented in hexadecimal format, it is essential to first transform the data into numerical form. This transformation can involve converting hexadecimal values into decimal or binary formats or labeling the data with specific numerical categories to facilitate analysis [13, 14]. Among the commonly used techniques, comparative analysis, statistical analysis, and correlation analysis stand out. In comparative analysis, patterns and characteristics are extracted from normal data and compared to attack data to identify anomalies. Statistical analysis focuses on evaluating data distributions and trends to detect deviations introduced by attacks [1]. Correlation analysis, typically employing Pearson correlation, examines the relationships between variables to uncover irregularities [15]. By integrating these transformation and analysis methods, researchers can build a robust framework for detecting and understanding abnormal behaviors within CAN networks.

4.2 Feature selection

4.2.1 Feature selection processes

Designing an IDS for IVNs presents unique challenges due to the limited power resources inherent in such systems. High computational demands can significantly hinder the feasibility of deploying IDS on IVNs, making efficiency a critical factor. At the same time, response time and model generalization are crucial requirements for effective intrusion detection, as delayed responses or overfitting can compromise vehicle safety and system reliability. Consequently, the design of an IDS must achieve a delicate balance between computational power demands, response time, and detection accuracy. A key step in attaining this balance is minimal feature selection, which ensures the IDS operates efficiently while maintaining high detection performance.

Feature selection is pivotal in reducing computational overhead and improving response time without sacrificing accuracy. Among various techniques, wrapper methods [16] are particularly effective due to their ability to iteratively evaluate and select the most relevant feature subsets for a given model. Wrapper methods are categorized into three main types:

- *Forward selection*: This method begins with an empty feature set and iteratively adds features one by one. At each step, the feature that most improves the model's performance is included in the set. The process continues until adding more features no longer enhances performance or meets the desired trade-offs. Forward selection is computationally efficient and well-suited for scenarios where lightweight models are required.

- *Backward elimination*: In this method, the process starts with the full feature set, and features are removed one at a time based on their significance. At each step, the least significant feature (i.e., the feature contributing the least to the model's performance) is excluded. This approach is useful when the dataset contains irrelevant or redundant features, but it can be computationally demanding, especially for larger feature sets.

- *Exhaustive search*: This method evaluates all possible combinations of features to identify the subset that yields the best performance. Unlike the other two methods, exhaustive search guarantees the optimal feature set by exploring every possible combination. While it is computationally expensive and often impractical for datasets with a large number of features, it becomes viable for smaller datasets, such as CAN data, which consists of manageable feature sets. Exhaustive search ensures that the selected subset delivers the highest possible accuracy, making it ideal when computational resources are available or when the feature set is limited.

In CAN frames, there are a total of eleven feature columns, including CAN ID, Data Length Code (DLC), eight payload bytes, and time intervals between frames [13]. Given this relatively small feature set, an exhaustive search emerges as the most suitable method for selecting the optimal combination of features. Based on exhaustive evaluation, the best combination includes CAN ID and time intervals [2]. These features are particularly effective in detecting anomalies, as they reflect the expected communication patterns, timing behaviors, and interaction sequences of ECUs. For example, the CAN ID sequence and time gap intervals are highly useful for identifying abnormalities. However, for ECU-specific attacks, relying solely on these features might lead to an increase in false positives, necessitating additional refinement to improve accuracy.

4.2.2 Chunk selection for categorical data in CAN networks

There are two ways to input data into the model: first, by inputting data in single instance input, and second, by using time series input by chunks. Inputting data in a single instance, input makes model deployment more complex and has a higher potential for false positive rates. On the other hand, time series input with an optimal chunk size makes the model more effective and generalized. Chunk selection for categorical data in CAN networks, particularly for analyzing CAN ID sequences, can be effectively performed using methods like Sliding Window with Overlap, Frequent

Pattern Mining, Mutual Information Analysis, and Change Point Detection [17–19]. Each of these methods serves a unique purpose in identifying meaningful chunks within the data.

- *Sliding window with overlap*: This method divides the CAN ID sequence into overlapping windows, ensuring that transitions between IDs are captured. For example, consider a sequence of CAN IDs: 0x100, 0x200, 0x300, 0x400, 0x500. Using a sliding window of size 3 with an overlap of 1, the chunks would be [0x100, 0x200, 0x300], [0x200, 0x300, 0x400], and [0x300, 0x400, 0x500]. This overlap ensures that transitional relationships between IDs, such as 0x200 to 0x300 and 0x300 to 0x400, are not missed.

- *Frequent pattern mining*: This method identifies recurring CAN ID subsequences within the data. For instance, in a dataset where the sequences 0x100, 0x200, and 0x300 frequently appear, it can be inferred that these IDs are often generated together due to the interaction of specific ECUs. This helps group chunks of IDs that represent repeated operational patterns, like a periodic status check between ECUs.

- *Mutual information analysis*: This method quantifies the dependency between adjacent CAN IDs to create meaningful chunks. For example, if CAN_ID 0x100 frequently precedes CAN_ID 0x200, this strong relationship will result in grouping them into the same chunk, such as [0x100, 0x200, 0x300]. This ensures that IDs with interdependent operations are analyzed together.

- *Change point detection*: This method identifies significant shifts in the CAN ID sequence that may signify a transition between operational states or an abnormal event. For example, if a normal sequence like 0x100, 0x200, 0x300, 0x400 suddenly changes to 0x100, 0x200, 0x999, 0x400, the presence of 0x999 (a potentially anomalous ID) could indicate a change point. The sequence can then be chunked as [0x100, 0x200] and [0x999, 0x400], isolating the abnormal region for further analysis.

Among these methods, Mutual Information Analysis is particularly effective for CAN data, as data generation often depends on dynamic driving activities and active functions. For instance, in the case of the Kia Soul, a chunk size of 10 to 20 is optimal for attack classification, capturing enough contextual information for effective intrusion detection. The optimal chunk size, however, varies by manufacturer, reflecting differences in communication patterns and ECU interactions. If the chunk size is too small, the IDS may lack sufficient information for analysis, leading to frequent activations and increased power consumption. Conversely, overly large chunks can adversely affect response time, delaying the detection of critical anomalies. Thus, selecting an appropriate chunk size is essential for achieving a balance between power efficiency and response time, ensuring an optimal IDS model tailored to the specific characteristics of the vehicle's CAN network.

4.3 Intrusion detection

There are two primary approaches to building an IDS: rule-based systems and machine learning-based systems. In a rule-based detection system, predefined rules are extracted and implemented as logic to identify anomalies [20]. However, these systems are highly prone to false positive rates due to the nature of in-vehicle network (IVN) attacks, which are often data- and frequency-agnostic [2]. Attackers can creatively inject data in unpredictable ways, making it challenging for rule-based systems to cover all dynamic situations effectively. In contrast, machine learning-based detection systems excel in adapting to dynamic and complex attack scenarios. These systems can analyze large datasets, identify hidden patterns, and learn from diverse scenarios to generalize effectively across various conditions. This adaptability enables machine learning models to handle the evolving nature of IVN attacks and significantly reduce false positive rates. Among the various machine learning approaches, deep learning stands out due to its superior performance in terms of efficiency, generalizability, and accuracy. Deep learning models leverage advanced architectures like neural networks to automatically extract high-level features from raw data, eliminating the need for extensive manual feature engineering. Additionally, their ability to learn hierarchical representations makes them highly effective in recognizing subtle patterns and correlations in complex datasets, which are critical for accurate intrusion detection. Furthermore, deep learning models are highly scalable, allowing them to handle large amounts of data and adapt to new attack vectors, making them the most robust option for intrusion detection in IVNs.

Deep learning offers several approaches, including supervised, unsupervised, semi-supervised, and reinforcement learning [2, 13, 21, 22], each suited for different types of problems. Below is a brief overview of these methods and their advantages and disadvantages:

- *Supervised learning*: This approach involves training a model on labeled data, where the input-output relationships are explicitly defined. The model learns to map inputs to the correct outputs, making it highly effective for classification and regression tasks. It is the most reliable and effective method due to its ability to achieve high accuracy when sufficient labeled data is available.

- *Unsupervised learning*: In this approach, the model is trained on unlabeled data to discover patterns or groupings within the dataset. Techniques like clustering and dimensionality reduction fall under this category. However, the lack of labeled data makes it challenging to validate the results, leading to potential inaccuracies and difficulty in interpreting the outcomes.

- *Semi-supervised learning*: This combines a small amount of labeled data with a large amount of unlabeled data to improve performance. While it bridges the gap between supervised and unsupervised methods, its disadvantage lies in the dependency on the quality and representativeness of the labeled data, which can limit its effectiveness.

- *Reinforcement learning*: This approach trains models to make sequential decisions by interacting with an environment and receiving feedback in the form of rewards or penalties. Although it is powerful for tasks like control systems and decision-making, reinforcement learning is computationally expensive, requires extensive trial-and-error, and can be unstable in complex environments.

Among these approaches, supervised learning stands out as the most reliable and effective for intrusion detection in IVNs. Its ability to leverage labeled data for precise training ensures high accuracy and robustness, making it the preferred choice for building dependable IDS models.

Neural networks can be broadly categorized into Deep Neural Networks (DNNs), Recurrent Neural Networks (RNNs), and Convolutional Neural Networks (CNNs), each designed for specific tasks. DNNs are the most basic form of neural networks, consisting of fully connected layers used for general-purpose tasks. RNNs are specialized for sequential data, as they have the ability to remember previous sequence patterns, making them highly effective for time series data. CNNs are designed for spatial data, particularly image and video processing, using convolutional layers to extract hierarchical features.

Among these, RNNs and CNNs have proven to be the most effective for various applications. RNNs excel at processing sequential data due to their memory capabilities, which allow them to capture patterns over time. Popular RNN variants include Long Short-Term Memory (LSTM), which addresses long-term dependency issues, and Gated Recurrent Unit (GRU), which offers a simpler and lighter architecture while maintaining similar performance. GRU is often preferred over LSTM due to its efficiency and reduced computational overhead.

CNNs, on the other hand, are highly effective for spatial data and have numerous architectures, such as AlexNet, ResNet, Inception, and MobileNet. Among these, MobileNet stands out for its lightweight design, making it ideal for resource-constrained environments like edge devices or IVNs. MobileNet uses depthwise separable convolutions, significantly reducing the computational complexity while maintaining high accuracy, making it the best choice for scenarios requiring efficiency.

In terms of architecture, both RNNs and CNNs can incorporate Autoencoders, which are designed to learn efficient representations of input data by compressing it into a lower-dimensional space and reconstructing it back. This is particularly useful for tasks like anomaly detection, where autoencoders learn to identify deviations from normal patterns.

Finally, while advanced architectures like CNNs and RNNs are effective, even a simple model can yield high accuracy when trained on precisely labeled data that covers dynamic situational variations, ensuring both efficiency and reliability in real-world applications.

Acknowledgements

The author acknowledges the use of QuillBot and ChatGPT for language polishing of the manuscript.

Author details

Mahdi Sahlabadi[1†], Md Rezanur Islam[2†], Munkhdelgerekh Batzorig[1†] and Kangbin Yim[1*†]

1 Department of Information Security Engineering, Soonchunhyang University, Asan-si, Korea

2 Department of Software Convergence, Soonchunhyang University, Asan-si, Korea

*Address all correspondence to: yim@sch.ac.kr

† These authors contributed equally.

References

[1] Lokman S-F, Othman AT, Abu-Bakar M-H. Intrusion detection system for automotive controller area network (CAN) bus system: A review. EURASIP Journal on Wireless Communications and Networking. 2019;**2019**(1):1-17

[2] Islam M, R et al. CF-AIDS: Comprehensive frequency-agnostic intrusion detection system on in-vehicle network. IEEE Access. 2023

[3] Koh Y et al. Real Vehicle-based attack dataset for security threat analysis in a vehicle. In: International Conference on Broadband and Wireless Computing, Communication and Applications. Cham, Switzerland: Springer; 2022. pp. 137-146

[4] Batzorig M et al. A novel attack scenario dataset collection for intrusion detection system in CAN network. In: International Conference on Network-Based Information Systems. Vol. 183. Springer; 2023. pp. 130-141

[5] Fugiglando U et al. Driving behavior analysis through CAN bus data in an uncontrolled environment. IEEE Transactions on Intelligent Transportation Systems. 2018;**20**(2): 737-748

[6] Aliwa E et al. Cyberattacks and countermeasures for in-vehicle networks. ACM computing surveys (CSUR). 2021;**54**(1):1-37

[7] Lee H, Jeong SH, Kim HK. OTIDS: A novel intrusion detection system for in-vehicle network by using remote frame. In: 2017 15th Annual Conference on Privacy, Security and Trust (PST). IEEE; 2017. pp. 57-5709

[8] Han ML, Kwak BI, Kim HK. Anomaly intrusion detection method for vehicular networks based on survival analysis. Vehicular Communications. 2018;**14**: 52-63

[9] Nowdehi N et al. CASAD: CAN-aware stealthy-attack detection for in-vehicle networks. In: arXiv preprint arXiv: 1909.08407. 2019

[10] Thien-Nu H et al. CANPerFL: Improve in-vehicle intrusion detection performance by sharing knowledge. Applied Sciences. 2023;**13**(11):6369

[11] Islam M, R, Insu O, Yim K. CANTool an in-vehicle network data analyzer. In: 2022 International Conference on Information Technology Systems and Innovation (ICITSI). IEEE; 2022. pp. 252-257

[12] Choi W et al. An enhanced method for reverse engineering CAN data payload. IEEE Transactions on Vehicular Technology. 2021;**70**(4): 3371-3381

[13] Hoang T-N, Kim D. Detecting In-vehicle intrusion via semi-supervised learning-based convolutional adversarial autoencoders. Vehicular Communications. 2022;**38**: 100520

[14] Jo H, Kim D-H. Intrusion detection using transformer in con-troller area network. IEEE Access. 2024

[15] Tomlinson A, Bryans J, Shaikh SA. Using internal context to detect automotive controller area network attacks. Computers & Electrical Engineering. 2021;**91**:107048

[16] Maldonado J, Riff MC, Neveu B. A review of recent approaches on wrapper feature selection for intrusion detection. Expert Systems with Applications. 2022; **198**:116822

[17] Miao R et al. Real-time defect identification of narrow overlap welds and application based on convolutional neural networks. Journal of Manufacturing Systems. 2022;**62**: 800-810

[18] Peng W et al. Global motion filtered nonlinear mutual information analysis: Enhancing dynamic portfolio strategies. PLoS One. 2024;**19**(7):e0303707

[19] Truong C, Oudre L, Vayatis N. Selective review of offline change point detection methods. Signal Processing. 2020;**167**:107299

[20] Bozdal M, Samie M, Jennions IK. WINDS: A wavelet-based intrusion detection system for controller area network (CAN). IEEE Access. 2021;**9**: 58621-58633

[21] Narasimhan H, Ravi V, Mohammad N. Unsupervised deep learning approach for in-vehicle intrusion detection system. IEEE Consumer Electronics Magazine. 2021; **12**(1):103-108

[22] Xiao L et al. Reinforcement learning-based physical-layer authentication for controller area networks. IEEE Transactions on Information Forensics and Security. 2021;**16**:2535-2547

Chapter 5

Investigation of Cyberattack and Intrusion: Methods and Tool

Tarana Aliyeva

Abstract

In modern times, due to the widespread use and use of cloud and web technologies, mobile and sensor environments, and social networks and online banking, cybersecurity is developing as a scientific field of interest to a large number of researchers. The rapid increase in Internet use day by day makes the solution and analysis of issues related to detecting intrusions into workstations or servers even more relevant. In order to ensure the confidentiality, integrity, and accessibility of data, it is necessary to eliminate vulnerabilities that could allow a successful attack on servers in a timely manner. The risks and consequences of vulnerabilities arising from the disruption of the function of the Server Message Block (SMB) protocol can significantly affect the security status of an organization. In this study, the Fake SMB Server Attack process as a means of capturing confidential information by taking advantage of the security vulnerabilities of Active Directory (AD) is studied using the Metasploit Framework tool and network traffic is analyzed using the Cyber Kill Chain (CKC) method. Following the recommendations given at the end of the section will help significantly reduce the risk of successful attacks by attackers who intrude into workstations and servers.

Keywords: cybersecurity, cyberattack, intrusion, detection and analysis, cyber kill chain

1. Introduction

In modern times, the existing tools for detecting and preventing cyberattacks are being replaced by newer and more sophisticated attack tools. In most cases, the current defense strategies applied are based on the attacker's "random attack on the network." If the attack is adequately prevented by the network, the attacker tries to reach his target by choosing another alternative attack strategy and in many cases succeeds. In the sphere of cybersecurity, when signs of malicious activity, unauthorized access, violation of security policies, or any signs of compromise are detected in networks or individual systems, the analysis of such intrusions by monitoring the input-output traffic is of great importance.

According to recent reports from reputable companies such as Micro and Report [1], the emergence of Advanced Persistent Threat (APT), a modern form of attack that has emerged as a means of destroying critical infrastructure such as power grids, once again confirms that the assumption of "random network attack" is no longer realistic.

APT operates continuously until it reaches its target, regardless of the defenses of the other party. Studying APT attacks by analyzing individual characteristics such as hash values, IP addresses, and indicators of compromise (IOC) attack tools [2] does not fully reflect the overall picture of these attack events. APT requires a more comprehensive approach, which is the main feature that distinguishes it from other cyberattack methods, since the period of stay of an APT in the targeted network can last for months or years. During this time, the attacker achieves his goals by consistently implementing selected tactics, techniques, and procedures (TTP). It is also possible to detect complex APT attacks through open source intelligence (OSINT). OSINT can help identify APT groups and their TTPs by collecting threat intelligence from open sources; in other words, it can provide organizations with information about how APT groups operate, the tools and techniques they use, and their ability to penetrate a target system. Thus, integrating OSINT into APT detection methods can help organizations better understand and protect themselves from such attacks [3]. It should be noted that in some cases, due to the lack of context in the information provided by OSINT, it may not be possible to fully understand the main goals of potential APT attackers. In this case, the use of popular MITER ATT&CK and cyberattack chain models overcomes this deficiency. Machine learning (ML) methods are widely used in modern times to combat and prevent cyber threats [4]. In order to scientifically substantiate the hypothesis that "illegal use of information and communication technologies can harm the country's infrastructure, national security, and economic development," the authors propose a statistical analysis of cybersecurity indicators on the example of Azerbaijan [5]. Several ML strategies applied for intrusion detection and pre-processing are discussed in Ref. [6]. Internal attacks are usually more difficult to detect, since security protocols have difficulty recognizing attacks coming from trusted sources in the network, including users. For this purpose, a new framework—a neural network model—is proposed to detect cyberattacks using ML combined with user behavior analytics [7]. As network traffic increases and attacks become more sophisticated, some researchers are looking at ways to improve intrusion detection systems by using ML algorithms in the intersection of these two areas [8]. It is known that malware attacks have become one of the major cybersecurity challenges today, as they have become one of the main tools used to collect confidential information or take over systems, attack other devices, send spam, and illegally obtain and share information [9]. With the increasing use of digital services, the recent evolution of malware has increased the possibility of data corruption, data theft, or other cybercrimes through malware attacks. Therefore, malware must be detected before it affects a large number of computers [10]. In security analysis, significant attention is also paid to studying software based on patch analysis [11]. It should be noted that the emergence of the Internet of Things (IoT) concept, in addition to revolutionizing a number of economic sectors, has also led to the emergence of cybersecurity risks in certain areas of human activity. Studies have discussed the nature of IoT devices, the harm caused to people as a result of their hacking, and the complicity of the owners of hacked IoT devices in cybercrimes, as well as the learning methods necessary to uncover cyberattacks on IoT infrastructure [12]. Internet use has increased exponentially in recent decades, and both individuals and businesses carry out many daily transactions in cyberspace. As a result of the widespread use of the digital environment, traditional crime has also moved to the digital space. Along with IoT, the introduction of new technologies such as cloud computing, social media, wireless communications, and cryptocurrencies has increased concerns about cybersecurity. This process has accelerated during the coronavirus (COVID-19) pandemic.

The study of the evolution of cyber threats aims to demonstrate the rapid dynamics of malware development and the importance of cybersecurity development for every business, organization, and individual [13]. As the number of devices connected to the network increases, as well as the number of interconnected devices, the number of cyberattacks also increases. Honeypot-based methods are also used as a type of security technology that screens devices to prevent attacks and unwanted activities [14]. In another study, the authors consider a method for capturing and analyzing network traffic during passive monitoring of a network segment, and also propose a method for processing multiple network traffic indices for further assessment of the security level of network data [15]. A unique deep learning-based defense mechanism for real-time threat detection is proposed to effectively identify and mitigate existing threats to Controller Area Network (CAN) networks, including spoofing, replay, and denial of service attacks [16]. The advantage of the improved EWMA model over abnormal traffic detection methods for setting dynamic thresholds for network traffic anomaly detection is substantiated [17].

As the value of information increases, the number of those interested in gaining unauthorized access to valuable information for profit is always increasing. Usually, attackers carry out cyberattacks by exploiting vulnerabilities in the servers where this information is processed within the organization. This study is dedicated to the description and analysis of the intrusion made by the attacker to detect cyberattacks in time and investigate their causes. The study explains the main objectives of the intrusion analysis and provides a step-by-step explanation of the Fake SMB Server Attack process, as one of the cyberattacks on AD, using the Metasploit Framework tool. Then, this intrusion was examined in Detection & Analysis, one of the main stages of the analysis process, by applying the CKC method. At the end of the section, it was recommended to implement certain cybersecurity measures in organizations to protect against intrusion risks.

2. Methodology

The basis of the analysis of the intervention is the study of issues such as the detection, investigation, and response to cybersecurity incidents. At the same time, it is desirable for the researcher to have individual intuition and critical thinking skills in preventing cyberattacks.

The main goals of the analysis of the intervention are as follows:

- Minimize the impact of cyberincidents on the organization or enterprise;
- Detect threats in a timely manner;
- Provide more effective protection against them in the future by obtaining information about the TTP used by the attacker;
- Achieve improvements in cyberattack defense and incident response processes based on the experience gained.

The analysis of the intervention is carried out in four stages: "Preparation," "Detection & Analysis," "Containment Eradication & Recovery," and "Post-Incident Activity" (**Figure 1**) [18]:

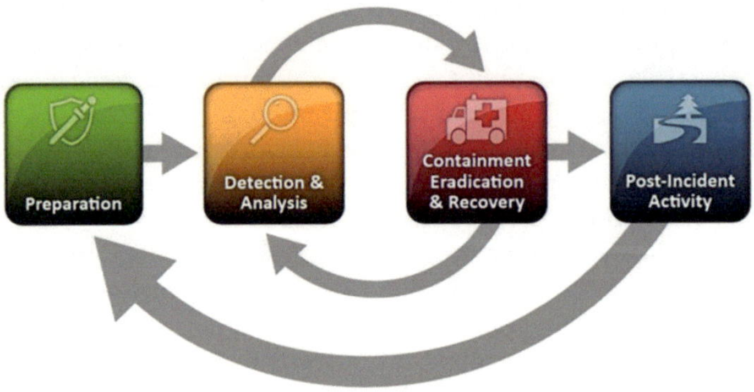

Figure 1.
Incident response life cycle.

1. Preparation: Tools and resources that can be useful in incident management are identified.

2. Detection and analysis: The incident is investigated and analyzed using various cybersecurity systems, methodologies, and analytical techniques.

3. Containment eradication and recovery: The consequences of the incident are localized, and appropriate decisions and strategies are prepared by determining acceptable risks.

4. Post-incident activity: Areas that need improvement are identified, and regular discussions called "Lessons Learned" are planned to be held to improve security measures and the incident management process itself.

It is known that information technologies that process valuable information are widely used by various organizations. For a comprehensive analysis of the intervention, the researcher must first be aware of the attack TTP.

- The research is conducted on detection and analysis, which is considered the most important of these stages. Here, Fake SMB Server Attack is applied as the most common attack method to capture valuable information by entering organizations' networks as a result of the opportunity created by security gaps in AD.

- Fake SMB (Server Message Block) Server Attack works at the network level, creates serious threats in the AD environment, and targets security systems with vulnerabilities over the network. The attacker creates a fake SMB server and tries to connect users and computers to network resources. The cyberattack process under study is carried out with Metasploit Framework, which is a powerful tool widely used by cybercriminals, "white hat hackers," as well as experts to detect vulnerabilities in networks and servers. Using tools such as the modern Metasploit Framework greatly benefits the intrusion analysis process. Metasploit allows you to obtain information about the target by scanning ports to find a way into the network, obtaining a digital footprint of the operating system, or using a vulnerability scanner. Metasploit is a tool consisting of hundreds of auxiliary modules that can perform functions such as listening to traffic, scanning ports, guessing passwords, searching for vulnerabilities. The following procedures should be taken into account before using this tool:

- The user should be aware that this tool will work with the local system protection disabled;
- The user should be aware of the potential risks, taking into account the framework's ability to create malicious code;
- This utility should be installed on any computer outside the system that has access to confidential information, if possible.

This process should be carefully analyzed and studied to minimize the impact of cyber threats, since most of the company's important data are located on servers.

There are a number of methods and tools for investigating large-scale security incidents. Each method and tool has its own advantages and disadvantages. The method used in the study for analyzing the intrusion is based on the CKC concept [19]. CKC describes an APT attack in stages, consisting of seven tactics—Intelligence, Weapons, Delivery, Operations, Establishment, Command and Control, and Objective Operations. CKC models cyberattacks as a sequence of adversary tactics. The CKC concept is based on the assumption that "adversary tactics must be changed sequentially for the success of a cyberattack"; the application of structured analytical methods such as CKS allows for a comprehensive and consistent analysis process.

In the construction of the CKC chain, both the Diamond model and the MITER ATT&CK framework are used in the study [20]. The Diamond model is one of the main tools for analyzing cyber threats (**Figure 2**). The main idea of the model is to analyze each attack event by linking it to four main components:

1. Adversary: The person or group that carries out the attack.
2. Capabilities: The tools or methods used by the attacker.
3. Infrastructure: The resources used to carry out the attack (e.g., botnets, C2 servers, email addresses, service accounts).

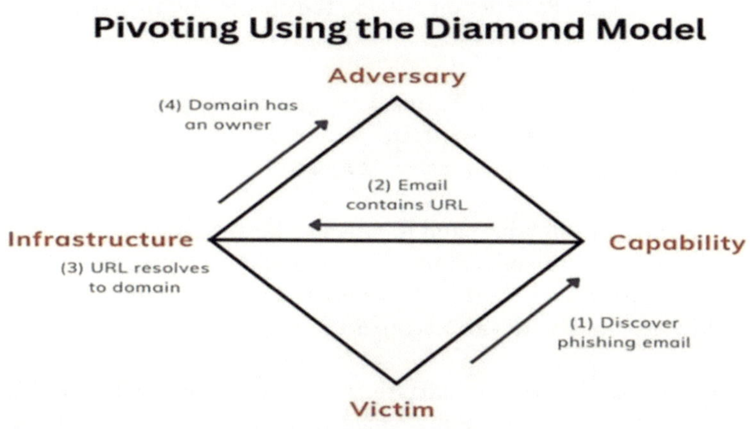

Figure 2.
Components of the Diamond model and the relationships between them.

4. Victim: The organization, individual, computer systems, networks, data that are the target of the attack.

MITER ATT&CK is a comprehensive concept that provides a framework for describing and classifying adversary TTPs based on real-world observations.

For example:

1. Tactics: Indicates the objectives of the attack (login capture, data theft).

2. Techniques: Specific methods used to carry out the attack (LLMNR Poisoning, Credential Dumping).

3. Procedures: The ways in which the techniques are applied (NTLM (NT LAN Manager) hash theft *via* specific malware).

While the MITER ATT&CK model includes the methods and techniques used during an incident or the infrastructure involved, it does not allow for connecting all the dots and obtaining tactical or strategic information. By showing only key indicators, the unified view of cyber threats offered by the Diamond model allows the analyst to better understand an intrusion, attack campaign, or attacker. It is important to identify as many indicators as possible to accurately track the attack process. Note that indicators are used to detect threats or find attackers using threat search queries.

3. Results on active directory attacks

In order to ensure the practicality of the research, this section comments on the results obtained in the direction of the research. It is a fact that any attack begins with the reconnaissance phase. The more information attackers can collect about the victim at this stage, the more potential attack vectors they have, including website attacks, attacks on terminal servers or VPNs, various types of physical penetration, etc. In this work, the process of attacking the attacker's network server by creating a fake SMB server and targeting its security vulnerabilities is described, and at the same time, analysis mechanisms are studied using CKC.

To implement the Fake SMB Server Attack, the operations are performed in the following sequence:

Step 1. a. Launch the Metasploit Framework and execute the msfconsole command in the terminal. As a result, the msfconsole interface opens and the msf prompt appears on the screen (**Figure 3**).

b. The msfconsole command is launched by entering msf > use auxiliary/ server/ capture/smb (**Figure 4**). Among the parameters of the module that appear on the screen, there is also the Johnpwfile stored in John the Ripper, along with various types of files.

Step 2. The command msf > auxiliary/server/capture/smb > set smbdomain server. local stores johnpwfile in the root domain hashes. This way, all files are hashed. The input file name is defined as NTLMv2_netntlmv2 and the run command is executed (**Figure 5**).

Figure 3.
Running the msfconsole command.

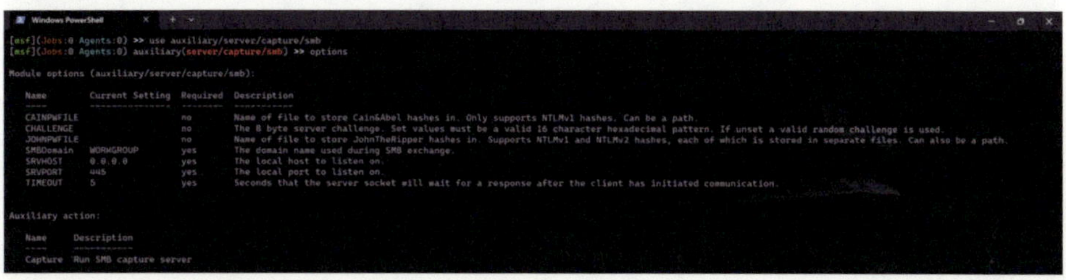

Figure 4.
Viewing the helper module settings.

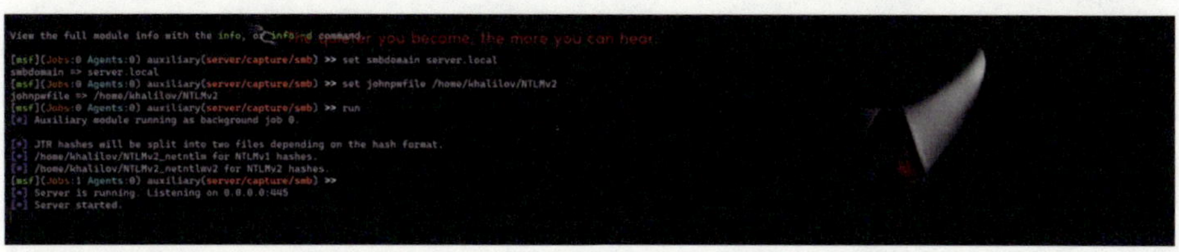

Figure 5.
Storing johnpwfile in the root domain hashes.

Step 3. The server and the module must be executed together, after step 2 the server is started, and to run the module together, the target computer must be connected to the local computer. For this, a Uncategorized Threat Group (UNC) must be sent to the target computer. Note that a UNC is a cluster of cyber-interference activities that includes observable artifacts such as adversary infrastructure, tools, and attack patterns. SMB requests from devices on the network are listened to by Metasploit's "listener" software modules that collect, filter, or perform other operations. The listening process allows us to identify vulnerabilities that can be exploited by monitoring requests made via the SMB protocol.

In order to perform a specific operation on the target computer and establish a connection, a password, and login must be entered in a window that opens on one of the possible servers (**Figure 6**).

Step 4. After the connection, the resulting hashes appear on the screen (**Figure 7**):

Step 5. To find out where the password you are looking for is located, change the directory by typing cd/server, and execute the ls command (**Figure 8**).

Step 6. To crack the NTLMv2_netntlmv2 file (**Figure 5**) containing the hashes defined above, use the hashcat tool to execute the hashcat -m 5600 -a 0 netntlmv2

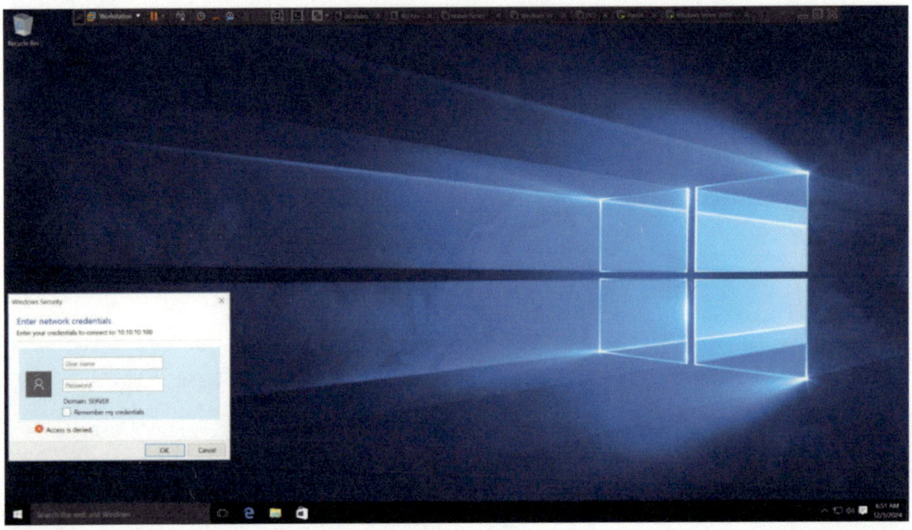

Figure 6.
Connecting to the target computer.

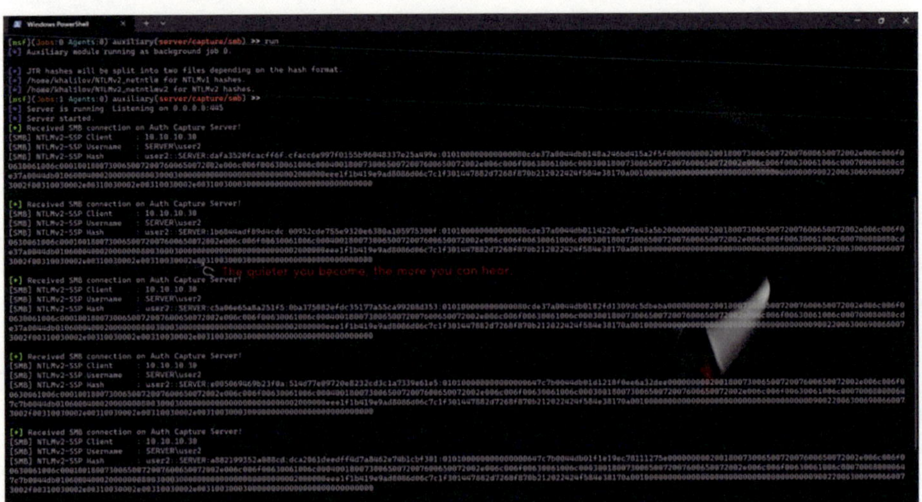

Figure 7.
Hash collection.

Figure 8.
Contents of NTLMv2_netntlmv2 file.

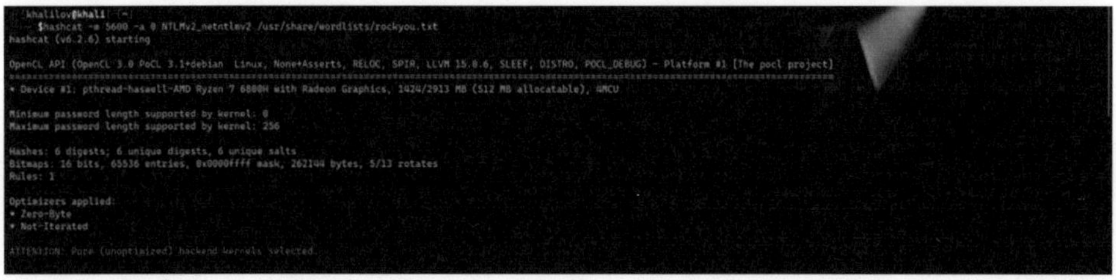

Figure 9.
Implementation of the Hashcat tool.

Figure 10.
Account hijacking.

/usr/share/wordlists/rockyou.txt command (**Figure 9**). Here, -m 5600 is the NetNTLMv2 type of hash, -a 0 is a dictionary attack, and /usr/share/wordlists is the directory where the wordlists are located. As a result, the user account is compromised (**Figure 10**).

Kill chain stage	What happened	Found where	Indicators	Action taken
KC1: Recon				
KC2: Weaponization				
KC3: Exploitation				
KC4: Delivery				
KC5: Install				
KC6: C2				
KC7: Actions				

Table 1.
Cauto_awesome structure of the cyber kill chain.

The procedure is shown in the video (*Video 1_Fake SMB Server Attack.mp4*). Thus, the successful completion of the Fake SMB Server Attack ends with the capture of the server password.

Let us apply the CKC method to investigate the Fake SMB Server Attack in depth. CKC provides a systematic approach to understanding the life cycle of a cyberattack. CKC is often used in the early stages of threat detection and prevention. It can help identify potential threats and eliminate them before they cause damage.

To create a CKC, you need to build a table (**Table 1**) as follows and fill in the appropriate cells. It is very convenient to identify and eliminate threats through the stages of the Kill Chain.

To build a 7-step chain, the type and location of the cyber incident that occurred should be indicated, as well as information about the appropriate action plan to be taken at each stage, identifying indicators of cybercrime, should be included in the table. At each stage, defenders have the opportunity to detect, prevent, or disrupt the attack. First, according to the Diamond model, the following components should be determined:

1. Adversary: The person or group that carried out the attack.

2. Capabilities: Tools such as Responder or Impacket.

3. Infrastructure: The IP address of the attacker

4. Victim: The IP address of the targeted web server.

Let us define the TTP as Scanning activities (T1595.002) based on the MITER ATT&CK framework. By filling in the row corresponding to each stage of the chain, it is possible to obtain detailed information about the attacker's goals, at the same time it will help determine how successful the attacker was and how it affected your organization. After the first 3 columns are filled, the 4th Action Taken column is filled from bottom to top. Each step of the chain must be completed.

As you progress through CKC, immediate actions can be taken to eliminate the threat, such as quarantining files or devices, resetting user accounts, or disabling network access. To prevent the intrusion under investigation:

- Ensure that SMB is only running on trusted systems on the network, and

Kill chain stage	What happened	Found where	Indicators	Action taken
KC1: Recon	Scanning SMB shares on the network	Network logs	Scanning activities (T1595.002)	Block IP address, enable strict SMB policies
KC2: Weaponization	Fake SMB server created to intercept data	EDR	Unauthorized SMB connections	Monitor and block unauthorized SMB traffic
KC3: Exploitation	Credentials captured via SMB communication	System logs	Plaintext password transmission	Reset credentials, enforce SMB encryption
KC4: Delivery	Captured credentials reused for lateral movement	Forensic analysis	Credential reuse patterns	Isolate affected accounts, monitor for anomalies
KC5: Install	Malware or tools installed on compromised systems	System changes	Unexpected file changes	Remove malicious tools
KC6: C2	Command communication over SMB traffic	Network monitoring	Unusual SMB activity	Terminate unauthorized sessions
KC7: Actions	Data accessed or manipulated from SMB shares	Data access logs	Unexpected file access	Restore data, notify impacted users

Table 2.
Fake SMB attack kill chain.

- Restrict use of NTLM and use the Kerberos protocol.

As can be seen in **Table 2**, CKC relies on following a specific sequence of tactics for all cyberattacks to succeed.

4. Conclusion

In modern times, the use of trusted technologies for processing, storing and transmitting confidential information, as well as cloud technologies, and the increasing digitalization of enterprises lead to an increase in the vulnerabilities of IT systems and, consequently, cybersecurity risks. The use of various mobile devices and Internet of Things, as well as a number of irresponsible actions of employees within the enterprise, also have an impact on these issues.

The methods and tools used in the course of the study and the results of the analysis conducted are very useful in organizing security services, building a cyberattack model to ensure cyber defense, developing more effective security policies and incident response plans. The Metasploit platform is an important tool for detecting hidden vulnerabilities; it allows you to use the same methods to conduct reconnaissance and penetrate networks and servers.

The application of CKC is of great importance in real-world scenarios such as infrastructure security and social engineering. In conjunction with the general defense security axiom, "intercepting" any step in CKC will successfully prevent the attacker from achieving his goal and ultimately protect the threatened party.

The risk of intrusion caused by unauthorized access, disruption, modification, or destruction of information systems and data faced by enterprises exposed to various attacks by attackers is a very serious problem. To this end, enterprises should:

Detect vulnerabilities and vulnerabilities in the organization's information systems in a timely manner by developing a risk management program within the framework of NIST;

- Be prepared to prevent any type of intrusion, in other words, have a response plan for identified incidents;

- Conduct constant monitoring and updating of detection systems to protect the enterprise from potential threats;

- Continuous training of analysts to recognize threats and be ready to respond to them;

- Assess cybersecurity risks and achieve risk reduction;

It is recommended to implement adequate cybersecurity measures, such as regularly exchanging information with other organizations about incidents that have occurred.

Acknowledgements

I express my deep gratitude to the young specialist in the field who contributed to the preparation of the section—student of the "Computer Engineering" specialty of Azerbaijan State Oil and Industry University Khalilov Aydin.

Author details

Tarana Aliyeva
UNEC Digital Research Center, Azerbaijan State University of Economics (UNEC), Baku, Azerbaijan

*Address all correspondence to: tarana.aliyeva@unec.edu.az

References

[1] Securing the Pandemic-Disrupted Workplace: Trend Micro 2020 Midyear Cybersecurity Report. 26 August 2020. Available from: https://www.trendmicro.com/vinfo/us/security/research-and-analysis/threat-reports/roundup/securing-the-pandemic-disrupted-workplace-trend-micro-2020-midyear-cybersecurity-report; https://documents.trendmicro.com/assets/rpt/rpt-securing-the-pandemic-disrupted-workplace.pdf

[2] Daly MK. The advanced persistent threat (or informationized force operations). Usenix. 2009;**4**:2013-2016. Available from: http://static.usenix.org/event/lisa09/tech/slides/daly.pdf

[3] Xing K, Li A, Jiang R, Jia Y. A Review of APT Attack Detection Methods and Defense Strategies. 2020 IEEE Fifth International Conference on Data Science in Cyberspace (DSC), Hong Kong, China. 2020. pp. 67-70. DOI: 10.1109/DSC50466.2020.00018

[4] Saini S, Kalia A. Detection of cyber attacks using machine learning. International Journal for Research in Applied Science & Engineering Technology (IJRASET). ISSN: 2321-9653; IC Value: 45.98; SJ Impact Factor: 7.538. Sep 2023;**11**(IX):1777-1785. DOI: 10.22214/ijraset.2023.55918

[5] Aliyeva T, Guliyeva A, Rzayeva U, Guliyeva G. Analysis of cybersecurity indicators: A case of Azerbaijan. In: Proceedings of the Seventh International Conference on Control and Optimization with Industrial Applications. Ministry Transport Commun & High Technologies Republic Azerbaijan. Vol. II. Baku State University, Institute of Applied Mathematics, ELECTR NETWORK; Aug 26-28 2020. pp. 89-91. Available from: https://www.webofscience.com/wos/woscc/full-record/WOS:000606324300026

[6] Al Moaiad Y, Tarshany YMA, Algeelani NA, Al-Haithami W. Cyber attack detection using big data analysis. International Journal of Computer Science and Information Technology Research. July 2022 - September 2022;**10**(3):26-33. DOI: 10.5281/zenodo.6924399

[7] Alshehri A, Khan N, Alowayr A, Alghamdi MY. Cyberattack detection framework using machine learning and user behavior analytics. Computer Systems Science and Engineering. 2023;**44**(2):1679-1689. DOI: 10.32604/csse.2023.026526

[8] Keegan N, Ji SY, Chaudhary A, et al. A survey of cloud-based network intrusion detection analysis. Human-centric Computing and Information Sciences. 2016;**6**:19. Available from: https://link.springer.com/article/10.1186/s13673-016-0076-z

[9] Akhtar Z. Malware detection and analysis: Challenges and research opportunities. Cryptography and Security. 2021. pp. 1-10. Available from: https://arxiv.org/abs/2101.08429

[10] Aboaoja FA, Zainal A, Ghaleb FA, Al-rimy BAS, Eisa TAE, Elnour AAH. Malware detection issues, challenges, and future directions: A survey. Applied Sciences. 2022;**12**:8482. Available from: https://www.mdpi.com/2076-3417/12/17/8482

[11] Alashjaee AM, Duraibi S, Song J. Dynamic taint analysis tools: A review. International Journal of

Computer Science and Security (IJCSS). 2019;**13**(6):231-243. Available from: https://www.cscjournals.org/manuscript/Journals/IJCSS/Volume13/Issue6/IJCSS-1518.pdf

[12] Bobrovnikova K, Lysenkoa S, Hurmana I, Kwiecieńb A. Machine learning based techniques for cyberattacks detection in the Internet of Things infrastructure. Intelligent Information Technologies & Systems of Information Security, Khmelnytskyi, Ukraine. March 23-25, 2022. pp. 411-420. Available from: https://ceur-ws.org/Vol-3156/; https://ceur-ws.org/Vol-3156/paper31.pdf

[13] Vasilyev A. A Brief History of the Evolution of Cyberattacks / A. Vasilyev // Mezhdunarodny'j nauchno-issledovatel'skij zhurnal [International Research Journal]. 2023:№11(137). Available from: https://research-journal.org/archive/11-137-2023-november/10.23670/IRJ.2023.137.39. DOI: 10.23670/IRJ.2023.137.39. [Accessed: February 7, 2025]

[14] Amal MR, Venkadesh P. Review of cyber attack detection: Honeypot system. Webology. 2022;**19**(1):5497-5514. DOI: 10.14704/WEB/V19I1/WEB19364

[15] Zhengbing H, Odarchenko R, Gnatyuk S, Zaliskyi M, Chaplits A, Bondar S, et al. Statistical techniques for detecting cyberattacks on computer networks based on an analysis of abnormal traffic behavior. International Journal of Computer Network and Information Security(IJCNIS). 2020;**12**(6):1-13. DOI: 10.5815/ijcnis.2020.06.01

[16] Aswal K, Pathak H. Advancing vehicle security: Deep learning based solution for defending CAN networks in the internet of vehicles. EAI Endorsed Transactions on Internet of Things. 2024;**10**:1-14. DOI: 10.4108/eetiot.652

[17] Yu H, Yang W, Cui B, Sui R, Wu X. Renyi entropy-driven network traffic anomaly detection with dynamic threshold. Cybersecurity. 2024;7:64. DOI: 10.1186/s42400-024-00249-1

[18] Cichonski P, Millar T, Grance T, Scarfone K. Computer Security Incident Handling Guide/Special Publication 800-61 Revision 2. NIST. U.S. Department of Commerce; 2012. Available from: https://csrc.nist.gov/pubs/sp/800/61/r2/final

[19] Nagar G, Kumar S. Cyber Security Kill Chain - Tactics and Strategies: Breaking down the cyberattack process and responding to threats. Mar 2025, 1st edition. Packt Publishing, eBook; 2025. 292 p. Available from: https://www.amazon.com/Cyber-Security-KillChain-cyberattack/dp/1835466095/ref=monarch_sidesheet_title

[20] Naik N, Jenkins P, Grace P, Song J. Comparing attack models for IT systems: Lockheed Martin's cyber kill chain, Mitre ATT&CK framework and diamond model. In: 2022 IEEE International Symposium on Systems Engineering (ISSE), Vienna. 24-26 October 2022:1-7. Available from: https://tinyurl.com/3y2u7h5m. DOI: 10.1109/ISSE54508.2022.10005490

Section 3

New-Age Solutions for Intrusion Detection

Chapter 6

Hunting the Invisible: Harnessing UEBA to Unmask Insider Threats

Subhash Parimalla, Chelumala Sreshta, M. Haarika, Ch. Likhitha Sowmya, Adiba Sania and Yagati Vaishnavi

Abstract

Insider threats pose a major threat to most organizations. It usually avoids all types of traditional cybersecurity controls and defenses. In this chapter, "Hunting the Invisible: Harnessing UEBA to Unmask Insider Threats," focus will be given on where AI, machine learning, and User and Entity Behavior Analytics (UEBA) are completely changing the mechanism of detection of insider threats. UEBA identifies real-time anomalous user behavior that signature-based systems miss. The chapter would discuss the kind of behavioral data that is analyzed by UEBA as well as the development of AI and machine learning in helping continuously improve detection. Using case studies in finance and healthcare, it explains the preventive activities regarding insider attacks and gives an overview of future roles of UEBA as an analytics tool and emerging strategy in security.

Keywords: user and entity behavior analytics (UEBA), insider threats, anomaly detection, machine learning in cybersecurity, behavioral analysis

1. Introduction

There are numerous definitions for the terms insider and insider threats. An insider is someone who has been legitimately empowered with the right to access, represent, or decide about one or more of the organization's structures or assets [1].

The insider threat is one who possesses privileges and misuses them or accesses security to the disadvantage of someone [1].

These impacts can be broken down into financial losses, disruption to the organization, loss of reputation, and long-term impacts on organizational culture. Such impacts can become very nuanced, with little measurement or accounting [1].

It is not clear how effective different prevention, detection, or response measures are to reduce insiders and, therefore, the threat. Conversely, they might be terribly important. The security domains might be misused by insiders in unexpected ways, triggering false alarms, with insiders either maliciously acting or working with legitimate credentials through illegal means and threats from non-malicious insiders who could be performing so either through negligence or ignorance [1].

Malicious insider threats comprise deliberate actions by insiders to harm the organization. For example, this might include a former employee leaking sensitive data to their competitors for compensation or out of personal reprisal. Edward Snowden notoriously leaked NSA classified information in the summer of 2013; he believed the U.S. government violated privacy rights before it happened [1].

Mischievous threats occur when an insider intentionally misuses those privileges, although they do not intend to cause actual harm to the organization. An employee may download non-approved software to make work easier or to avoid management restrictions, not intending to disable or harm an organization but to introduce security gaps. These acts, although not malicious, may expose the organization to vulnerabilities [1].

Negligent insider threats arise when insiders inadvertently undermine security because of some careless misjudgment. For example, an employee may forget to update a password or corrupt some software and thereby expose the organization to potential risk from external attackers. These cannot be categorized as crimes against the organization but rather as careless mistakes that can have disastrous consequences [2].

Accidental insider threats involve those situations where insiders act outside the bounds of the law by mistake rather than malice. For example, they might inadvertently send a sensitive email to an unintended recipient or wrongly delete files. Such incidents happen mostly out of error or failure to adhere to established security guidelines and can have considerable repercussions despite no malicious intent [2].

1.1 Real-life examples of insider attacks

Examples of high-profile insider attacks discarded severe consequences arising from such threats. The most serious of these incidents involved financial losses, tarnished reputations, and regulatory inquiry. Notable examples include:

Edward Snowden (NSA whistleblower): Edward Snowden was a former contractor in the National Security Agency, and in 2013, he leaked highly classified information about the agency's surveillance programs. As a malicious insider, he would have gained access to confidential information and released it. His actions instigated an international debate on privacy concerning government surveillance [3].

Target data breach: In 2013, hackers were able to enter Target's internal network through credentials stolen from a third-party vendor. The attackers utilized these credentials legitimately in establishing malware on Target's point-of-sale systems, which led to the stealing of credit or debit card details involving 40 million accounts. Target was vulnerable due to poor internal security practices, while compromised third-party credentials were the specific cause of that breach [4].

The Capital One Data Breach (2019): A former employee of Amazon Web Services (AWS) hacked into and stole Capital One's consumer data on AWS servers. This revealed more than 100 million customer accounts, including credit scores, credit card applications, and social security numbers; the alleged hacker, a former employee of AWS, had knowledge of the system and exploited a vulnerability, thus accessing the information [5].

The Google Project Zero Insider Attack: In 2019, a Google employee was found to have misused his access to the internal systems and exfiltrated intellectual property. Though the cow was tended to early, concerns regarding the supply chain have been related to rising indirect threats even in high-security environments [6].

1.2 Why traditional defenses fail softer against insider threats

Traditional cyber defense strategies have long focused on keeping outside threats from attacking the organization's periphery. However, insider threats, be they malicious, negligent, or even compromised, dictate a different approach that those old model systems just cannot offer. Key reasons traditional defenses have failed against insider threats are as follows.

Perimeter-centric security models: Traditional security systems focus on preventing external attacks with the help of firewalls, intrusion detection systems (IDS), and antivirus applications. These defenses operate under the premise that internal users are trusted; hence, they are permissible for getting by undetected by security systems for compromising insiders.

Research insight: About 78% of insider threats bypass traditional perimeter defenses such as firewalls and IDS, according to a 2021 cybersecurity study. This reveals how vulnerable such arrangements are, considering that malicious or compromised insiders are well able to go beyond perimeter defenses based on trust levels, all while carrying out hostile activities.

Example: A particularly notorious case occurred in 2021 when an employee's stolen credentials were used by the attacker to launch an attack against sensitive systems belonging to Colonial Pipeline. Due to the traditional defenses failing to notice the attack until considerable damage was done, these soft-attack dangers may unfold.

No behavioral analytics and context-aware security: Traditional defensive systems tend to operate on static, signature-based detection methods. The mode of detection is based upon attitudes toward identifying known threats or patterns, not on detecting behavior that constitutes anomalies and which would not readily conform to established signature patterns. From this, it poses the threat that insiders may or may not set alerts, especially when modifying their activities slightly from routine ones and their behavior is not overtly suspicious.

Key problem: Static security models struggle to detect subtle insider activities, such as gradual data exfiltration, unusual login times, or the use of privileged access.

Research: A 2022 paper in Cyber Defense Review demonstrates that legacy systems fail to recognize "normal" behavior deviations, which are often characteristic of insider threats.

Improved solution: User and Entity Behavior Analytics (UEBA) allows machine learning and artificial intelligence techniques to track and analyze behavior patterns, helping them to alert unusual activities. Therefore, the UEBA could reveal dangerous insider threats—like an employee accessing data they do not usually work with or uploading massive amounts of data—before the organization even notices something is wrong.

Insufficient privilege and access management: Old systems do not detect and limit user privileges properly, necessarily creating insults where employees are allowed to perform more actions than prescribed. Excessive access rights provide insiders an avenue to perform major havoc, either intentionally (malicious insider) or unintentionally (negligent insider).

Research insight: As reported in a 2023 study, 56% of insider threats related to insiders misusing their legitimate access rights have been highlighted as a major flaw in traditional practices of access management [7].

Example: An employee at a financial institution plundered sensitive customer data in 2022 by leveraging their administrative access. This activity was, however, under wraps for a few months on the basis that nobody managed privilege dynamically.

False alarms and alert fatigue: Traditional security systems often generate alerts based on heuristics and signatures. They tend to undergo a problem of false positives. Also, this will strain out the security teams, thus reducing their effectiveness, creating delays, and creating a situation in which insider threats can be overlooked.

Impact: A 2021 paper published in IEEE Transactions on Security found that false positives overwhelm security teams, causing them to exhaust themselves and allowing threats to escape through fireworks [8].

Example: A user intentionally initiating a login may be wrongfully interpreted as an attack, drawing security attention away from subtler and more grave insider actions like unauthorized data download.

Delayed detection and response time-to-time: Traditional systems are not meant for real-time detection of insider threats. As they are based on periodical scans or manual reviews, these systems might take a couple of hours or even days to sift through an insider breach. This is even if the insider has already had his chance to cause damage and exfiltrate sensitive data.

Research insight: In a 2021 study by Gartner, it was observed that insider threats go unnoticed for an average of 77 days, a time period significantly longer than for an external threat, where it shortens to 56 days [9].

Going back to an example, one case in 2019 involved a malicious insider causing exfiltration for an entire 6 months before detection.

Insufficient monitoring of insider behavior: Traditional methods of defense focus on endpoint security and the detection of external threats rather than internal behavior. Such limited focus thus creates huge gaps wherein malicious or negligent insiders may bypass detection by utilizing their IoT access.

Major problem: Standard systems are incapable of detecting information being accessed by an insider unless comprehensive contextual analysis of user behavior is informed (e.g., when, where, and how sensitive data get accessed).

Research insight: A 2022 research paper on insider threat detection reported that 67% of insider attacks were undetected due to a lack of continuous monitoring of user behavior happening in real time [10].

2. What is UEBA and how does it work?

User and Entity Behavior Analytics refers to a cybersecurity solution depending on the analysis of machine learning and algorithms-based user and entity behavior in a network. It helps pinpoint any form of anomalous behavior that will deviate from the normal, such as when the user in a day is downloading 20 MB and suddenly downloads about 4 GB.

Such anomalies are flagged as potential threats for some investigational action [1]. UEBA also tracks machine behavior. An unexpected spike in requests to a server could indicate a Distributed Denial of Service (DDoS) attack. UEBA systems can spot these anomalies and inform IT administrators, who take the necessary actions [1].

2.1 Operation of UEBA

To work efficiently, UEBA should be installed on all devices connected to the corporate network, including personal devices used for work. The system collects data that, in turn, would establish norms during its first learning stage. The normal behavior is used in flagging any threat of hazard through the detection of anomalous events [1].

DOI: http://dx.doi.org/10.5772/intechopen.1008799

2.2 Essentially UEBA comprises three components

2.2.1 Analytics

The analytics component collects and organizes data to define behavioral norms for users and entities. Statistical models are utilized to detect deviations that could require alerts for potential threats [2].

2.2.2 Integration

Integration with existing security systems makes UEBA much stronger by combining the data from different sources, including logs and network packets, presenting a complete picture of possible threats [2].

2.2.3 Presentation

Findings are reported to the IT teams or acted upon automatically. An alert will then prompt a manual investigation, while automation would isolate any suspicious user or device from the network to prevent further damage [2].

2.3 Differentiating UEBA from legacy systems

User and Entity Behavior Analytics (UEBA) distinguishes itself from legacy systems of security in that it incorporates advanced analytics, machine learning, and contextual data in offering much more superior threat detection. Legacy systems basically run off static rules and known threat patterns but employ a dynamic behavior-based methodology to detect anomalies and contextual understanding.

2.4 Key differences

2.4.1 Variety of data sources

Legacy systems: Depend on a handful of data sources, for example, web proxy, firewall logs, and system event logs.

UEBA: Integrates numerous data sources such as application use, network activity, email interactions, and user access patterns to create a complete picture of user behavior (The Role of User Entity Behavior Analytics to Detect Network Attacks in Real Time).

2.4.2 Behavioral analysis

Legacy systems: Rely on static, rule-based detection.

UEBA: Generates dynamic user profiles that leverage machine learning in detecting deviations from normal behavior; therefore, this system is suitable for detecting emerging or insider threats (The Role of User Entity Behavior Analytics to Detect Network Attacks in Real Time).

2.4.3 Proactive threat detection

Legacy systems: Responds reactively to known threats through pre-configured rules.

UEBA: Proactively monitors the anomalies and identifies possible threats in real time, thereby allowing for precautionary measures to be set to on (What is UEBA and Why It Should Be an Essential Part of Your Incident Response?).

2.4.4 Contextual understanding

Legacy systems: Analyze events in isolation.

UEBA: Explores contextual factors such as user location, time of access, and device used to understand and analyze the risk in a complete way (What is UEBA and Why It Should Be an Essential Part of Your Incident Response?).

2.4.5 Score on risk

Legacy systems: Do not provide comprehensive scoring systems.

UEBA: Applies an aggregated risk score that provides the security team with a frame of reference for prioritizing investigations of any incident where anomalies were detected (The Role of User Entity Behavior Analytics to Detect Network Attacks in Real Time).

2.4.6 Example of application

Legacy system: Alert triggered when a sensitive file is accessed from an odd IP based on a location anomaly—however, it could be legit.

UEBA: These contexts plug the user's access into normal patterns, new logins, and the latest device activities, and then work out whether that behavior deviates from normal established norms, and this reduces chances of false positives (What is UEBA and Why It Should Be an Essential Part of Your Incident Response?).

Thus, in conclusion, the combination of machine learning, big data analytics, and dynamic behavior profiling has facilitated the migration of organizations from a reactive to a proactive security strategy. This helps the Authorized User Behavioral Analytics address most gaps in legacy systems through contextual user activity and probabilistic models that are essential for modern cybersecurity infrastructure.

3. The role of AI and ML in UEBA

User and Entity Behavior Analytics (UEBA) refers to the use of artificial intelligence and machine learning for next-generation cyber defense, proactive detection, and mitigation of threats. Unlike traditional rule-based systems, UEBA is focused on the analysis of behavioral patterns of users and entities like devices and applications to detect anomalies that can indicate possible malicious intent, insider threats, or compromised accounts.

UEBA has become the much-needed safeguard against increasingly complex computer threats because traditional firewalls, antivirus programs, and human monitoring are grossly inadequate. This system is based on dynamic baselines created from learning by AI and ML algorithms. Overall, UEBA systems are dynamic systems and will, therefore, offer flexible protection and defense against active assailants [10].

AI and ML basically constitute UEBA's backbone for performing concretely deep analysis on substantial heterogeneous domains comprising datasets on par with even the most minute anomalies. The basic building blocks and methods incorporate:

Supervised learning: Here, the models are designed based on labeled data to discriminate between normal behavior and anomalous behavior [10]. Example scenario: Employees accessing unauthorized systems or files.

Unsupervised learning: This identifies patterns in unlabeled data, thus effectively indicating unknown or succeeding lurking threats [10].

Example scenario: Sudden data transfer spikes or unusual login activities.

Deep learning: Involves the use of neural networks to capture complex patterns from very large unstructured datasets, for example, emails, network logs, or user communications [10].

Example models: Convolutional Neural Networks (CNN) on image-based data, Recurrent Neural Networks (RNN) on time-series analysis.

Natural Language Processing (NLP): Analyzes textual data such as emails, chats, or documents to identify phishing, inappropriate communication, or sensitive data exposure [10].

Example scenario: Phishing emails and unauthorized sharing of top-secret documents.

Graph analytics: Graphs the relationships of users, devices, and applications to uncover unusual ties or data flows [10].

Example scenario: Detecting privilege escalation attacks or unauthorized access chains.

3.1 List of advantages of AI-powered UEBA

- *Threat reduction*: Detection of advanced persistent threats (APTs), insider threats, and zero-day vulnerabilities. Enter example: An employee trying to exfiltrate sensitive data using atypical access patterns [11].

- *Reduce false positives*: The AI-performed risk scoring differentiates the serious threat from benign anomalies to dramatically reduce repetitive alerts and analyst fatigue [11].

- *Scale and efficiency*: Ability to invariably process voluminous data flows from multiple sources, with a constant performance level as the organization grows. Example: Monitoring millions of endpoints across the world [11].

- *Continuous learning and adaptation*: ML models are capable of adjusting their baselines for user and entity behavior as they evolve with time [11].

- *Better visibility and better insights*: Holistic picture of network activity, which helps to spot weak points and determine security policies [11].

3.2 Challenges in deploying AI-driven UEBA systems

- *Data quality and availability*: Need huge and great datasets for proficiently trained models. If inconsistent data or missing data is there, then will not get an accurate result [12].

- *Privacy and compliance*: User data accessed by a UEBA will always be sensitive, and hence, it must follow privacy and regulatory laws (GDPR, HIPAA) [12].

- *Algorithmic biases*: Generally, ML models directly learn from the training datasets well, so they sometimes have standards of bias, which may produce skewed results or let discrimination happen. Example Mitigation: Regular audits and diverse datasets to minimize biases [12].

- *Skill gaps*: It requires appropriate skills in cybersecurity, data science, and AI/ML, and knowing how to deploy a UEBA system or proceed with its management could require heavy investment either in training or recruiting [12].

- *Integration with existing systems*: Integration with Security Information or Event Management (SIEM) and SOAR and other security tools could be challenging and time-consuming [12].

3.3 Use cases for AI-powered UEBA financial services

Insider threats, fraud activity, and unauthorized access to sensitive financial information are detected.

Example: This could entail flagging unusual transfer patterns of broad amounts indicative of possible money laundering [10].

3.3.1 Healthcare

To monitor the access of EHRs and compliance with regulations like the Health Insurance Portability and Accountability Act, access to the electronic health record (EHR) system will need constant monitoring.

Example: A medical staff member is flagged when he/she accesses patient records outside of his/her department [10].

3.3.2 Enterprise and technology

Protection of intellectual property through monitoring sensitive data access and transfer patterns. Example: Detecting unauthorized attachment downloads of proprietary source code.

3.3.3 Critical infrastructure

Securing OT networks for energy, transportation, and utility sectors.

3.3.4 Retail and e-commerce

Tracking user activity for the sake of protection against account takeover, payment fraud, and customer data breaches.

3.4 Future of AI and ML in UEBA

Multimodal analytics—combines diverse data sources (e.g., physical access logs, endpoint telemetry, cloud activity) for comprehensive anomaly detection.

Explainable AI (XAI)—enhances transparency by providing insights into why certain behaviors are flagged, thus aiding trust and validation for the analyst.

Automated response systems—it can integrate with SOAR platforms to automatically quarantine compromised accounts or block suspicious traffic in real time.

IoT and edge computing—extend UEBA capability to monitoring and securing connections for IoT devices and edge networks, which is critical as attack surfaces expand.

Collaborative threat intelligence—the sharing of threat patterns and behaviors across organizations enhances collective defense.

3.5 Case studies

3.5.1 Financial institution

Problem: Weak monitoring of a vast range of users across global operations.

Solution: Artificial Intelligence-based UEBA, using supervised and unsupervised learning methods and algorithms, with graph analytics.

Outcome: Detected insider threats. An employee attempting to sell customer data was halted from doing so, saving the organization from a huge financial and reputational loss [13].

3.5.2 Healthcare organization

Problem: Need to comply with HIPAA and prevent unauthorized access to data. Solution: NLP was used to analyze communication logs supervised for access patterns.

Outcome: Flagged and mitigated inappropriate access to patient records, thus reinforcing compliance and data security.

4. Behavioral analysis and applications in UEBA

Behavioral analysis is the process by which the patterns of action and interaction of users and entities within a system are established [14]. In the sphere of User and Entity Behavior Analytics, it comes to the great importance of enhancing cybersecurity. UEBA systems utilize big behavioral data to unveil deviations from standard patterns, allowing for automated detection of security threats and the prevention of suspected risks by either an insider attack or malware activity. Advanced analytics methodologies, such as statistical modeling and machine learning, are exploited to continuously assess and monitor the behavior of users and systems.

UEBA's primary consensus value for behavioral analysis is its ability to set baselines for "normal" behavior, thus allowing organizations to spot subtle anomalies that could be overlooked by traditional rule-based systems. For instance, the detection system of static rules only raises concerns for the expressly unauthorized actions taken by an end-user, while behavioral analysis generates a higher level of vigilance for any user- or system-initiated activity that, despite being permissible per se, is out of the given limitations. The proactive detection capability makes UEBA a robust contributor in the fight against both outside attacks, such as compromised accounts, and insider risks, such as insider misuse.

4.1 Data collected: logs, patterns of access, mode of system usage

4.1.1 Logs

Logs form the basis of UEBA and generally describe any kind of data being captured or sought after to audit the activities on various systems. The composition of the typical log includes:

1. *Event logs*: Detailed interactions between users and systems with respect to file access, command execution, and configuration changes. Clustering techniques can be utilized to illustrate logs into meaningful sequences in order to isolate anomalies associated with users deviating from the standard action sequences.

2. *Authentication logs*: Contain information regarding login attempts and origin IP addresses and devices used. Constant failures at sign-ins in strange locations or from odd devices could be taken as an indicator of maybe a brute-force attack or other user-attributed security violations.

4.1.2 Access patterns enable UEBA systems to know how users interact with resources

Key insights include:

1. *File access logs*: Tracking which files are accessed, by whom, and how frequently. A user consistently accessing restricted data, such as financial records instead of their usual HR files, is flagged as suspicious.

2. *Network access patterns*: Tracks the connections of the systems or servers. Frequent high or long-duration connections may indicate lateral movement by the attackers as they attempt privilege escalation or obtain access to sensitive information.

4.1.3 System usage

Metrics that describe how the user interacts with the system:

1. *Session data*: Tracks the length of the session, login time, and what activity has been done. Lengthy sessions that occur late at unorthodox hours reflect suspicious activities.

2. *Activity metrics*: Measures application usage, document edits, and other system interactions. Deviations, such as new application access or high-volume activities, are considered threats.

All these data types allow the UEBA systems to build a strong sense of normal behavior and provide a basis for anomaly detection.

4.2 Anomaly detection in user and entity behavior

Identifying anomalies in user and entity behavior focuses on locating deviations in established baselines to discover potential threats [15]. The following discusses some of the methods and techniques used to identify anomalies.

DOI: http://dx.doi.org/10.5772/intechopen.1008799

4.2.1 Building behavioral baselines

The UEBA systems generate baselines of "normal" user and entity behavior based on historical analysis, including login time, access patterns, and system usage. These dynamically shift according to changes in user behaviors. For example, if a person accessed an HR file all day long, the usual time is during business hours. Any access to a financial record at midnight is recorded as unusual behavior. This process guarantees that UEBA has something to compare with its determinations of what represents deviances [9].

4.2.2 Statistical and threshold-based detection

Statistical methods can be used by applying averages, standard deviations, and thresholds to detect outliers. For instance,

- *Variance monitoring*: This detects spikes in activity, for example, excessive access to files or repeated login failures.

- *Time-series analysis*: This monitors activities over time to detect unusual activity patterns, such as attempting to log in from remote locations during off-hours.

Threshold-based rules can be particularly useful for certain applications, like identifying brute-force attacks when several failed login attempts exceed a defined threshold [16].

4.2.3 Machine learning techniques

Machine learning enhances anomaly detection through complex pattern discovery within data. The most important approaches include:

- *Unsupervised learning*: Techniques such as K-means clustering and Isolation Forests identify anomalies in unlabeled data. For example, it can find an employee who suddenly accesses resources [10].

- *Supervised learning*: Models that are trained from historical labeled data classify the activities as normal or suspicious [10].

- *Deep learning*: Neural networks are used for finding slight yet consistent changes in the pattern of access, say, files over a period of time [10].

These methods work best in dynamic behavior environments or very large datasets where traditional techniques may not be able to capture the subtlety of anomalies [10].

4.2.4 Real-time detection and contextual analysis

Real-time monitoring provides for instant response to anomalies by continuously analyzing the log data and activity streams, thus alerting the activities, such as sudden spikes in data access or logins from geographically disparate locations. False positives are reduced through contextual analysis, including consideration of certain role changes or environmental variables like the reputation of an IP address or device fingerprint.

This amalgamation of approaches ensures that security teams identify and resolve the threats without being swayed by nonsensical alerts.

4.3 Key takeaway

UEBA systems identify threats such as insider misuse, compromised accounts, and malware activity through behavioral baselines, statistical models, machine learning, and contextual analysis. This advanced technique ensures proactive protection against a wide range of cyber risks.

4.4 Sample data analysis scenarios

4.4.1 Insider threat detection

Any employee accessing financial records above and beyond his normal job function would indicate insider misuse. Also, the logs and access patterns might reveal constant deviations, and thus, security teams might have to probe deeper.

4.4.2 Account compromise detection

If an account owned by a legitimate user is accessed from a strange location or at weird hours, then the UEBA system will look to check up on the login time, IP address, and type of device utilized for possible account compromise. It is made feasible because of the behavioral baselines.

Malware entering the system usually does things such as lateral movement across the servers or accessing files that are restricted. A UEBA system detects and prevents malware threats by comparing current patterns of system use to historical data.

4.4.3 Undocumented data exfiltration

Unusual data transfer from a user, especially during off-peak times or with some other sites, could raise suspicion of data exfiltration. This is detected by a UEBA system through access patterns and usage in the system.

4.4.4 Privilege escalation

Attackers often escalate privileges to access sensitive resources. By monitoring log data, UEBA systems can flag unusual behavior that suggests an escalation of privileges.

5. UEBA systems implementation

User and entity behavior analytics (UEBA) is an approach to enhancing the detection and mitigation of insider threats, such as account compromises, and the organization's other security-related vulnerabilities. It uses different analysis techniques that include machine learning-based and behavioral analytics and has used advanced threat detection to notice these anomalies in behavior patterns within those organizations, thus enabling them to take preemptive measures.

5.1 Steps for implementation of UEBA in an organization

The successful implementation of UEBA systems requires a structured approach compatible with the organization's security goals and infrastructure [17].

5.1.1 Step 1: Define objectives and scope

- *Objective setting*: Organizations should determine the primary goals of deploying UEBA, including the detection of insider threats, unusual access patterns, and sensitive data leak prevention.

- *Scope identification*: It is essential to identify the assets and areas of the network to be monitored, including user access to critical systems, application logs, and network traffic flows. This clarity ensures targeted and efficient deployment.

5.1.2 Step 2: Data collection and integration

- *Data sources*: UEBA systems require comprehensive data collection from diverse sources, such as user activity logs, endpoint data, network traffic, and existing SIEM platforms.

- *Normalization*: Data, which is gathered from various sources, needs to be normalized so that it can be uniformly analyzed by the UEBA system. This step covers preprocessing and arranging raw data for compatibility.

5.1.3 Step 3: Configure baseline behavioral models

- *Behavioral profiling*: Using the historical data, machine learning algorithms create profiles of normal user and entity behaviors. These profiles form the basis on which anomalies are detected that diverge from expected activity.

- *Behavioral analytics*: This system uses analytics and compares behaviors in real time against pre-defined baselines, thereby pinpointing threats such as uncommon login hours, access to sensitive files, and escalations of privilege.

5.1.4 Step 4: Install UEBA solution

- *Pilot testing*: In preparation for full-fledged rollout, pilot test the UEBA in a controlled environment. Testing enables it to fine-tune the configuration so that the system does not trigger a lot of false positives during actual operation.

- *Full deployment*: After testing, the system is deployed throughout the organization to ensure continuous monitoring and real-time anomaly detection.

Paper: Building an Overall Framework for User and Entity Behavior Analytics (UEBA): Combination of Sophisticated Machine Learning and Contextual Information Garima Sharma1, Ambika Thakur2, Chetna Tiwari.

5.2 Well-known tools and platforms for UEBA [18]

1. Exabeam

   - Overview: Exabeam is a security operations platform that is AI-driven and utilizes machine learning and behavioral modeling for real-time detection and response to cyber threats.

   - Key features:

     o Real-time threat detection and risk-based alerts

     o Machine learning and behavioral modeling

     o Cloud-native, user-friendly platform

     o Streamlined threat detection, investigation, and response (TDIR)

2. Splunk User Behavior Analytics

   - Overview: Splunk User Behavior Analytics can be described as the detection of insider threats, fraud, and targeted attacks, correlating data from several sources that give an extensive view of user behavior.

   - Key features:

     o Data from multiple sources correlation

     o Deployment on-premises, cloud, hybrid

     o Detection of insider threats, fraud, and targeted attacks

3. IBM Security QRadar

   - Overview: IBM Security QRadar is the network and user activity visibility of security teams that can identify threats in a timely and effective manner.

   - Key features:

     o Real-time visibility of network activity and user behavior

     o Integration with threat intelligence

     o Centralized dashboard management of security posture

4. Microsoft Sentinel

   - Overview: Microsoft Sentinel is a cloud-based SIEM and SOAR solution that uses advanced analytics and AI to detect and respond to threats, prioritizing alerts based on risk.

- Key features:

  - Real-time threat detection and prioritization

  - Centralized dashboard for monitoring and management

  - Integration with Microsoft's Security Graph

6. Practical use cases of UEBA

6.1 Real-time threat detection in action

Real-time threat detection encompasses the act of using advanced security tools to detect and respond to threats as they occur. This includes identifying compromised accounts, spotting insider threats, and preventing data breaches. It is achieved by monitoring user behavior, comparing actions against those of their peers, and much more, all in an effort to quickly detect suspicious activities. A strategy is to take rapid actions, such as blocking high-risk users or escalating investigation processes, while integrating with other security systems like SIEM in bolstering overall security [19].

6.1.1 Account compromise detection

Indicators:

- Improbable authentication patterns (e.g., dormant account use).

- Concurrent Logins from Multiple Locations.

- Account activity from unusual locations or times.

- Customer peer group behavioral deviations.

- Using peer group information to identify abnormal password behaviors, such as abnormal numbers of authentication errors or account lockouts.

Actions:

- Detection of compromised credentials used for malicious purposes.

- Identify generic account abuse.

6.1.2 Data exfiltration detection

Indicators:

- USB data transfers after accessing private documents.

- Blacklisted attempts at communication.

- Abnormal traffic patterns that indicate unauthorized data movement.

Actions:

- Detection of malicious attempts to remove sensitive data from the network and its prevention.

6.2 Real-time anomaly detection techniques

Behavior analysis: Create a baseline of user behavior to identify unusual activity (e.g., unauthorized access to sensitive files).

Peer group analysis: Comparison of user activity against peers in similar roles to flag exceptional behavior (e.g., accessing records outside of standard group permissions).

Event rarity analysis: Detection of unprecedented or unusual events (e.g., login attempts during odd hours).

As for the analysis of sequences of actions, the basic principle is simple: opening a password-protected document followed by an upload to an external host might raise suspicion.

6.3 Risk-based real-time actions

Block a high-risk user immediately (disabling access to critical applications, for instance). Continuous monitoring and alerting of suspicious activity. Improved investigation workflows for flagged anomalies.

Integration with security operations:

These tools function in conjunction with existing systems, such as Security Information and Event Management, for investigation purposes.

Provides multi-layered defense strategies through continuous correlation of data from logs, network traffic, and applications used.

6.4 Insider attack prevention in finance

The finance sector is damagingly exposed to insider threats due to the general nature of its sensitive data and elevated levels of access that employees are granted. Insider threats might come from malicious insiders who abuse access for personal financial gain, negligent insiders, or individuals who intentionally wreak havoc. In view of the volume of data and transactions managed on an hourly and daily basis, the challenge of identifying and preventing these threats is huge for most financial institutions.

UEBA will, therefore, assist an organization in identifying anomalous activities that could indicate insider threats to allow for timely intervention to prevent breaches [20].

6.4.1 Use case 1: Detection of insider fraud attempts

6.4.1.1 Scenario

Andrew, a financial adviser with Goldguard Holdings, has been trying to use dormant bank accounts for money laundering [21]. His plan is to stop notifications from the account, use small amounts of illicit funds to make apparently legal deposits, reroute the deposits to external accounts, and erase any transactions in order not to be discovered. Such fraud is difficult to detect manually because it appears regular.

6.4.1.2 Detection

Goldguard Holdings is integrating a UEBA system to continuously monitor worker behavior. In Andrew's case, the UEBA system raises some unusual activities, such as abnormal queries in the database with high-frequency deactivations of the notifications for certain accounts. The deviations from normal working behavior and role responsibilities are high.

6.4.1.3 Reaction

UEBA alerts notified the security personnel of the suspicious behavior for closer investigation. With an intensive investigation, the team was able to uncover Andrew's nefarious scheme. Real-time termination of his access privileges to sensitive systems leaves him with little opportunity to hinder further action, as everything is acted upon with no other transaction being done.

Furthermore, they reported the issue to the appropriate authorities to help avert financial loss, legal liability, and damage to the reputation of the organization.

6.4.2 Use case 2: Prevention of spear phishing attacks

6.4.2.1 Scenario

A marketing manager at Alpha Financial receives an email that appears to come from a legitimate advertising agency [20]. The email contains an attachment—a Word document—formulated to perform the task of stealing sensitive customer data through a malicious macro.

6.4.2.2 Detection

The UEBA system of Alpha Financial analyzes user and system activity in real time, catching some anomalies ranging from multiple PowerShell commands being executed from Margaret's computer to quick access to sensitive customer data files. This behavior strays away from her normality, and the automatic alert is triggered on the rise of her risk score.

6.4.2.3 Action

The UEBA system informs the security operators that they were given an approach to block Margaret's computer—it was disconnected from the network to stop any extent of loss. The latter on the probe affirmed the attack as phishing, and after measures were taken to have those files made safe, it became the organization's initiative to train Margaret and company on recognizing phishing attempts and lessening the chances of yet another occurrence.

6.4.3 Use case 3: Stopping data exfiltration by a disgruntled employee

6.4.3.1 Scenario

A disgruntled employee in a financial institution is attempting to exfiltrate sensitive customer data [22]. This employee goes ahead to download several files within a very short time and later encrypts them with unauthorized software so as to send them out.

6.4.3.2 Detection

The UEBA system of the shop keeps an eye on and analyzes user behavior continuously, with red flags like large-scale file downloads occurring in a very short time, access to files outside the ambit of an employee's duties, and improper usage of encryption software—that is, compared to the employee's baselines.

6.4.3.3 Action

The UEBA solution alerted, and the security team reacted by suspending access with immediate effect from critical systems. Investigations were conducted, confirming that it was an exfiltration operation. Necessary steps were undertaken to ensure the data was secured, the employee was taken through the disciplinary procedure, and new access policies were stated to corral such practices in the future.

These situations demonstrate how financial institutions can mitigate insider threats with the aid of UEBA systems. These technologies detect anomalous employee behavior that may portend trouble, watching in real time for suspicious activities before they can create serious problems. Timely interventions and consciousness-raising efforts are also key to protecting sensitive financial data, thereby putting financial institutions in compliance with GLBA in the long run. By combining Data Loss Prevention (DLP) technologies, advanced UEBA analytics, and employee awareness training, financial organizations can effectively defend against insider threats, minimizing the risk of data breaches and financial losses.

6.5 Mitigating data breaches in healthcare

The ongoing increase in the attacks on healthcare institutions by cybercriminals is primarily due to the highly marketable value of personal health information (PHI) that can be utilized for identity theft or sold on the black market. User and Entity Behavior Analytics (UEBA) is indispensable in behavioral deviation detection that would trigger an alert about a possible data breach, allowing mitigation controls for that particular breach [23].

6.5.1 Use case 1: Preventing insider threats in patient data exfiltration

6.5.1.1 Scenario

A young medical student working for a hospital, Mark has access to patient records on a need-to-know basis directly related to his studies [20]. He attempts to copy the sensitive information to transfer it out on the black market to pay off some of his debts—a crime he committed in some hours of the night after working hours.

6.5.1.2 Detection

Mark's unusual behavior is deftly picked up by the medical organization's UEBA system, monitoring all user activities. Mark has the required access powers, but in light of what was customary behavior for him, the system annotated his behavior—much as that Mark hardly ever accessed patient records outside normal hours. His huge volume of records being copied late at night creates an aberration, triggering a suspicion.

6.5.1.3 Action

Once the UEBA system raises the alarm and locks out Mark's account, the IT Security team investigates at great speed, recovers the USB device, and determines that Mark's intention was to exfiltrate sensitive patient data. Revoked user access; an investigation is done against him as well. The access controls will be reviewed and tightened by the hospital to avert further incidents.

6.5.2 Use case 2: How to stop unauthorized access to PHI after device theft

6.5.2.1 Situation

Dr. Sarah Jones, a pediatrician, has her laptop stolen, which has access to an online portal that collects patient data for the hospital [24]. Although the laptop was password-protected, it remained logged into the hospital system, leaving sensitive information vulnerable to an attacker.

6.5.2.2 Detection

The hospital's UEBA system detects such unusual activity immediately upon its commencement. The system noted several unsuccessful login attempts from the device, and this anomalous behavior indicates a risk score spike in Dr. Jones's account. The system correlates the access attempts with the laptop's theft, which had been reported by Dr. Jones, and flags the activity as a breach risk.

6.5.2.3 Response

Once the system identifies the anomaly associated with the theft, it automatically locks Dr. Jones out of her account in order to stop any further transmissions. The hospital IT team wipes the laptop of sensitive data from afar. The hospital also files a police report with respect to the stolen laptop and implements corrective actions involving stronger two-factor authentication and enhanced security training.

These scenarios describe how UEBA is able to identify and interdict risks associated with unauthorized access, insider threats, or data breaches in healthcare to protect patient data while ensuring compliance with regulatory requirements such as HIPAA.

7. Overcoming challenges in UEBA implementation

The prospect of possible use is laced with challenges that have to be attended to. The barriers are few, however, that can be flashing between and within environments for widespread and meaningful adoption of UEBA:

7.1 Managing data quality and preprocessing

UEBA effectiveness is proportional to the input data quality. Noisy, incomplete records or stale baselines yield subpar results. Solutions include robustly established preprocessing pipelines and automated feature extraction to minimize human error and data inconsistency [25].

7.2 False positives—managing alerts

False positives remain as one of the most overbearing challenges besetting them. In fact, this overwhelms security teams and, to some extent, lose their ability to respond effectively. The detection can be refined by merging machine learning models with contextual analysis—e.g., where alerts nephrology-hospital—that is, known threat vectors, or real-world use cases would be correlated with some threat [26].

7.3 Activity of privileged user and developer

Irregular patterns associated with privileged users and developers offer unique challenges for the UEBA systems. They can also employ advanced role-based profiling and adaptive baselines that can customize the thresholds of the detections specific to the roles or job functions [25].

7.4 Scalability and computational overhead

As organizations tend to grow, UEBA systems also need to scale up toward the continuous quantities of data to process without losing performance. The scalability can be ensured, and the achieved cumulated computation costs can be minimized when resources available through a cloud-based and distributed processing models like Apache Kafka and Spark are used [26].

7.5 No standardized rules across vendors

Being no standardized frameworks for UEBA tools by which procuring customers will be exposed to inconsistencies in implementation and integration, one would need advocacy for industry-wide best practices and open standards as a means of facilitating interoperability and improving the overall efficiencies.

8. UEBA and future directions

The future of User and Entity Behavior Analytics (UEBA) is geared toward addressing increasingly sophisticated threats by leveraging cutting-edge technologies and methodologies.

8.1 Integration with AI and big data

Over the past few years, UEBA systems have increasingly completed AI and Big Data Analytics to enhance actionable insights regarding behavioral anomalies. AI models such as Deep Neural Networks and Ensemble learning techniques will enable the processing of large-scale and unstructured datasets for more accurate anomaly detection. Big data capability allows a UEBA solution to feed, in real time, extensive logs, traffic, and user activity [25].

8.2 More effective countering of insider threats

Insider threats are likely to continue being the forefront of UEBA advancement focus areas. In future systems, one expects the inclusion of context-aware mechanisms capable of making the distinction between benign anomalies and malfeasance. This might include better role-based baselining with the addition of sentiment analysis found to detect disgruntled or potentially malicious insiders [26].

8.3 Hybrid models like improved SIEM collaboration

The integration of UEBA systems with Security Information or Event Management (SIEM) platforms is likely to continue. A hybrid approach would mean that organizations would be able to track behavior against that of other security events in the broader context of threat. While SIEM can greatly aid UEBA by providing the enriched data needed for more accurate threat detection, UEBA adds an additional layer of anomaly detection capabilities [26].

8.4 Automation and continuous learning

Future UEBA systems will emphasize automation in such a way that they will self-update malintent behavior profiles and automatically resolve anomalies, which involves deploying reinforcement learning algorithms to update detection procedures genuinely during ongoing operations and performing this with minimal manual intervention [25].

8.5 Explainable AI (XAI) adoption

As UEBA systems get more intricate, embracing Explainable AI will become paramount. The capability of the system would enable security officers to comprehend the reasons behind detection results more convincingly, which would garner trust that would turn prediction results from being mere crystal balls into platforms for knowledge-based actions for AI models [26].

Author details

Subhash Parimalla*, Chelumala Sreshta, M. Haarika, Ch. Likhitha Sowmya, Adiba Sania and Yagati Vaishnavi
Vallurupalli Nageswara Rao Vignana Jyothi Institute of Engineering and Technology (VNRVJIET), India

*Address all correspondence to: subhash.parimalla@gmail.com

References

[1] Prabhu A, Thompson N. Insider Threats: Malicious, Negligent, and Compromised. Nikthompson.com. 2022. Available from: https://nikthompson.com/PDF/Prabhu-Thompson-2022-Primer.pdf

[2] IEEE. Understanding Insider Threats: A Comprehensive Study. IEEE Xplore. 2023. Available from: https://ieeexplore.ieee.org/stamp/stamp.jsp?arnumber=10445123

[3] The Guardian. The Edward Snowden Leaks: What Happened and Why It Matters. 2013. Available from: https://www.theguardian.com/world/2013/jun/09/edward-snowden-nsa-whistleblower-surveillance

[4] Target Data Breach Update. Target Corporate Report. **56**(3):12-15. Available from: https://corporate.target.com/press/release/2014/01/target-provides-update-on-data-breach-and-financial-performance

[5] Neto NN, Madnick S, de Paula AMG, Borges NM. Capital One Data Breach Incident. Capital One Security Report. 2019. Available from: https://cams.mit.edu/wp-content/uploads/capitalonedatapaper.pdf

[6] Thomas K, Moscicki A. Project Zero Insider Threats. Google Security Blog. 2019. Available from: https://security.googleblog.com/2019/05/

[7] Sharma G, Thakur A, Tiwari C. Developing a Comprehensive Framework for User and Entity Behavior Analytics (UEBA): Integrating Advanced Machine Learning and Contextual Insights. 2024. Available from: https://research-reels.com/wp-content/uploads/2024/08/Developing-a-Comprehensive-Framework-for-User-and-Entity-Behavior-Analytics-UEBA.pdf

[8] Osoro S. Security Threat Detection in the Workplace: A Behavior-Based Artificial Intelligence Approach. University of Nairobi; n.d. Available from: http://erepository.uonbi.ac.ke/bitstream/handle/11295/161091/Osoro_Security%20Threat%20Detection%20in%20the%20Workplace%20-%20a%20Behaviour-based%20Artificial%20Intelligence%20Approach.pdf?sequence=1

[9] Petri Enberg P. Leveraging AI and UEBA for Cybersecurity. Theseus.fi. 2024. Available from: https://www.theseus.fi/bitstream/handle/10024/869703/Enberg_Petri.pdf?sequence=2

[10] Ripla A. Leveraging AI for User and Entity Behavior Analytics (UEBA). LinkedIn. 2024. Available from: https://www.linkedin.com/pulse/leveraging-ai-user-entity-behavior-analytics-ueba-andre-ripla-pgcert-7aeme/

[11] CrowdStrike. User and Entity Behavior Analytics (UEBA). n.d. Available from: https://www.crowdstrike.com/en-us/cybersecurity-101/identity-protection/user-and-entity-behavior-analytics-ueba/

[12] CertiSec. What is User and Entity Behavior Analytics and Why Does It Matter? n.d. Available from: https://certisec.org/what-is-user-and-entity-behavior-analytics-and-why-does-it-matter/

[13] Securonix. Financial Services Organization Case Study. 2022. Available

from: https://www.securonix.com/wp-content/uploads/2022/03/Financial-Services-Organization-Case-Study-Securonix.pdf

[14] UPC. Advancements in UEBA-Based Threat Detection. Upcommons.upc.edu. n.d. Available from: https://upcommons.upc.edu/handle/2117/369769

[15] Raguvir S, Babu S. Detecting Anomalies in Users – A UEBA Approach. Proceedings of the International Conference on Industrial Engineering and Operations Management. UAE: Dubai; 2020. Available from: https://www.ieomsociety.org/ieom2020/papers/632.pdf

[16] Exabeam. What is UEBA and Why It Should Be an Essential Part of Your Incident Response? n.d. Available from: https://www.exabeam.com/explainers/ueba/what-is-ueba-and-why-it-should-be-an-essential-part-of-your-incident-response/

[17] Sharma G, Thakur A, Tiwari C. Developing a comprehensive framework for user and entity behavior analytics (UEBA): Integrating advanced machine learning and contextual insights. Journal of Communication Engineering & Systems. 2024;**14**(2):20-31. Available from: https://research-reels.com/wp-content/uploads/2024/08/Developing-a-Comprehensive-Framework-for-User-and-Entity-Behavior-Analytics-UEBA.pdf

[18] Exabeam. UEBA Tools: Key Capabilities and 7 Tools You Should Know. n.d. Available from: https://www.exabeam.com/explainers/ueba/ueba-tools-key-capabilities-and-7-tools-you-should-know/

[19] Raj G, Savai C. Cyber Security: Combating Attacks with Automation & UBA. Tata Consultancy Services; 2020. Available from: https://www.tcs.com/content/dam/global-tcs/en/pdfs/insights/whitepapers/ai-ueba-cyber-security.pdf

[20] ManageEngine. Cybersecurity in Financial Services. ManageEngine.com. (n.d.).. Available from: https://www.manageengine.com/log-management/cyber-security/cybersecurity-in-financial-services.html

[21] Votiro. Securing the Vault: Preventing Insider Threats in Financial Institutions. 2024. Available from: https://votiro.com/blog/preventing-insider-threats-in-financial-institutions/

[22] Emma Leit. The Threat Within: How Finance Organisations Can Mitigate Rising Insider Risks. 2023. Available from: https://www.europeanfinancialreview.com/the-threat-within-how-finance-organisations-can-mitigate-rising-insider-risks/

[23] Zac Amos. Best UEBA Use Cases to Implement in Healthcare. 2023. Available from: https://readwrite.com/best-ueba-use-cases-to-implement-in-healthcare/

[24] ManageEngine. Data Security in Healthcare with UEBA. ManageEngine.com. n.d. Available from: https://www.manageengine.com/log-management/cyber-security/data-security-healthcare-ueba.html

[25] Datta J, Dasgupta S, Dasgupta R, Reddy KR. Real-time threat detection in UEBA using unsupervised learning algorithms. In: IEEE International Conference on Electronics, Materials Engineering & Nano-Technology (IEMENTech). 2021

[26] Salitin MA, Zolait AH. The role of user entity behavior analytics to detect network attacks in real time. In: IEEE International Conference on Innovation and Intelligence for Informatics, Computing, and Technologies (3ICT). 2018

Chapter 7

Smart Detection: Reinforcement Learning for Network Intrusion Defense

Faheem Yar Khuhawar, Tayyaba Shaikh, Abdul Latif Memon, Irfan Halepoto, Fahim Umrani, Rizwan Ali Shah, Hyder Bux Mangrio and Omar Bani Fayyad

Abstract

As cyber threats grow in complexity, the demand for intelligent and adaptive intrusion detection systems (IDS) is more critical than ever. Traditional machine learning models, while effective, often struggle to keep up with the dynamic and evolving nature of cyberattacks. This chapter presents an advanced approach to network intrusion detection using reinforcement learning (RL), a machine learning paradigm that enables systems to learn optimal actions through trial and error without the need for extensive retraining. Specifically, the proposed IDS leverages Q-learning, enhanced by dueling deep Q-learning (DQL) and double deep Q-networks (DDQN), to autonomously monitor and protect networks. By learning from its environment and making decisions based on real-time feedback, the system continuously improves its detection capabilities, even as new threats emerge. When tested on the CIC-IDS 2018 dataset, the DQL-based IDS achieved an impressive accuracy of 94%, significantly outperforming traditional machine learning algorithms such as Decision Trees, Random Forest, and XGBoost. Unlike conventional models constrained by static feature sets and predefined learning, the RL-driven IDS adapts dynamically to changing environments, offering robust detection of sophisticated intrusions. Despite its strong performance in simulated environments, the practical application of this approach to real-world scenarios presents challenges, such as ensuring scalability and handling diverse network conditions. Nonetheless, this research demonstrates the transformative potential of reinforcement learning in network security, paving the way for systems capable of autonomously detecting and responding to complex cyber threats in an efficient and adaptive manner.

Keywords: intrusion detection system (IDS), reinforcement learning (RL), Q-learning, dueling deep Q-learning (DQL), double deep Q-network (DDQN)

1. Introduction

1.1 Rise of big data

Big data has become a popular concept with the technological advances in the past decade. Before then, it was extremely costly to store the data because acquiring the needed disk space was not as easy as today. Cloud systems were expensive and not common; therefore, to store data, companies needed to have their own storage facilities which required time, space, and money, much more than compared to today. In the present day, we have unlimited storage, especially provided by cloud services, at our disposal. With the competition between service providers, the prices of these services are decreasing, whereas the quality of the services is rising. Moreover, many different frameworks and tools exist to handle different types of big data. All these advancements have recently made big data one of the most popular concepts in computer science.

The capability of storing and retrieving data sheds light on big data. In real time, it is important to highlight the fact that it could be of great help in detecting any attacks on systems. We worked on a big data analytics approach for intrusion detection in networks using deep reinforcement learning, incorporating the system's time feature during anomaly detection, which aligns with the goals of most intrusion detection tasks. In this regard, as the system is planned to act in near real time, it utilizes streaming big data from the network. On the contrary, the processing of streaming data is done in real time, so real-time queries on the side are also possible. For this reason, stream processing has been selected as the relevant mode of processing in our case.

1.2 Machine learning for intrusion detection

Over the last few years, there has been a huge leap in the machine learning domain and it started being employed in several areas. One of the popular areas, which have been utilizing machine learning-based solutions, is the cybersecurity domain for detection of malicious activities. Due to signature-based approaches now considered to be inadequate for the detection of current cyber threats, machine learning approaches have attained enormous relevance to address this shortfall.

In the survey [1], the machine learning techniques used in intrusion detection systems are of three broad categories, namely supervised learning, unsupervised learning, and reinforcement learning.

- *Supervised learning*: This technique of learning is also referred to as classification and in this technique, the model is presented with a given dataset that contains labeled instances to train the model. For that reason, supervised learning algorithms seek to estimate the output values of new data points by building dependencies and relations that exist between the features of the inputs and the labels of the dataset that will become the outputs after the model has been trained. Boosting, Ensemble classifiers (Bagging, Boosting), Linear classifiers (Logistic regression, Fisher Linear discriminant, Naive Bayes classifier, Perceptron, SVM), Quadratic classifiers, etc. are some of the commonly used supervised learning techniques.

- *Unsupervised learning*: In contrast to supervised learning, the model is provided with an unlabeled dataset in this unsupervised learning. The algorithms operating on pattern detection and descriptive modeling are among the most common methods employed in this strategy. Since there are no labels to learn, algorithms that fall under this category explore the unlabeled input data by clustering, summarizing, and detecting patterns in order to extract useful information to make predictions. Some of the most commonly used unsupervised ones are: Cluster analysis (K-means clustering, Fuzzy clustering), Hierarchical clustering, Self-organizing map, Apriori algorithm, Eclat algorithm, and Outlier Factor (Local Outlier Factor).

- *Reinforcement learning*: Additionally, while belonging to Machine Learning kinds of techniques, reinforcement learning can also be considered a type of artificial intelligence. In this strategy, the algorithm keeps on learning in cycles from the environment it is operating in with respect to a reward framework. The overarching objective behind this is to increase the total sum of the rewards as the complete set of states is able to be reached. Commonly used reinforcement learning algorithms are: Q-Methods, T-D learning, and deep adversarial networks.

Mishra et al. [2] discussed a survey on the pattern of analysis in machine learning for intrusion detection. In this survey, they have discussed a few of the approaches of machine learning with examples of the related works completed. Using this survey, the general framework for network anomaly detection is employed for machine learning. First, it was decided that the labeled or unlabeled dataset will be the input into the selected technique. Following that, in the operation convenience, in the data processing phase, the dataset is reorganized and processed. Depending on the selected machine learning technique, anomaly detection can be performed using either supervised or unsupervised learning. The process results in an output that serves as a prediction from the model. Finally, the calculated scores or labels determine the model's efficiency and effectiveness

Recent advances in the uptake of network mean that critical applications are executed over the computer networks, hence enhancing the need to embrace network security [3]. With continually increasing network traffic, attacks on military, government, and commercial networks have intensified [4, 5]. Intrusion detection includes the practice of watching a number of, or all, the operations that take place within a network environment for the first signs of security threats. Various attacks over the internet present a real menace to computer users and organizations. Intrusion detection in a system is the process of identification of unauthorized attempts to break the system to affect the CIA triad of confidentiality, integrity, and availability [3].

1.3 Framing the problem

The detection of network intrusion is important when it comes to protecting networks. With deep learning-based IDS, the current research has acquired significant detection performance; however, it faces two important limitations: the problem of imbalanced datasets and the inability to effectively detect minority and other unknown invasion types. Numerous studies employ various machine learning algorithms to identify network intrusions, yet, these algorithms often fall short against intelligent attackers. Traditional IDS, whether signature-based or anomaly-based, necessitates continuous updates to their databases to remain effective.

To address these challenges, we develop a reinforcement learning (RL) model capable of automatically adapting to new traffic patterns, thereby improving intrusion detection capabilities. This approach using the RL is designed to improve the current solutions to above-mentioned problems by offering a better model to use in network security.

The proposed reinforcement learning model, an intrusion detection method with feature selection based on deep reinforcement learning, is a solution to the current issues faced by intrusion detection systems (IDS), such as large computation and poor recognition of unknown network attacks. DDQN model is a method for detecting intrusions based on deep reinforcement learning.

Using correlation-based feature selection method, we first pick the ideal feature subset that best captures the deep information of the original dataset, and then we utilize the Mini-Batch module to generate the data to accommodate the DDQN model. Then, we create an effective network intrusion detection model. We utilize the CSE-CIC-IDS2018 dataset to train and evaluate the performance of the DDQN model, and the experimental results are compared to other well-known Machine Learning Models, which demonstrate that our proposed strategy can successfully pick the best feature subset of the original dataset and further enhance the model's performance.

2. Review of previous relevant work

2.1 Intrusion detection in cloud networks

Deshpande et al. [6] proposed an intrusion detection model for cloud environments. The model consists of a data logging module, a preprocessing module, an analysis and decision engine, and a management module. Logs are obtained using the Linux audit framework. After logs are ready for processing, a k-nearest neighbor classifier comes into play and decides if there is an anomaly or not. In Ref. [7], Maiero and Miculan suggested that with the usage of virtualization techniques, intrusion detection monitors can be deployed in a guest VM or virtual machine monitors. Beyond host or network device monitoring, distributed collaborative monitoring approaches are also utilized to catch system-wide attacks as described by Bharadwaja et al. [8].

2.2 Big data approaches for IDS

In Ref. [9] Mahmood and Afzal stated that threat detection and monitoring is the largest field in security analytics for financial and defense institutions. Big data analytics helps in this area by predicting and detecting malicious or dangerous network traffic patterns, as well as unusual user behaviors. Additionally, it will help unveil sudden changes—which typically are suspicious incidents—in network servers. Recent works have proposed using big data processing approaches to solve the problem of intrusion detection in cloud environments [10].

One of these solutions was introduced by Casas et al. [11]. They developed a system called Big-DAMA, which utilized Apache Spark for both batch data processing and streaming data processing. Then, they combined their solution with five different supervised machine learning algorithms. To detect a possible attack using intrusion detection systems (IDS), Alavizadeh et al. [12] stated that basically two techniques can be used: In misuse detection, the IDS knows about previous attack patterns and tries to catch an attack by comparing the collected data to previous patterns. In anomaly detection, the IDS does not know about any previous attacks and tries to find anomalies in the network data, which could be possible signs of attacks. In recent years, machine learning approaches have been used successfully for both of these techniques [13].

2.3 Machine learning solutions for intrusion detection

With the advancements in machine learning in recent years, most of the anomaly-based intrusion detection systems have started benefiting from machine learning algorithms. One of the successful solutions, Beehive was introduced by Badr [14]. In their solution, they used logs to detect network intrusions. They separated their features into four categories:

- Destination-Based Features
- Host-Based Features
- Policy-Based Features
- Traffic-Based Features.

By using these four different feature types, they have been able to apply an unsupervised learning algorithm, k-means clustering, to detect suspicious activities. Although the Beehive solution is simple yet effective, it does not work in real time, whereas the solution described in this chapter works near real time.

A combination of k-means clustering and K-Nearest Neighbor was proposed by Sharifi et al. [15]. They first applied k-means clustering to define clusters and their centers. The clustering process is applied multiple times in order to achieve the best structure. Then, this structure is used to classify the data using KNN. Their solution is somewhat similar to Razaq et al. 's solution. Rather than tweaking k-means like them, they combined it with KNN. Their overall accuracy was around 90%, which should be improved in order to establish a secure system.

Another deep learning solution is proposed by Behera et al. [16], which is implemented using convolutional neural networks (CNN). In CNN, there are neurons with learnable weights and biases. CNN has five types of layers, namely, input layer, convolution layer, rectified linear unit, pooling layer, and output layer.

Different than standard neural networks, the convolution layer uses dot product of weights and local regions to calculate inputs for the next layer. Rectified linear unit is used for better gradient propagation and effective processing. The authors had successful results with their experimentations using the NSL-KDD dataset. Their solution proves the usability of deep learning for network intrusion detection. The solution proposed in this chapter combines deep learning with reinforcement learning for creating a system, which can adapt to zero-day attacks.

2.4 Deep reinforcement learning solutions in different fields

Deep reinforcement learning is being used in many different fields. Although it is especially common in AI solutions such as robots, game-playing agents, there are various approaches implementing it for distinct purposes. Playing Atari is one of the classic examples, which is implemented by Mnih et al. [17]. In their solution, similar to the solution in this thesis, a convolutional neural network is combined with reinforcement learning. They have used a modified Q-learning algorithm to train the network. In Ref. [18], Cuayahuitl et al. implemented a DRL solution for playing a strategic board game (Settlers of Catan). Their solution had significant success over other random, rule-based or supervised-based solutions. Giraffe, a chess engine developed by Lai [19], implements deep reinforcement learning to play chess. MathDQN, proposed by Wang et al. [20], used DRL to solve arithmetic word problems. Again, similarly, they have used a two-layer feed-forward neural network in order to find out the potential Q-value.

DRL is used in the biology field as mentioned by Mahmud et al. [21] in their paper. It is being used to extract features from biological sequence data (DNA, RNA, and amino acids) and perform predictions on them. Also, it is mentioned that DRL is used for bioimaging as well for pixel-level, cell-level, and tissue-level analyses.

Additionally, it is stated that DRL is implemented in many medical imaging applications for analyzing medical images obtained from different scans (MRI, CT, PET, etc.) [22].

3. Proposed work

The following section presents the work that will be carried out in relation to the aims of this chapter with the work progressing in a methodical sequence corresponding to the process flowchart outlined below (**Figure 1**). The process flowchart illustrates the key steps in developing a reinforcement learning (RL) model, starting from dataset preprocessing and feature engineering to data splicing, RL model development, training and testing, and finally, model evaluation.

3.1 Overview

The main contributions of our work are summarized as follows:

1. We present the network intrusion detection methods of this new generation that came from the integration of Q-learning-based reinforcement learning with a deep feed-forward neural network method. Our proposed model is equipped with the ongoing auto-learning capability for a network environment it interacts with and can detect different types of network intrusions. Its self-learning capabilities allow our model to continuously enhance its detection capabilities.

2. We provide intrinsic details of the best approaches employed in tuning the various hyperparameters of improved deep learning RL algorithms such as learning rates dislike the discount factor to facilitate optimal self-learning and interaction with the underlying network environment for even more optimized network intrusion detection tasks.

3. The empirical findings for the test case on the CSE-CIC-IDS 2018 dataset reveal that our proposed DDQN is conceivably useful in identifying various intrusion classes and is superior to other comparable machine learning techniques

Figure 1.
Process flow diagram includes; (1) dataset preprocessing, (2) feature engineering, (3) data splicing, (4) RL model development, (5) training and testing, (6) model evaluation.

that yield more than 90% accuracy in the classification tasks related to multiple network intrusion classes.

3.2 Reinforcement learning-based intrusion detection system (IDS)

3.2.1 Reinforcement learning

An agent is designed to carry out a specific task independently without guidance. That agent engages in trial and error through interaction with that particular environment to reach its ultimate objective. After that, the agent gets a reward representing how well the performance was executed. The agent swiftly adapts its strategy in light of the incentives and focuses on raising the reward value (**Figure 2**).

Starting with an analogy, say our goal is to teach a child the behavior of returning items after usage instead of punishing the child when they do not or directly instructing the child on how to do this. We will instead reinforce the child's behavior at any point in which they use the item and return with the reinforcement "good girl plus clap." The behavior initially may not be stable as it may take the child several trials to meet reinforcement contingencies. Any time the child does not return items after use, they will be ignored, that is, no reinforcement (good plus clap) will follow. Eventually, the child realizes that putting things back in their rightful place after use produces support (good girl plus bangs). This way, the child begins to return stuff after use. The agent will not be taught what to do or how to do it in an RL situation but instead will be rewarded for each action it does. If the agent takes a reasonable effort, we will reward it positively; if it takes a wrong step, we do otherwise. As a result, reinforcement learning can be compared to a learning process where the agent tries out several behaviors and finds the one that produces a favorable reward. In the child example, the child stands as the agent, and rewarding the child by clapping when it successfully returns the item after usage is a positive reward, while failing to do so is Harmful [23].

3.2.2 Deep Q-network (DQN) and its variants

DQN is a variation of the Q-learning technique that approximates the long-term benefits connected to various actions in a given state using a neural network instead

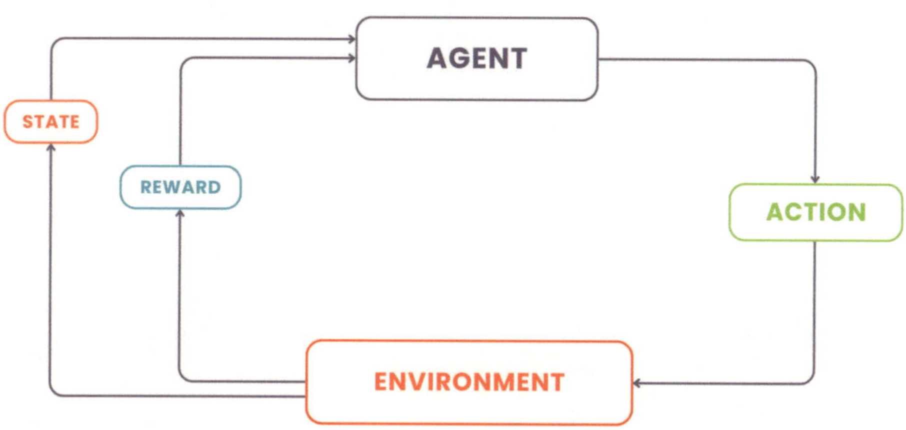

Figure 2.
An image of a reinforcement concept.

of a Q-table. Due to the difficulty of utilizing a Q-table to express high-dimensional and continuous state spaces, DQN is now equipped to handle them. The replay buffer is used to store and sample previous experiences for training, and using a variety of stochastic gradient descents, the neural network is trained. This enhances the stability and convergence of the learning process and enables the agent to learn from a broad range of events.

3.2.3 Dataset and data preprocessing

3.2.3.1 CIC ids 2018

Different benchmark datasets have also been used to compare the intrusion detection model. The work performed on the various datasets is to display higher classification accuracy and detection rate. In the CIC-IDS 2018 dataset, there are 15 different classes: 14 representing attack types and 1 representing benign traffic. The dataset contains a total of 16,233,002 instances (approximately 16 million). The CSE-CIC-IDS2018 dataset used in this study is obtained from the Canadian Institute for Cyber Security Research at the University of New Brunswick. Data was emulated in the CIC test environment with 50 attacking machines, 420 victim PCs, and 30 victim servers in the time period of February 14 to March 2, 2018. Fresh 14 attacks were identified, and the dataset is labeled and comes with anonymized PCAP files in one place. Altogether, 80 network traffic features were identified and computed from packets using the CICFlowMeter. There are 10 CSV files that are provided for machine learning, which include records of 16,232,943. In **Table 1**, the class representation of this dataset is shown in summary.

The diverse environment was developed with the AWS computing platform. The overall structure was further bifurcated as the attacking and victim organization. The

File/day	Normal instances	Attack instances
Wednesday-14-02-2018	667,626	FTP-BruteForce (193,360), SSH-BruteForce (187,589)
Thursday-15-02-2018	996,077	DoS attacks-GoldenEye (41,508), DoS attacks-Slowloris (10,990)
Friday-16-02-2018	446,772	DoS attacks-SlowHTTPTest (139,890), DoS attacks-Hulk (461,912)
Thursday-20-02-2018	7,372,557	DDoS attacks-LOIC-HTTP (576,191)
Wednesday-21-02-2018	360,833	DDOS attacks-LOIC-UDP (1730), DDOS attack-HOIC (686,012)
Thursday-22-02-2018	1,048,213	Brute-Force-XSS (79), Brute-Force-Web (249), SQL Injection (34)
Friday-23-02-2018	1,048,009	Brute-Force-XSS (151), Brute-Force-Web (362), SQL Injection (53)
Wednesday-28-02-2018	544,200	Infiltration (68,871)
Thursday-01-03-2018	238,037	Infiltration (93,063)
Friday-02-03-2018	762,384	Bot (286,191)

Attack instances for each file/day with corresponding normal instance counts.

Table 1.
Data distribution of CSE-CIC-IDS2018.

attacking organization consisted of 50 machines. The victim organization has 420 machines and 30 servers. This dataset was formed from the accumulated network traffic and system logs of those machines. The following are the six different attack scenarios that were performed during the experiments:

- DDoS
- DoS
- Brute-force
- Botnet
- Infiltration
- Web Attack

Thus, as illustrated in **Figure 3** from Ref. [24], in order to emulate all the attacks, various operating systems with different versions and different services (Windows, Ubuntu, and Mac) were integrated into the environment: Ubuntu versions: 12.04 and 16.04; Windows versions: Vista, 7, 8.1, and 10, etc.

The information regarding the distribution of the network traffic on this dataset is illustrated in **Table 2** from Ref. [24]. All 14 attack types are associated with the attack scenarios.

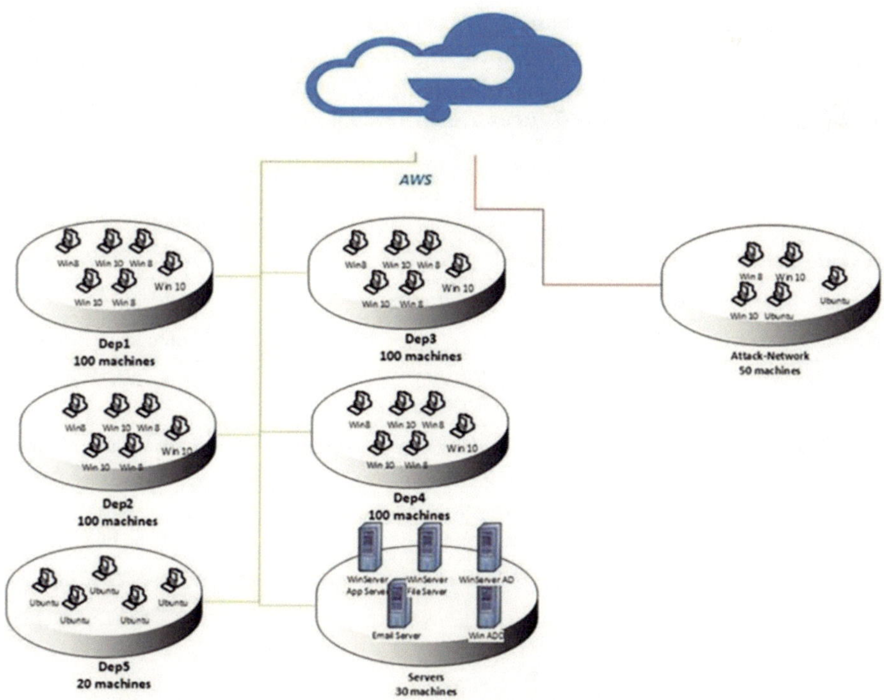

Figure 3.
CSE-CIC-IDS2018 network attack topology.

Attack scenario	Attack name	Distribution (%)
Benign	None	83.07
DDoS	DDoS attacks-LOIC-HTTP DDOS-LOIC-UDP DDOS-HOIC	7.786
DoS	DoS-GoldenEye DoS-Slowloris DoS-SlowHTTPTest DoS-Hulk	4.031
Brute-force	FTP-BruteForce SSH-BruteForce	2.347
Botnet	Bot	1.763
Infiltration	Infiltration	0.997
Web Attack	Brute-Force-Web Brute-Force-XSS SQL Injection	0.006

Table 2.
Attack scenario distribution.

This collected raw network traffic data is distributed day by day among 10 CSV files which have been collected and stored in the AWS cloud and can be downloaded. When using CICFlowMeter-V3 as a network traffic flow generator and analyzer, over 80 features can be derived from network traffic data. Using CICFlowMeter, we can generate bidirectional network flows. This is very advantageous for the detection of cyberattacks since it provides results such as Duration, number of packets, number of bytes, and packet length in both the forward direction and backward direction (from destination to source). The attack tools and victim environments used to execute each attack are presented in **Table 3** of Ref. [24]. detailing the types of attacks in the CSE-CIC-IDS2018 dataset on AWS.

The distribution of the classes in the dataset can be seen in the figure below, refer to **Figure 4** in Ref. [25]. As for data capturing and feature selection, we use the CIC-IDS-2018 dataset, which is composed of 16,232,943 instances. The normal instances are 13,484,708 and the attack instances are 2,748,235.

Attack	Tools	Victim
Brute-force attack	FTP-Patator SSH-Patator	Ubuntu 16.4 (Web Server)
DoS attack	Hulk GoldenEye Slowloris Slowhttptest	Apache
DoS attack	Heartbleed	Ubuntu 12.4 (Open SSL)
Web attack	Damn Vulnerable Web App (DVWA) In-house selenium framework (XSS and Brute-force)	Ubuntu 16.4 (Web Server)
Infiltration attack	First level: Dropbox download in a Windows machine Second level: Nmap and portscan	Windows Vista, Macintosh
Botnet attack	Ares (Python): remote shell File upload/download Capturing screenshots, keylogging	Windows Vista, 7, 8.1, 10 (32-bit, 64-bit)
DDoS+PortScan	Low Orbit Ion Canon (LOIC) for UDP TCP, or HTTP requests	Windows Vista, 7, 8.1, 10 (32-bit, 64-bit)

Table 3.
Tools and victims for different attacks.

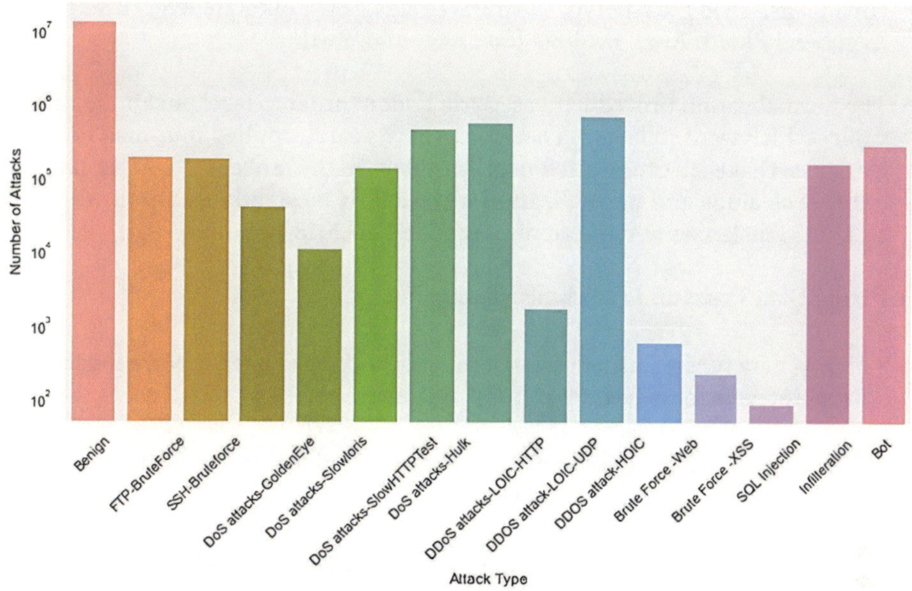

Figure 4.
Bar charts showing the class distribution in the dataset.

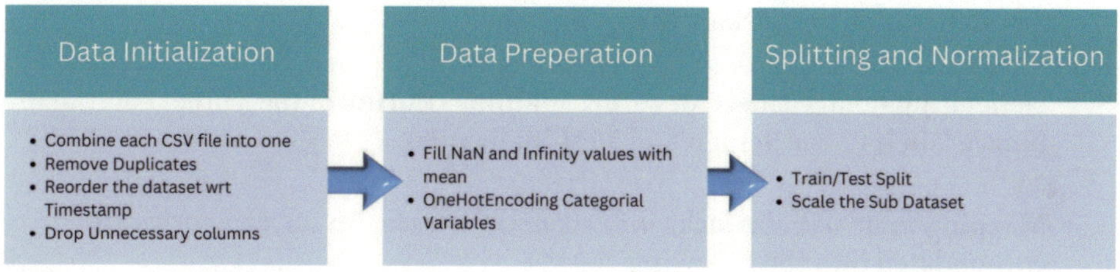

Figure 5.
Data preprocessing methodology.

3.2.3.2 Data preprocessing

Data are preprocessed and normalized before any training is carried out on the same data. This phase is used for filtering out the data noise and retaining only meaningful and important information. In the proposed model, preprocessing involves the following main tasks (**Figure 5**):

- New features without NaN values.
- Timestamp column and correspondent record duplicates were deleted as no time series-dependent machine learning methods have been selected in this study. Subsequently, eight features initiating with 'Bwd' and 'Fwd' were eliminated because they were all empty and provided no useful information namely, 'Bwd

URG Flags,' 'Bwd Pkts/b Avg,' 'Bwd PSH Flags,' 'Bwd Blk Rate Avg,' 'Fwd Byts/b Avg,' 'Fwd Pkts/b Avg,' 'Fwd Blk Rate Avg,' and 'Bwd.'

- The normalization procedure was carried out in order to level out all the data values which were collected. Therefore, this research applied min-max normalization so that each of the attributes has values in the range [0,1]. After carrying out data cleaning and normalization, particularly by standardization, we got 16,137,183 instances with 70 attributes. [CIS IDS 2018]

1. Fixing Data Types and Handling Missing Values

    - Fixing data types: Ensure each column in the dataset has the correct data type (e.g., integers for labels, floats for continuous variables).
    - Handling infinity values: Replace any infinity values with null values to avoid inconsistencies during data analysis.
    - Dropping null values: Eliminate all rows containing null values, ensuring that only complete data points are used for analysis.
    - Dropping unnecessary columns: Remove the Timestamp column as it is not needed for the model.

2. Label Generation and Attack Mapping

    - Generating binary labels for threat column: Transform the Threat column into binary labels (0 for Benign and 1 for Malicious).
    - Mapping multi-label attacks into six main classes: Attack categories are consolidated into the following classes:
    - Brute-Force, Web Attack, DoS Attack, DDoS Attack, Botnet, Benign.
    - Creating label column: Assign labels to each class to reflect the transformation.
    - Train-test split and balancing the data.
    - Preparing data for training and testing (X, y): Split the dataset into feature matrix (X) and label vector (y) for training and testing.
    - Using RandomUnderSampler: Apply undersampling to balance the class distribution in the training set.
    - Sanity check: Evaluate the label distribution before and after applying the RandomUnderSampler to ensure balance in the training data.

3. Combining Data and Removing Unnecessary Features

- Combining all data frames: Merge multiple data frames into a single one for a unified dataset.
- Removing constant features: Calculate the variance of each feature and drop those with zero variance (constant values).
- Dropping duplicates: Eliminate duplicate rows (using axis = 0), as they may distort model performance.

4. Feature Correlation and Selection

- Plotting Heatmap: Generate a Pearson correlation heatmap to visualize correlations between features.
- Implementing correlation-based feature selection (CFS):
- Calculate the correlation matrix and select highly correlated features (threshold greater than 90%).
- Drop highly correlated features from both the training and testing datasets.
- Feature selection logic: Ensure that correlation-based feature removal is done only after the train-test split and before applying the RandomUnderSampler.
- MinMaxScaler: Use the MinMaxScaler to scale features between 0 and 1 based on the training set, and apply the same transformation to the testing data.

5. Label Encoding and Class Weight Calculation

- Generating a List of Unique Labels: Extract unique class labels from the dataset, such as ['Benign,' 'Brute-force,' 'Infiltration,' 'Web attack'].
- Computing Class Weights: Compute class weights to account for imbalanced data, assigning higher weights to underrepresented classes.
- Mapping Class Weights to Class Indices: Create a dictionary where each class label is mapped to its corresponding class weight.

3.2.4 Feature engineering

When performing feature selection, SelectKBest acts only on the largest classes; hence, there can be an enhancement of the conjecture to perform a feature selection in the pipeline approaches selecting the most significant features first of all, for the specific class with the minimum samples and then use selective features for other classes. Feature selection will account for the proper performance of the classifier and generally assist in improving the IDS performance. The additional and non-contributing factors complicate the overheads and the classifier [26].

3.2.4.1 Feature selection using pre-trained model

Feature selection is done by feeding the pre-trained model to the SelectFrom Model and using the learned feature importance for selecting the features. Some of the features that were selected include 'Dst Port,' 'Flow Byts/s,' 'Bwd IAT Tot,' 'Bwd IAT Min,' and 'Bwd Pkts/s,' 'Init Fwd Win Byts,' 'Fwd Seg Size Min.'

- Feature importance: The feature importances from the model are pulled out and ordered and only the high priority features are employed for the training at the end.

- Feature reduction: It aids in eliminating the extraneous features that do not positively contribute to the training process or improve the final model.

3.2.5 Training/testing ML models

3.2.5.1 Decision tree classifier

A Decision Tree is a supervised, non-parametric model where nodes represent features and end nodes represent classes or labels. It is used for classifying DDoS attacks by partitioning data based on the most informative features. The tree structure is built to predict outcomes, considering probabilities and factors like costs. In this study, the decision tree classifier is trained on 85 features, with feature importance ranked using ExtraTreesClassifier. To enhance efficiency, 20 features are selected for training. The model is evaluated on the test set using metrics such as accuracy, precision, recall, F1-score, and confusion matrix.

Decision trees are effective, interpretable classifiers, commonly used in tasks like fraud detection, disease diagnosis, and credit risk assessment (**Figure 6**).

3.2.5.2 Random Forest classifier

The Random Forest Classifier is employed in this research from the Scikit-learn ensemble module. Random Forest is one type of ensemble learning best known for its process of generating the decision tree as many numbers of times as the number of data samples. The model used in this case is decision trees, and to further divide this model, each decision tree will have the features and data points randomly selected. In this implementation, the Random Forest Classifier is created with its default attributes for training models, using the gini impurity measure for feature importance, and maintaining 100 decision trees in the forest. Random Forest Classifier is developed using the hyperparameters that are set at default and they include the number of trees in the forest as well as maximum depth of each tree run. After that, the trained model is used to select churn status of the test data. Last but not the least, we also measure the model's accuracy, precision, recall value, and F1-score for its performance. The model is fit with the training data through the fit () method after which the model is ready for testing (**Figure 7**).

3.2.5.3 Extreme gradient boosting (XGB) classifier

XGBoost is one of the most used machine learning algorithms for classification, regression, or rank purposes. It is in the family of boosting algorithms which are

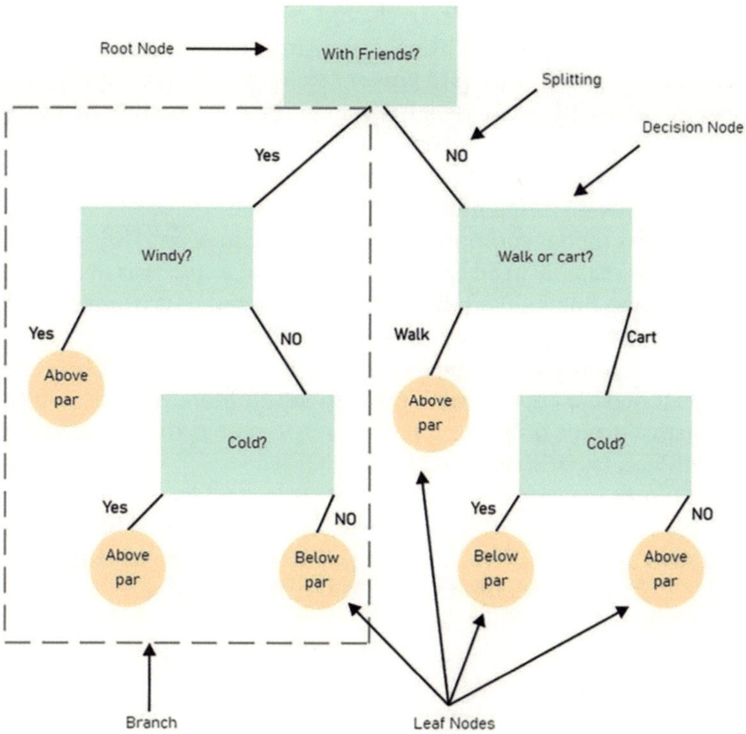

Figure 6.
Example of decision tree classifier.

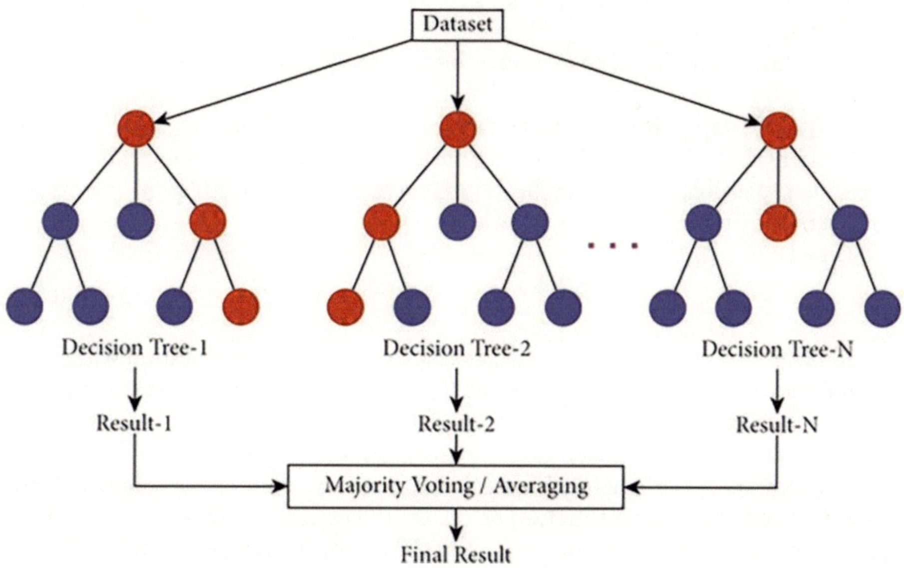

Figure 7.
Example of Random Forest Classifier.

learning algorithms that are built iteratively and are made up of weak models. The XGBoost algorithm differs from traditional boosting algorithms in two main ways: First, a stricter model formalization to prevent overfitting is employed, which is attained through the addition of a penalty term to the loss function that is optimized during training. Second, it employs second-order approximation of the objective function so as to enhance the rate of convergence to the optimal solution and enhance the performance of the resulting model.

This approach has higher computational efficiency in several low-memory environments and is scalable in all cases. The quality of a split was inspected by the 'friedman mse' parameter, *viz.*, the average of squared deviations of each split's effectiveness from the overall average of all splits. To generate the performance score, Friedman's percentage is added to the Mean Squared Error (MSE). This criterion provides the most reliable approximation in this study. Moreover, the identification of using probabilistic outputs is made by adopting deviance as the loss function, which is, as a matter of fact, logistic regression.

All in all, XGBoost is a very efficient and versatile machine learning tool, which demonstrates good results on different datasets and tasks. Radial basis functions are widely used due to their capability of dealing with large-scale and complicated data, and the regularization and second-order optimization approaches. **Figure 8** shows the schematic illustration of the XGboost model.

3.2.6 DDQN model description

This section outlines the DRL model used in this study alongside providing more information on it. The agent interacts with its environment by executing actions, observing their outcomes in terms of rewards, and predicting subsequent states. These experiences, which consist of states, actions, rewards, and the ensuing state—are stored in a replay buffer. This buffer enables the random sampling of batch experience for training, preventing the agent from becoming overly dependent on recent events.

A Q-function is employed to estimate the expected maximum reward achievable from a given state by taking a specific action. Therefore, the Q-value, which is represented as Q(s, a), depends on the state s and the action a. Whenever the Q-function is defined, fixing the policy function which prescribes which action should be made in a given state is possible. The policy function is directly influenced by the state and is computed based on the learned Q-values.

$$\text{Policy}(s) = \arg\max \max_{a} Q(s,a) \tag{1}$$

The epsilon-greedy policy is a training process that supports exploration while exploiting known information at the same time. The agent makes a random move with probability and otherwise, it chooses a move that it considers best for the high expected reward. A policy is used to designate a stochastic choice mechanism for an action at each state. After a policy has been set, one can predict what follows in terms of rewards. The action-value function estimates the expected future cumulative reward when an action is taken in a state and the policy is then pursued. The policy is one that leads to the maximum expected cumulative reward over the states. This optimal policy is a fixed point of the Bellman optimality equation, which is considered in its properties in the next section.

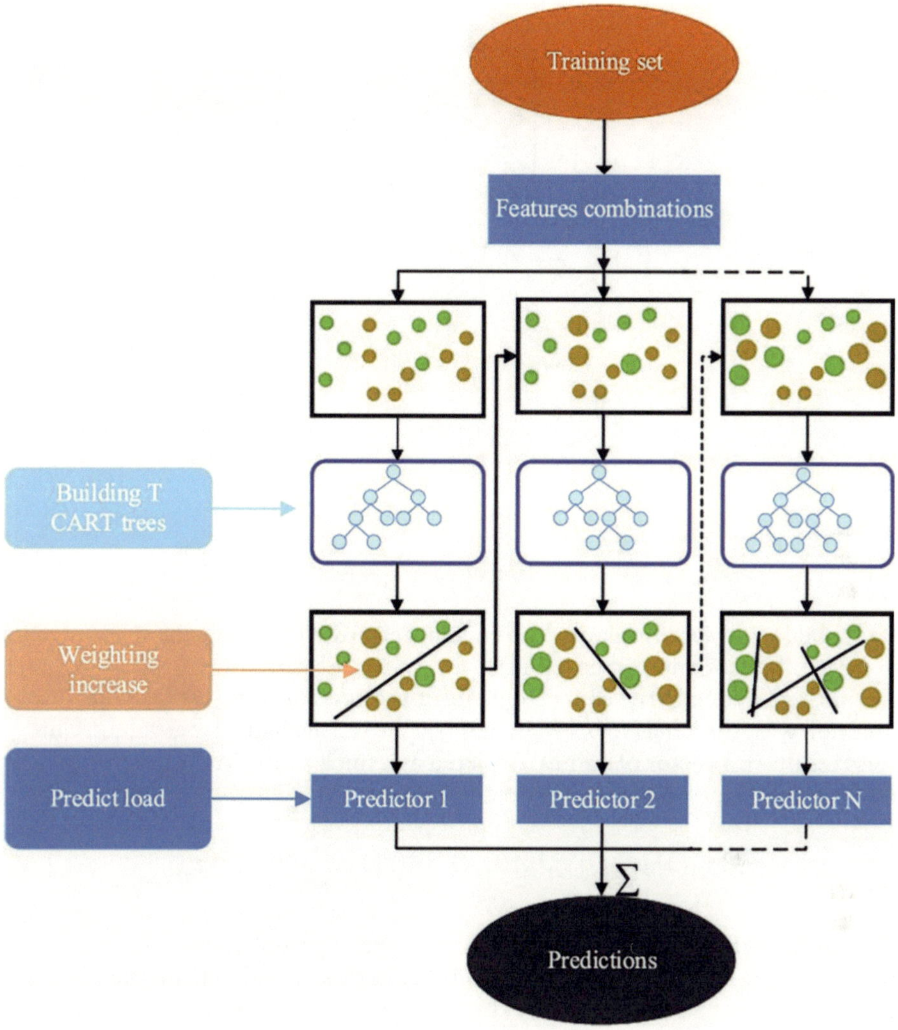

Figure 8.
Example of XGBoost Classifier.

$$Q^*(a,s) = R(a,s) + \gamma \int_{s'} T(s' / s,a) \max_{a'} Q^*(a',s') \quad (2)$$

The Q-value was updated iteratively in order to optimize. With each training, iteration starts a sample of the current state, its label, and the following state. This sample belongs to a random sub-sampling of a group of mini-batches; in other words, a mini-batch has a random selection of samples from the specified dataset. To diversify the space, the dataset is first randomly permuted before generating each mini-batch.

The action-value function is then approximated by a neural network containing three hidden layers. Softmax and tanh are generally known to give negative Q-values at the output layer, but the output layer herein employs a linear function to allow positive Q-values only. The network is taught using the Huber loss function, which determines the loss between the predicted Q-value and a reference value. This reference

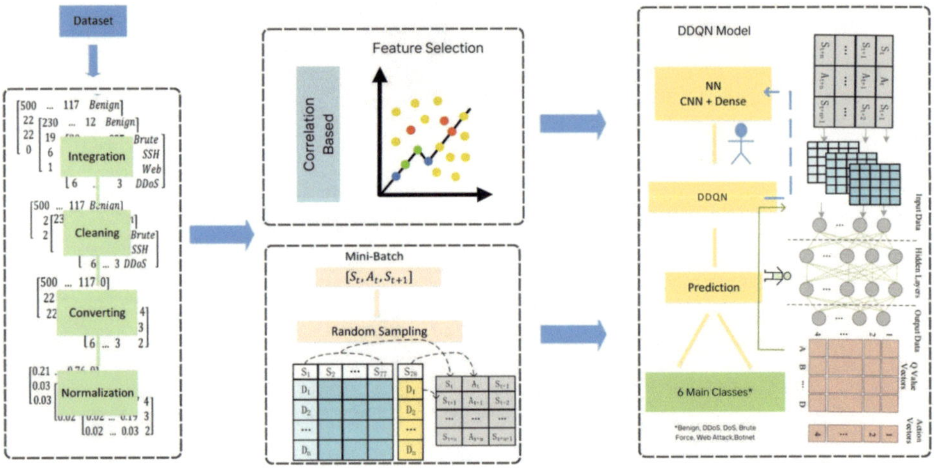

Figure 9.
Proposed model.

value is obtained by accumulating the current reward, Q-value of the successive state with discount factor and correct label.

In this way, to obtain the expected value of the current state, we take the Q-function with the labels to be evaluated equal to all available label values. This process results in a vector of values, depicted as a thick arrow in the graphic presentation of the model introduced in **Figure 9**.

$$Q\left(s_v,\{a\}\right)=\left[Q\left(s_v,\{a\}0\right), Q\left(s_v,\{a\}1\right),\ldots,Q\left(s_v,\{a\}p\right)\right] \quad (3)$$

The universal set of actions is expressed by the symbol a, with its size indicated by the symbol p. The best action from this set exhibiting the highest Q-value is chosen using the argmax function. This chosen action is then fed into the epsilon-greedy algorithm which then decides whether to take the action epsilon*p or take a random action 1-epsilon*p. The action that is expected when applying the functionalities of the decision-making process is referred to as expected action.

Using a similar approach, the next action for the next state is predicted without the inclusion of epsilon-greedy exploration.

The reference Q-value is computed from the predicted action as well as the next state of the game and then used to arrive at the action during the learning process. This can be easily done by direct maximization of the Q-value for the next state and all the possible actions.

To stabilize training, two neural networks are employed in the DDQN framework: one for the current Q-function and a separate target network, which is updated periodically during each iteration. The target network is an outdated copy of the primary network and thus slows down the changing of Q-values in the target. This mechanism contributes to solving the shifting target problem. The model was trained to 300 epochs; epoch is defined as one complete run of all the data through the model.

4. DDQN analysis and results

The states (s_t) represent the random sample from the input data that the RL agent uses to make predictions, and the actions (a_t) variable corresponds to the RL agent's forecasts for the binary classification task. The environment selects a new state (s_{t+1}) randomly from the dataset, such that it has the same intrusion label as the action chosen by the environment, and the agent chooses an action based on its policy and the new state. The reward (r_{t+1}) is computed based on the agent action and the true intrusion label of the new state. Using the transition (s_t, a_t, s_{t+1}, r_{t+1}), the environment and the agent update the Q-function, then the new state (s_{t+1}) becomes the current state (s_t) for the next iteration. In our case, the input data is the dataset with the selected features from our feature selection process. Actions can take on values 0 or 1, where 0 typically represents a prediction of 'no attack' or 'normal,' and 1 illustrates a projection of 'attack.' The reward variable represents the immediate reward the RL agent receives for its actions (i.e., based on the correct and incorrect predictions). The reward is calculated based on the correctness of the agent's predictions. If the forecast is correct (the predicted activity matches the actual label), the reward is set to 1; otherwise, it is set to 0. The total reward by episode variable accumulates the total compensation obtained during an episode. It represents how well the agent is performing in terms of correct predictions.

The agent and environment interact by choosing actions (predictions) depending on its current state (input data), and rewards are collected based on its predictions' correctness. The agent then uses these rewards to update its Q-values and improve its prediction accuracy.

4.1 Setting up the experiment and parameters used

Firstly, the dataset was preprocessed and features were selected using the Kaggle Notebook. Then, the selected features were used by the model/code. The DDQN was performed in Python using the Kaggle Notebook T4 GPU, TensorFlow, and Keras framework version 2.13.0 and 2.6.0, respectively. The DQN model has specified three main components: a data class, a neural network class, and a DQN agent class. The data class is responsible for loading, formatting, and preprocessing the dataset. The neural network class is accountable for constructing, training, and evaluating the model, processing input data, and generating Q-values for different actions. The other class of DQN is in charge of the DQN algorithm that plays the game and learns from the rewards and penalties. The neural network feature requires a specific formation of the layers of the neural network; in this case, it has two total dense layers, which make the hidden layer. The model contains hidden size neurons in each Dense layer, and Rectified Linear Unit (ReLU) as an activation function that imparts nonlinearity in the model. The dataset's features correspond to the neural network input layers, and the count of input features determines its shape. The model output consists of two Q-values, one for each possible action (regular or attack). There are two neurons in the output layer, one for each Q-value. The final layer employs sigmoid activation to normalize it to a probability distribution of the actions, assisting in the selection of the best Q-value action and quantifying the uncertainty of the model.

Several significant parameters were determined and examined during the training to obtain the optimum values that are adequate and perfect for the model. The exploration rate or Epsilon (ϵ) of 0.1 is selected to allow the execution exploration of the agent based on a certain amount of randomness with a 0.7 decay rate, which is used

Dst Port TotLen Fwd Pkts Fwd Pkt Len Std	Bwd Pkts/s Init Fwd Win Byts Fwd Seg Size Min

Figure 10.
Names of selected features.

Parameters	Values	Parameters	Values
Number_Episode	100	Minimum Epsilon	0
Hidden_layers	3	Gamma	0.001
Number_iteration	100	Decoy rate	0.99
Number_units	3 × 124	Learning_rate	0.001
Activation_function	ReLU	Batch-size	100
Initial Weight Value	Normal	Optimizer	Adam
Epsilon	1		

Table 4.
List of selected features.

to decrease the exploration rate (ϵ) over time. The tables below provide the selected features and the values for other parameters, including batch size and discount factor (γ).

The following table illustrates the features that are crucial for attack detection (**Figure 10**).

Table 4 below outlines the parameters set for the environment creation, which will guide the Neural Network and DQN Agent in optimizing their performance for the given task.

4.2 Metrics evaluation

The parametric for the measurement of the performance of our model is derived from the characteristics of the dataset and our performance indicators. First of all, if looking at the distribution of the dataset as shown in terms of percentages in **Figure 11**, we conclude that there is a major problem of class imbalance within our dataset.

The ratio assigned to the majority (System, Malware in our case) as compared to the rest (Benign in our case) is provided as follows:

$$Imbalance\ Ratio = \frac{13413990}{2263160} = 5.927$$

This part builds the model's learning needs using the confusion matrix, to illustrate the effectiveness of our model's categorization and give the confusion matrix. The confusion matrix highlights those forecasts that were accurate, as well as those that were false. In machine learning models, the outcome of the predictions for the existence of malicious traffic has four possible outcomes.

The following defines the evaluation metrics:

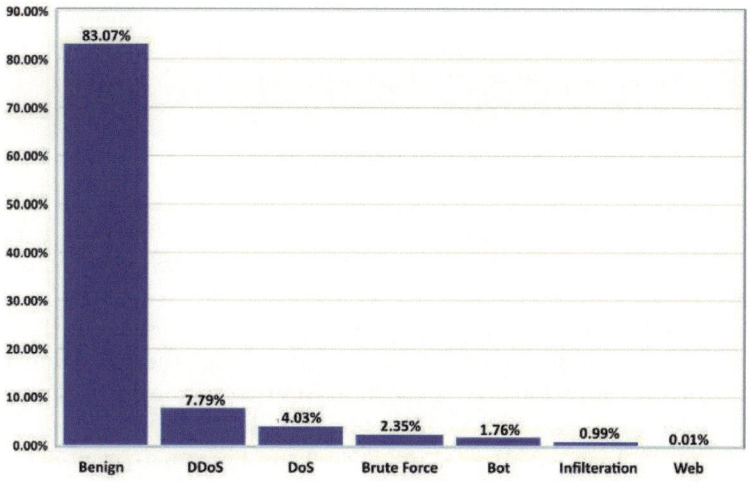

Figure 11.
Class distribution of the dataset in terms of percentage.

True Positive (TP): The number of DDoS attacks that are correctly identified as attacks.

True Negative (TN): The number of legitimate network traffic instances correctly classified as normal.

False Positive (FP): The number of normal network traffic instances incorrectly classified as attacks.

False Negative (FN): The number of DDoS attacks that are mistakenly identified as normal traffic.

Our proposed model is also evaluated using several common metrics used in intrusion detection systems. Below are the formulas for accuracy, precision, recall, and F1-score:

Accuracy: Accuracy measures the overall percentage of correct predictions (both true positives and true negatives) in the IDS model. It indicates the model's general performance and is calculated as:

$$\text{Accuracy}\left(\text{A}\right)=\left(TP+TN\right)/\left(TP+TN+FP+FN\right).$$

TP = True Positive, TN = True Negative, FP = False Positive, and FN = False Negative.

Precision: Precision, also known as the positive predictive value, calculates the ratio of correctly identified attacks to all instances labeled as attacks. It reveals the accuracy of positive predictions:

$$\text{Precision}\left(\text{P}\right)=\left(TP\right)/\left(FP+TP\right).$$

Recall: Also called the detection rate (DR) or true positive rate (TPR), recall measures the proportion of actual attacks that are correctly identified by the model. It indicates the effectiveness of detecting harmful events:

$$\text{Recall}\left(\text{r}\right)=TP/\left(FN+TP\right)$$

F1-score: The F1-score is a crucial metric that balances precision and recall, especially in situations where the data is imbalanced. It reflects the model's performance by considering both false positives and false negatives.

$$\text{F1} - \text{Score} = 2 \times (\text{Precision} \times \text{Recall}) / (\text{Precision} + \text{Recall})$$

Support Score: In the scikit-learn module, the support score is used to evaluate the frequency of each class in the dataset. It helps measure how often each classification is accurate.

Confusion Matrix: The confusion matrix is a key tool for assessing the model's performance. After training and predicting with the model, the confusion matrix is calculated using the confusion matrix function from sklearn.metrics. This function compares the true labels (y test) and the predicted labels (y pred).

The resulting confusion matrix is visualized using a heatmap generated by the heatmap () function from the seaborn library. The heatmap shows the number of true positives, false positives, false negatives, and true negatives for each class.

The diagonal elements represent the number of correct predictions, while the off-diagonal elements highlight misclassifications.

4.3 Analyzing the results

A comprehensive analysis of the results obtained from the experiment is presented in **Table 5**, comparing the performance of traditional machine learning models with the proposed reinforcement learning model. This comparison is based on key evaluation metrics, including accuracy, precision, recall, and F1-score.

4.3.1 Machine learning models

The following tables present the performance measures and classification reports of various machine learning models, including the Decision Tree Classifier, Random Forest Classifier, and XGBoost Classifier, along with their respective confusion matrices (**Table 6**). The binary classification results are shown in **Table 7**, while the performance details of the Decision Tree Classifier, Random Forest Classifier, and XGBoost Classifier are provided in **Table 8–10**), respectively.

Metric	Random forest classifier	Decision tree classifier	XG boost classifier	Double deep Q-network
Accuracy	**93.48%**	**94.39%**	**95.90%**	**94.68%**
Precision	93.48%	94.40%	95.91%	94.13%
Recall	93.48%	94.39%	95.91%	94.13%
F1 - Score	94.47%	94.39%	94.91%	93.74%

Table 5.
Comparison of machine learning model and proposed reinforcement learning model.

Dataset files	Normal	Malicious/Attack
2/14/2018	663,808	380,943
2/15/2018	988,050	52,498
2/16/2018	446,772	601,802
2/20/2018	7,313,104	576,191
2/21/2018	360,833	687,742
2/22/2018	1,042,301	362
2/23/2018	1,042,301	566
2/28/2018	538,666	68,236
3/1/2018	235,778	92,403
3/2/2018	758,334	286,191

Table 6.
Binary classification results.

		Confusion matrix for binary classification		
		Normal	**Attacks**	**Total**
Actual	Normal	2,676,761	2058	2,678,819
	Attacks	34,180	514,438	548,618
Total		2,710,941	56,496	3,227,437

Table 7.
Confusion matrix for binary classification.

Decision Tree Classifier				
Classes	**Precision**	**Recall**	**F1-Score**	**Support**
Normal	0.94	0.99	0.96	452,999
DDoS attack	1	0.93	0.96	57,238
DoS attack	0.78	1	0.88	76,189
Brute-force	0.99	1	0.99	187,405
Botnet	1	0.79	0.88	99,854
Infiltration	0.75	0.19	0.3	32,128
Web attack	0	0	0	185
Accuracy			0.94	905,998
Macro Avg	0.78	0.7	0.71	905,998
Weighted Avg	0.94	0.94	0.93	905,998

Table 8.
Performance measures of Decision Tree Classifier.

Random forest classifier				
Classes	**Precision**	**Recall**	**F1-Score**	**Support**
Normal	0.94	0.99	0.96	452,999
DDoS attack	1	0.93	0.96	57,238
DoS attack	0.78	1	0.88	76,189
Brute-force	0.99	1	0.99	187,405
Botnet	1	0.79	0.88	99,854
Infiltration	0.75	0.19	0.3	32,128
Web attack	0	0	0	185
Accuracy			0.94	905,998
Macro Avg	0.78	0.7	0.71	905,998
Weighted Avg	0.94	0.94	0.93	905,998

Table 9.
Performance measures of random forest classifier.

XG Boost Classifier				
Classes	**Precision**	**Recall**	**F1-Score**	**Support**
Normal	0.94	0.99	0.96	452,999
DDoS attack	1	0.93	0.96	57,238
DoS attack	0.78	1	0.88	76,189
Brute-force	0.99	1	0.99	187,405
Botnet	1	0.79	0.88	99,854
Infiltration	0.75	0.19	0.3	32,128
Web attack	0	0	0	185
Accuracy			0.94	905,998
Macro Avg	0.78	0.7	0.71	905,998
Weighted Avg	0.94	0.94	0.93	905,998

Table 10.
Performance measures of XGBoost Classifier.

4.4 DDQN results

This section presents the results and analysis of the DDQN model, highlighting its performance and effectiveness in the given task. Detailed insights and evaluations are provided based on the experimental outcomes.

4.4.1 DDQN reward and loss values

Figure 12 below shows the reward and loss values derived from discount factor values throughout the DQN training procedure. The complete episode reward on the top graph sums up all the rewards the DQN agent achieves in each episode. The reward is

DOI: http://dx.doi.org/10.5772/intechopen.1008896

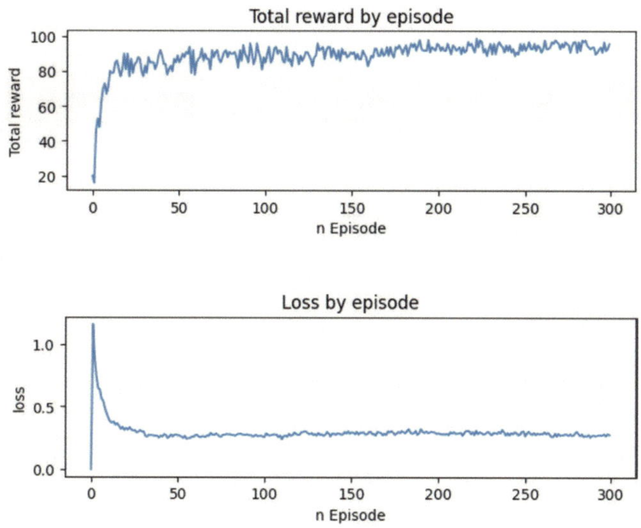

Figure 12.
Reward-Loss Graph by each episode.

	Estimated	Correct	Total	Accuracy
Benign	475,394	448,664	452,999	99.043044
Botnet	57,691	57,188	57,238	99.912645
Brute-force	86,079	72,787	76,189	95.534788
DDoS attack	188,281	186,994	187,405	99.780689
DoS attack	90,838	86,730	99,854	86.856811
Infiltration	7715	5441	32,128	16.935383
Web attack	0	0	185	0

Table 11.
Evaluation metrics for DDQN model.

1 for each correct action and − 1 for each incorrect action. The total reward by episode reflects how well the DQN agent performs on the task of network intrusion detection. The performance improves as the overall reward increases. The above graph of reward loss in **Figure 12** illustrates the loss by episode, showing the mean squared error between the target Q-values and the predicted Q-values by the constructed neural network for each episode. The Q-values represent the future possible rewards of action and state expected. The loss by episode reflects how well Q-values are approximated by the neural network. The lower the loss, the better the approximation.

4.4.2 DDQN analysis and results

The evaluation metrics of the proposed DDQN model using the CIC-IDS 2018 dataset are analyzed to assess its effectiveness in detecting network intrusions (**Table 11**). The test set score distribution across various classes of normal and attack traffic illustrates the model's classification performance (**Figure 13**), while a detailed

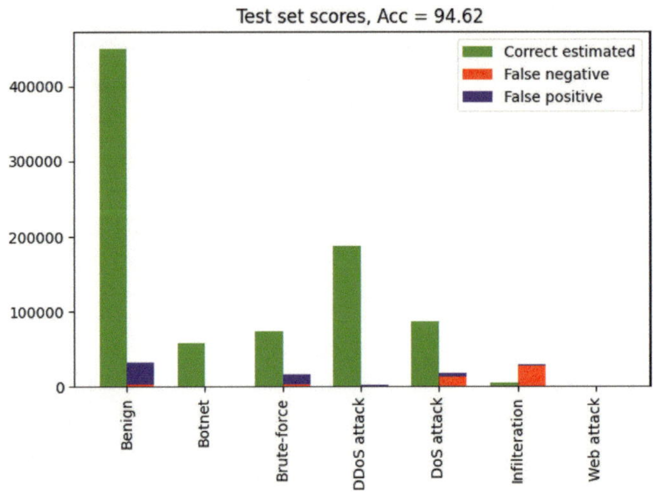

Figure 13.
Distribution over six classes.

classification report highlights key metrics such as accuracy, precision, recall, and F1-score (**Table 12**).

4.4.2.1 Confusion matrix for all models

The following presents the confusion matrices for all models, including Decision Tree, Random Forest, XGBoost, and DDQN (**Figure 14**).

4.4.3 Summary of results

The DDQN model (which is the DRL model that presents the best results in this article) achieves almost equal or slightly better detection performance (accuracy, F1,

DDQN algorithm				
Classes	**Precision**	**Recall**	**F1-Score**	**Support**
Normal	0.95	0.96	0.95	452,999
DDoS attack	0.99	1	0.99	57,238
DoS attack	0.76	1	0.86	76,189
Brute-force	0.98	1	0.99	187,405
Botnet	0.98	0.78	0.87	99,854
Infiltration	0.4	0.25	0.31	32,128
Web attack	0	0	0	185
Accuracy			0.93	905,998
Macro Avg	0.72	0.71	0.71	905,998
Weighted Avg	0.93	0.93	0.92	905,998

Table 12.
Classification report for DDQN model.

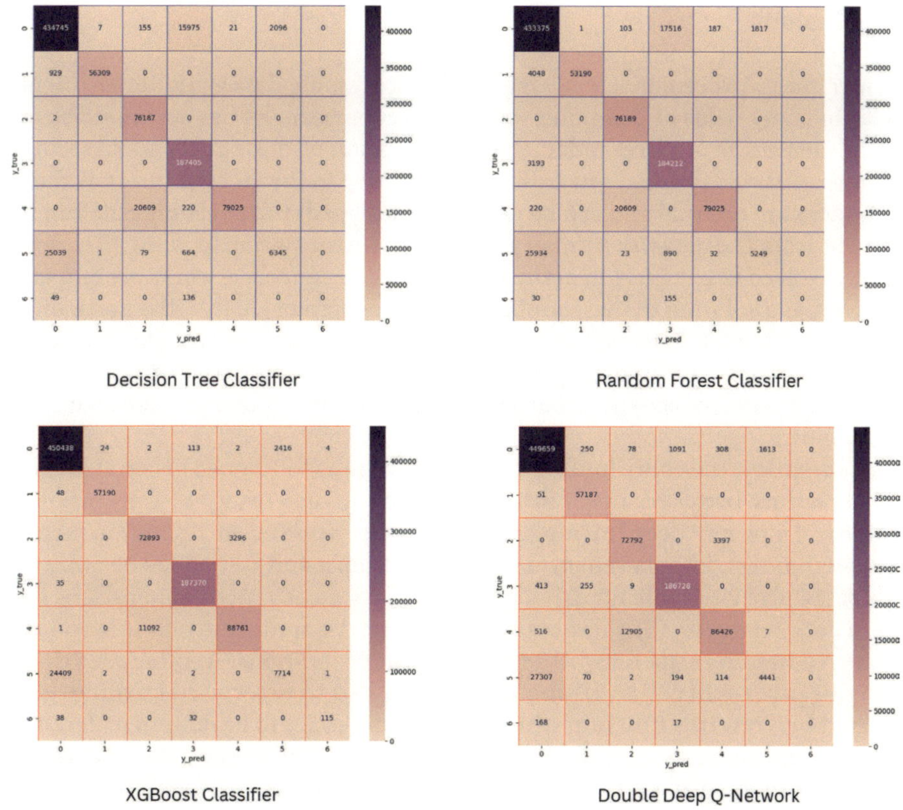

Figure 14.
Confusion matrix for all models.

precision, recall, etc.) as compared to other benchmark SOTA ML models such as Random Forest, Decision trees, XGBoost, etc. The results were achieved utilizing the CIC-IDS 2018 dataset, and the proposed model based on the DDQN is in the list of the best solution models.

Thus, the conclusion made is that it is our model that offers a more effective solution in a range of circumstances. Of particular importance is the observation of the recall metric in which DDQN performs exceptionally well since for an intrusion detection algorithm, false negatives must be kept to the barest. Besides showing that DRL models can be applied to intrusion detection problems with access to a labeled dataset, the classifiers that are derived (once they are trained) are a simple and fast neural network that can work efficiently on modern high-performance, or distributed computing environments like TensorFlow. For example, the DDQN model at the test time results in much smaller prediction times compared to the best SOTA models explored for this study.

Therefore, for the situation with the use of DRL models, one can conclude that their application to the described scenario with a set of labeled data highly depends on the choice of the value of the discount factor. This is quite a surprising and large finding, for it appears that when one does not engage with a live environment (which means that the feedback loop resulting from interactions with the environment due to the actions taken is severed), then in updating our policy function, we have to be more cautious, thus making the convergence slower but more stable.

5. Conclusions

Due to the enhancements in big data technologies, big data analytics are highly popular in many fields of computer science. As cybersecurity has become such an essential element in our lives today, the incorporation of these analytics in security solutions is unavoidable and rewarding. Besides, due to the fact that most of the cyberattacks are internal and can be easily camouflaged, relatively big data can be pulled out from the network by querying traffic data or system logs, etc [27]. As they become involved extensively in many learning tasks, neural networks are employed extensively as a solution to these problems (or part thereof). Thus, the usage of a learning mechanism is a must in order to handle zero-day attacks. Since today, almost all networks are exposed to threats from zero-day vulnerabilities, a solution that should be able to recognize that potential threats being of a previously unseen type is a must.

As a summary, the contributions of the paper are as follows: (1) New algorithm that can produce better results of intrusion detection than using the conventional machine learning and deep learning techniques. (2) Another such solution intrusion detection algorithm based on an extremely simple and fast policy network that is particularly suitable for driving ultra-fast-paced advanced applications in modern data networks. (3) The obtained model can be applied to online learning, which is required for data networks with changing conditions. Another idea that is new to this paper is in point (4) where DRL is applied to supervised learning. It is motivated by a rewards function which gives no necessity to be definitely derivable and can uniformly be used in all kinds of optimization. As a result, we perform a comparative analysis of a DRL algorithm (DDQN) and its possible implementation on a dataset containing intrusions, rather than in interaction with a live network environment. Additional analysis is provided, comparing this algorithm to several alternative machine learning models, considering three performance aspects: (1) the prediction scores, (2) the training time, and (3) the prediction time of the model using CIC-IDS 2018 Dataset.

The best DRL algorithm (DDQN) has a detection performance (measured by several performance metrics) that ranks similarly to or even higher than a full range of the state-of the-art ML models, including random forest, decision trees, XGboost for the same metrics such as accuracy, F1, precision, and recall.

Furthermore, it should be noted here that, as to DDQN and, in general, DRL methods, the advantage of significantly less prediction time is evident, making them suitable for online detection and new highly demanding network services types, such as IoT networks.

As future work, we hope to explore new DRL architecture and that is new DRL architectures for DRL specifically multi-agent and adversarial models for DRL which can be practical for intrusion detection systems. Furthermore, the minority classes in our dataset can also be expanded by providing CICFlowMeter with its own generated captures.

Author details

Faheem Yar Khuhawar[1*], Tayyaba Shaikh[1], Abdul Latif Memon[1], Irfan Halepoto[2], Fahim Umrani[1], Rizwan Ali Shah[1], Hyder Bux Mangrio[1] and Omar Bani Fayyad[3]

1 Department of Telecommunication Engineering, MUET, Pakistan

2 Department of Electronic Engineering, MUET, Pakistan

3 Bahrain Polytechnic, Bahrai

*Address all correspondence to: faheem.khuhawar@faculty.muet.edu.pk

References

[1] Haq N, Avishek M, Shah F, Onik A, Rafni M, Md D. Application of machine learning approaches in intrusion detection system: A survey. International Journal of Advanced Research in Artificial Intelligence. 2015;**4**:10. DOI: 10.14569/IJARAI.2015.040302

[2] Mishra P, Varadharajan V, Tupakula U, Pilli E. A detailed investigation and analysis of using machine learning techniques for intrusion detection. IEEE Communications Surveys & Tutorials. 2018;**21**:1-1. DOI: 10.1109/COMST.2018.2847722

[3] Nguyen H, A, Choi D. Application of data mining to network intrusion detection: Classifier selection model. In: Asia Pacific Network Operations and Management Symposium (APNOMS) 2008. Berlin, Heidelberg: Springer; 2008. pp. 399-408. Available from: https://dblp.org/db/conf/apnoms/index.html

[4] Tan. Dimensions of cybersecurity risk management. In: Advances in Cybersecurity Management. Cham, Switzerland: Springer International Publishing; 2021. pp. 21-30. Available from: https://link.springer.com/book/10.1007/978-3-030-71381-2

[5] Ahsan MK. Increasing the Predictive Potential of Machine Learning Models for Enhancing Cybersecurity [Thesis]. USA: North Dakota State University; 2021

[6] Deshpande P, Sharma SC, Peddoju SK, Junaid S. HIDS: A host based intrusion detection system for cloud computing environment. International Journal of Systems Assurance Engineering and Management. 2018;**9**(3):567-576. DOI: 10.1007/s13198-014-0277-7

[7] Maiero C, Miculan M. Unobservable intrusion detection based on call traces in Paravirtualized systems. Proceedings of the International Conference on Security and Cryptography. 2012:300-306. DOI: 10.5220/0003521003000306

[8] Bharadwaja S, Sun W, Niamat M, Shen F. Collabra: A xen hypervisor based collaborative intrusion detection system. In: Proceedings - 2011 8th International Conference on Information Technology: New Generations, ITNG 2011. Piscataway, NJ, USA: IEEE; 2010. pp. 695-700. DOI: 10.1109/ITNG.2011.123

[9] Mahmood T, Afzal U. Security analytics: Big data analytics for cybersecurity: A review of trends, techniques and tools. In: 2013 2nd National Conference on Information Assurance (NCIA), Rawalpindi. Vol. 2013. Piscataway, NJ, USA: IEEE; 2013. pp. 129-134. DOI: 10.1109/NCIA.2013.6725337

[10] Nieles M, Dempsey K, Pillitteri V. Nist Special Publication 800-12 Revision 1 an Introduction to Information Security. Gaithersburg: National Institute of Standards and Technology; 2017

[11] Casas P, Soro F, Vanerio J, Settanni G, D'Alconzo A. Network security and anomaly detection with big-dama, a big data analytics framework. In: Proceedings of 2017 IEEE 6th International Conference on Cloud Networking (CloudNet). Piscataway, NJ, USA: IEEE; 2017. pp. 1-7. DOI: 10.1109/CloudNet.2017.8071525

[12] Alavizadeh H, Alavizadeh H, Jang-Jaccard J. Deep Q-learning based reinforcement learning approach for network intrusion detection. Computers. 2022;**11**(3):41

[13] Nygard KE, Rastogi A, Ahsan M, Satyal R. Dimensions of cybersecurity risk management. In: Advances in Cybersecurity Management. Springer; 2021. pp. 369-395

[14] Badr Y. Enabling intrusion detection systems with dueling double deep Q-learning. Digital Transformation and Society. 2022;**1**(1):115-141. DOI: 10.1108/DTS-05-2022-0016

[15] Sharifi AM, Amirgholipour SK, Pourebrahimi A. Intrusion detection based on joint of K-means and KNN. Journal of Convergence Informa- tion Technology. 2015;**10**(5):42

[16] Behera S, Pradhan A, Dash R. Deep neural network architecture for anomaly based intrusion detection system. In: 2018 5th International Conference on Signal Processing and Integrated Networks, SPIN 2018. Piscataway, NJ, USA: IEEE; 2018. pp. 270-274. DOI: 10.1109/SPIN.2018.8474162

[17] Mnih V, Kavukcuoglu K, Silver D, Graves A, Antonoglou I, Wierstra D, et al. Playing Atari with deep reinforcement learning. arXiv. 2013;**abs/1312.5602**:1-9. Available from: http://arxiv.org/abs/1312.5602

[18] Cuayhuitl H, Keizer S, Lemon O. Strategic dialogue management via deep reinforcement learning. arXiv. 2015;**abs/1511.08099**:1-10. Available from: http://arxiv.org/abs/1511.08099

[19] Lai M. Giraffe: Using deep reinforcement learning to play chess. arXiv. 2015;**abs/1509.01549**. Available from: http://arxiv.org/abs/1509.01549

[20] Wang L, Zhang D, Gao L, Song J, Guo L, Shen HT. MathDQN: Solving arithmetic word problems via deep reinforcement learning. In: 32nd AAAI Conference on Artificial Intelligence, AAAI 2018. Palo Alto, CA, USA: AAAI; 2018. pp. 5545-5552

[21] Mahmud M, Kaiser MS, Hussain A, Vassanelli S. Appli- cations of deep learning and reinforcement learning to biological data. IEEE Transactions on Neural Networks and Learning Systems. 2018;**29**(6):2063-2079. DOI: 10.1109/TNNLS.2018.2790388

[22] LaBar J, Chowdhury M, Jochen M, Kambhampaty K. Honeypots: Security by deceiving threats. In: The Midwest Instruction and Computing Symposium 2019. Host Institution; 2018

[23] Yen T-F, Oprea A, Onarlioglu K, Leetham T, Robertson W, Juels A, et al. Beehive: Large-scale log analysis for detecting suspicious activity in enterprise networks. In: Proceedings of the 29th Annual Computer Security Applications Conference (ACSAC '13). New York, NY, USA: Association for Computing Machinery; 2013. pp. 199-208. DOI: 10.1145/2523649.2523670

[24] Bilgisayar Ağ larında Saldırı Tespiti için Makine Ö ğ renme Yö ntemleri: Karşılaştırmalı Bir Analiz - Scientific Figure on ResearchGate. Machine Learning Methods for Intrusion Detection in Computer Networks: A Comparative Analysis. Available from: https://www.researchgate.net/figure/Network-Topology-25$_f ig1_3$74694982 [Accessed: December, 17, 2024]

[25] Chimphlee W, Chimphlee S. Network intrusion detector using multilayer perceptron (MLP) approach. Turkish Journal of Computer and Mathematics Education (TURCOMAT). 2022;**13**(03):488-499. DOI: 10.17762/turcomat.v13i03.13018

[26] Short-Term Load Forecasting Method Based on Feature Preference Strategy and LightGBM-XGboost - Scientific Figure

on ResearchGate. Available from: https://www.researchgate.net/figure/Schematic-illustration-of-the-XGboost-model$_f$ $ig2_3$62100649 [Accessed: December, 17, 2024]

[27] Ciaravino E, Chowdhury M, Jochen M, Kambhampaty K. Security issues of scada systems. In: The Midwest Instruction and Computing Symposium 2019. Host Institution; 2018